IMAGES
of America

SHIPPENSBURG

I0807656

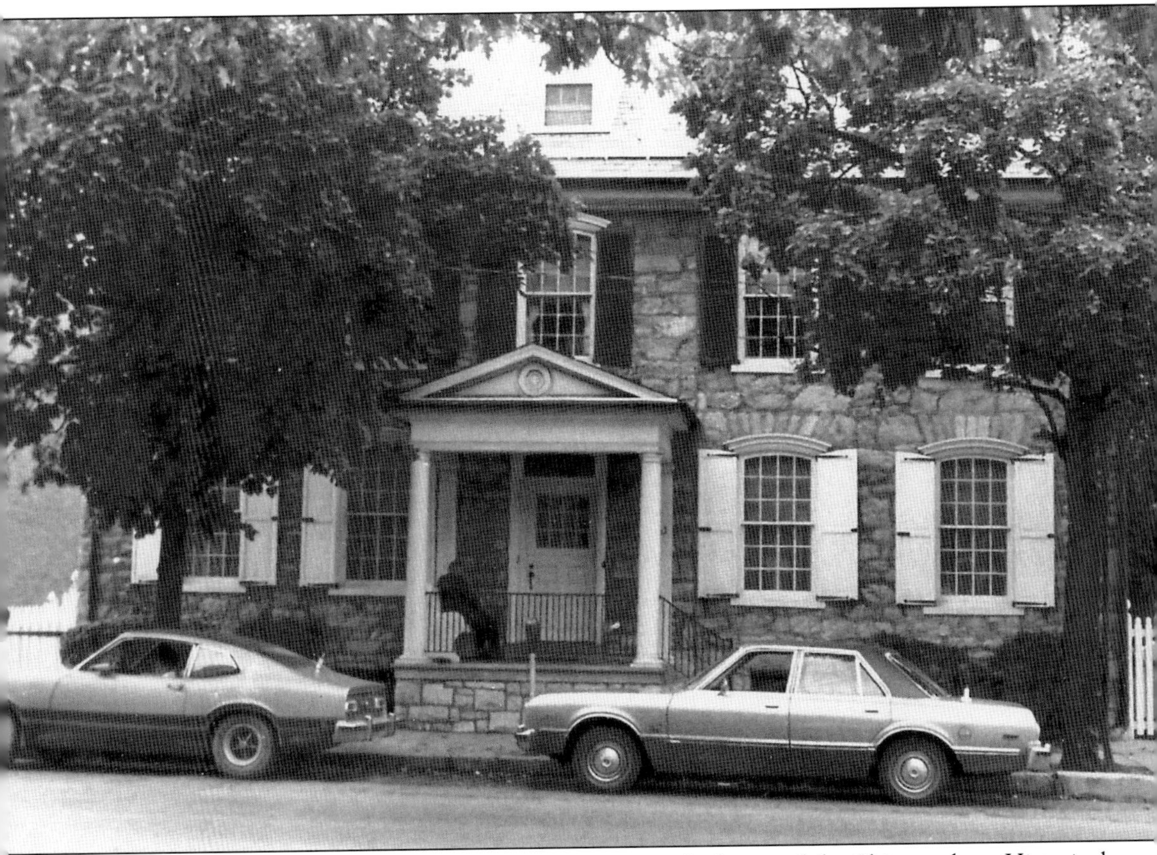

The former residence of Dr. Alexander Stewart, now the home of the Shippensburg Historical Society, is located at 52 West King Street. The current house consists of two distinct stone structures that were consolidated in the 1930s by Dr. Stewart. The original house was built in 1784 by John Redott and measured 28 feet by 32 feet. Redott's initials and the date of construction are chiseled into a stone next to the front window.

On the Cover: This photograph was taken at Devil's Den on the Gettysburg National Battlefield by M.F. Williams, a Gettysburg photographer, sometime in 1914. The young people in the bed of G. Raymond "Shorty" Fogelsonger's Republic truck are students from the Cumberland Valley State Normal School (now Shippensburg University of Pennsylvania), enjoying a battlefield tour. Fogelsonger is standing at the rear of the truck. Fogelsonger's first such excursion to Gettysburg was in 1910 when he took a group of African American youth on a similar tour. (Courtesy of Shippensburg Historical Society.)

IMAGES
of America

SHIPPENSBURG

Paul E. Gill with the
Shippensburg Historical Society
Publication Committee

ARCADIA
PUBLISHING

ISBN 978-0-7385-7699-2

Published by Arcadia Publishing
Charleston, South Carolina

Printed in the United States of America

Library of Congress Control Number: 2011943546

For all general information, please contact Arcadia Publishing:
Telephone 843-853-2070
Fax 843-853-0044
E-mail sales@arcadiapublishing.com
For customer service and orders:
Toll-Free 1-888-313-2665

Visit us on the Internet at www.arcadiapublishing.com

This book is respectfully dedicated to the memory of William "Bill" Burkhart, whose contributions to preserving the history of his hometown and surrounding regions are legion. Many of the photographs in this work were collected by Bill, who thoroughly researched each one.

Contents

ACKNOWLEDGMENTS

At the outset, great thanks must be given to the Shippensburg Historical Society for allowing me to use the facilities for the preparation of this work. Next, I want to acknowledge the contributions of the members of the historical society's Publication Committee. John Fague led me to many of the photographs and provided information for the chapter on businesses, manufacturing, and transportation. David Ferry was charged with working with the Laughlin collection of postcards, as well as the chapter on schools. John McCorriston, who served as president of the society when this project began, provided photographs and captions for the chapter on historic and unusual buildings of Shippensburg. Gail Runshaw scanned all the photographs and also contributed to the chapter on churches. My own work consists of the chapter on veterans and military affairs and putting the final product together. I wish also to render my thanks to the several acquisitions editors with whom I worked on this project—including Erin Vosgien, Darcy Mahan, and Abby Henry—who guided me through the final phases of the publication process. This was most assuredly a team project. Finally, I must acknowledge the encouragement and moral support of my wife, Donna, during the many frustrating periods that always accompany the preparation of any book. Unless otherwise noted, all photographs are courtesy of the Shippensburg Historical Society.

Introduction

The history of what would become Shippensburg begins in the early 1730s when cabins were built along the Virginia Path, a Native American path leading southwestward through the Kittochtinny Valley in Pennsylvania and Virginia. This area was settled first by Scots-Irish Presbyterian immigrants seeking religious freedom and lands to farm. The Middle Spring Presbyterian Church, founded by Scots-Irish near modern-day Shippensburg, was established in 1738.

In March 1737, Edward Shippen purchased 1,312 acres of land from the family of William Penn, who had been given the land comprising Pennsylvania by King Charles II of England in settlement of a debt owed to Penn's father. The town that lay within the boundaries of Shippen's purchase was named for the owner, thus Shippensburg—although he never lived there.

When the course of the "Great Road" was laid out from Harris Ferry (Harrisburg) to the Potomac River in 1744, it followed the Virginia Path. Shippensburg was the only village or town on its entire course.

In July 1755, after British general Edward Braddock suffered defeat at the hands of the French and Indians near present-day Pittsburgh, the Cumberland Valley became the target of attacks, causing a provincial fort, named after Pennsylvania governor Robert Hunter Morris, to be built at Shippensburg as part of a Colonial defense system. After two centuries of debate over the location of this fort, an archaeological dig sponsored by the Shippensburg Historical Society during the summers of 2008 and 2009 reached the near certain conclusion that it was located on the property at modern-day 333 East Burd Street. In 1758, British general John Forbes spent three weeks at Fort Morris while on his way to capture Fort Duquesne from the French. Once again, Shippensburg was located along a road, this one being constructed westward across the Allegheny Mountains, a road to be known as Forbes Road.

Following the defeat of the French and Indians, the roads leading through Shippensburg became the way to the West for settlers eager to settle the frontier. Shippensburg became a jumping-off point for waves of pioneers heading west over the Appalachian Mountains. This rush to the west created an atmosphere of entrepreneurism in Shippensburg for wagon makers, carpenters, chair makers, merchants, etc., to supply the travelers as well as the residents of the town. The Cumberland Valley Railroad came through Shippensburg in 1836.

Shippensburg has provided soldiers, sailors, and Marines for all of the wars from the French and Indian through the present conflicts in the Middle East. This book will provide photographs of selected enlisted men and women and officers from Shippensburg, as well as the town's only general, Brig. Gen. Samuel Sturgis, who served with credit throughout the entire American Civil War and continued in the Army until his discharge in 1886. He was at Antietam and Gettysburg as well as many other important battles. His son Richard was killed at the Little Bighorn along with the rest of Custer's men from the 7th Cavalry. The little town of Sturgis, South Dakota, named in honor of Richard, has become a mecca for tens of thousands of motorcyclists who descend upon it every summer.

Inseparable from the town of Shippensburg is the institution of higher learning which began in the northwest part of town in 1871 as the Cumberland Valley State Normal School. In the 1930s, it became known as Shippensburg State Teachers College. In the 1960s, it was renamed Shippensburg State College as a liberal arts program was added to the curriculum. Finally, in 1983, its name was changed to Shippensburg University of Pennsylvania. During the academic year, there are more students on campus than residents of the borough of Shippensburg. *US News & World Report* ranked Shippensburg University among the top public universities in the North in its 2009 report on America's "best colleges." It was named one of the 100 best values among public colleges in *Kiplinger's Personal Finance*. Shippensburg was also included in the 2007 edition of the Princeton Review's *The Best Northeastern Colleges*.

Shippensburg has a history of distinction, and this book will attempt to illustrate through words and pictures some of the features of that history that are the town's claims to fame among the many interesting communities that have been featured in companion volumes of the Images of America series.

One

The Photographs and Postcards of Clyde A. Laughlin

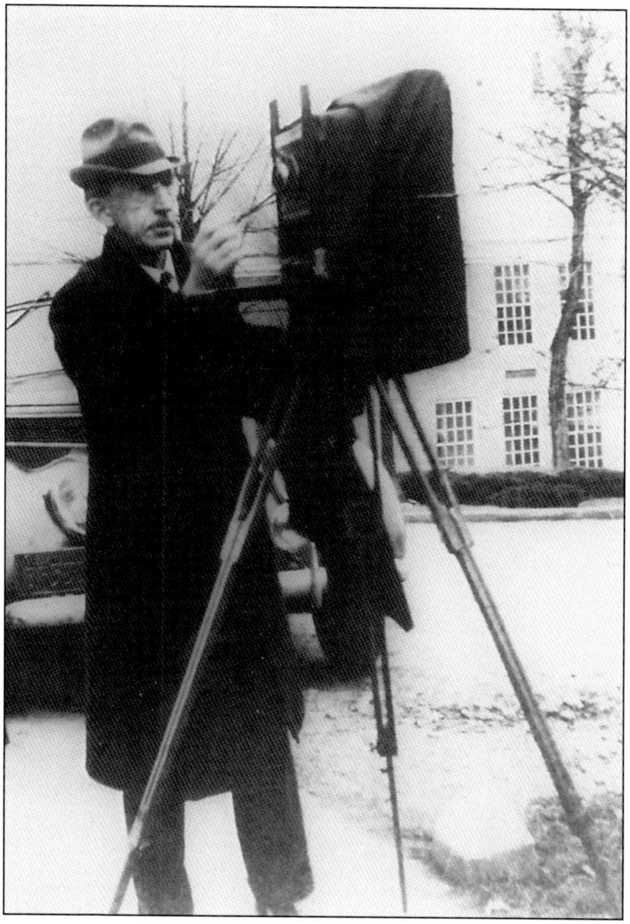

This photograph shows Clyde A. Laughlin on the job. Laughlin was born on July 11, 1881, in Newburg, Pennsylvania. On May 2, 1897, he took his first photograph with a Kodak camera that he purchased for less than $1. His photography and postcard-making career spanned the years from 1906 until 1945, and while no one knows just how many postcards Laughlin produced, there might have been more than 3,000. Laughlin took the photographs and created the postcards himself. Many of his postcards were of everyday scenes in Shippensburg and neighboring communities. Laughlin has been called the "Postcard King of the Cumberland Valley." (Courtesy of Walter L. Cressler Jr.)

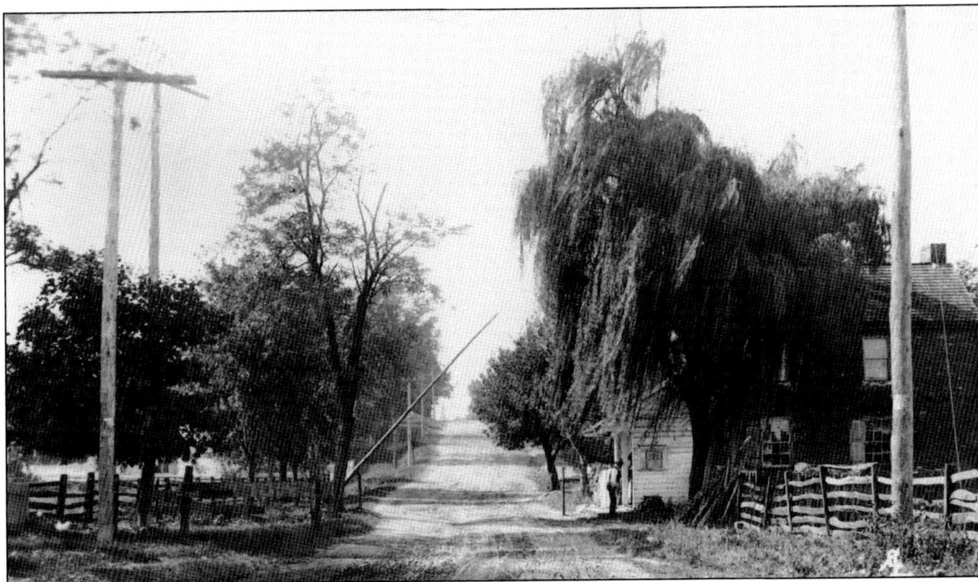

When entering Shippensburg on the turnpike, travelers had to pass through the toll gate and pay a toll. Tolls were collected on wagons, buggies, sleighs, bobsleds, riders on horseback, and drovers of livestock, but not on pedestrians or people going to church by vehicle. The collected tolls paid back the private investment that financed the road and also provided a small maintenance budget. This toll gate operated from around 1814 until 1914.

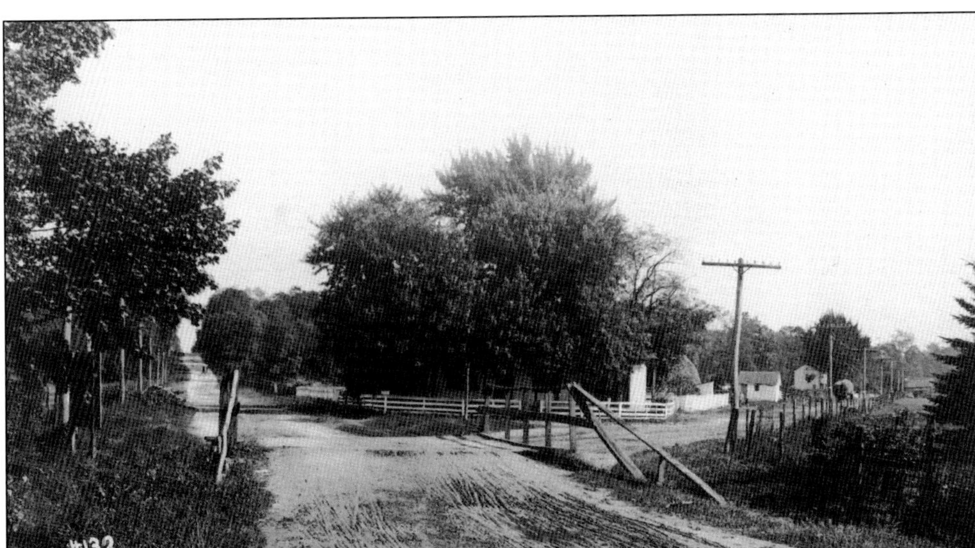

Travelers leaving Shippensburg who were headed to Carlisle and points north had a choice of continuing on the turnpike (present-day Route 11) or turning right onto Walnut Bottom Road. Either way, they traveled on dirt roads.

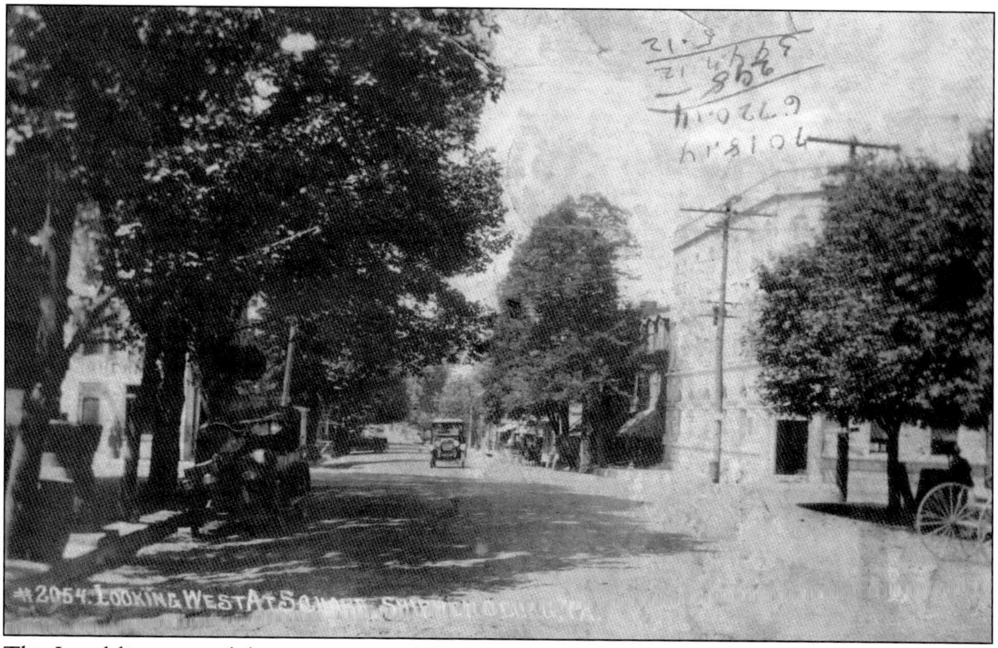

This Laughlin postcard shows an unpaved West King Street. In 1911, prompted by the Shippensburg Civic Club, the borough covered the streets with road oil. Property owners on both sides of the street were charged 8¢ per front foot for the improvement.

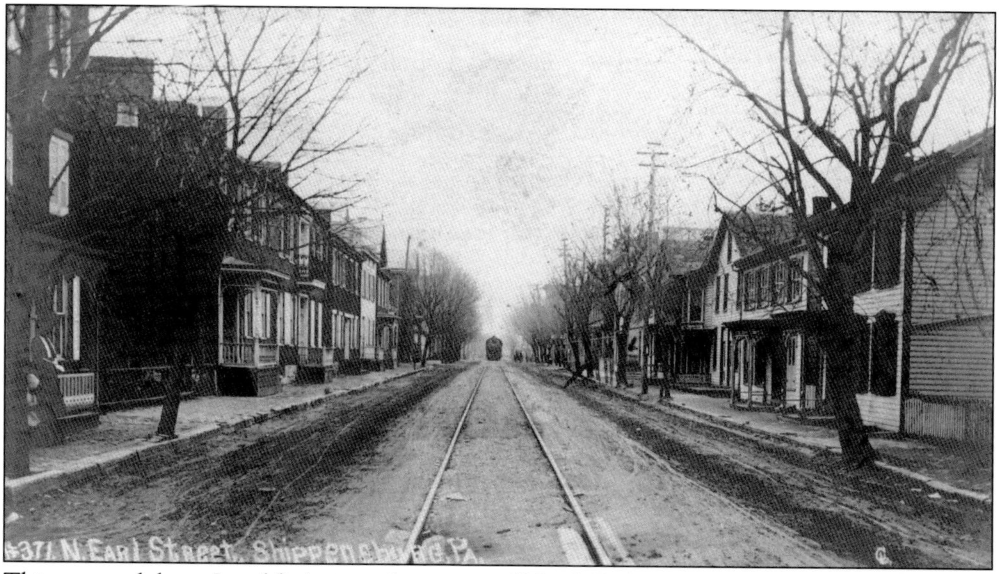

This postcard shows Laughlin's view of an unpaved North Earl Street with railroad tracks running down the center. The tracks were built by the Cumberland Valley Railroad and became part of the Pennsylvania Railroad system in 1919. Passenger service ended in 1962, and Conrail discontinued all freight traffic on these tracks in 1981. In 1985, the tracks were removed.

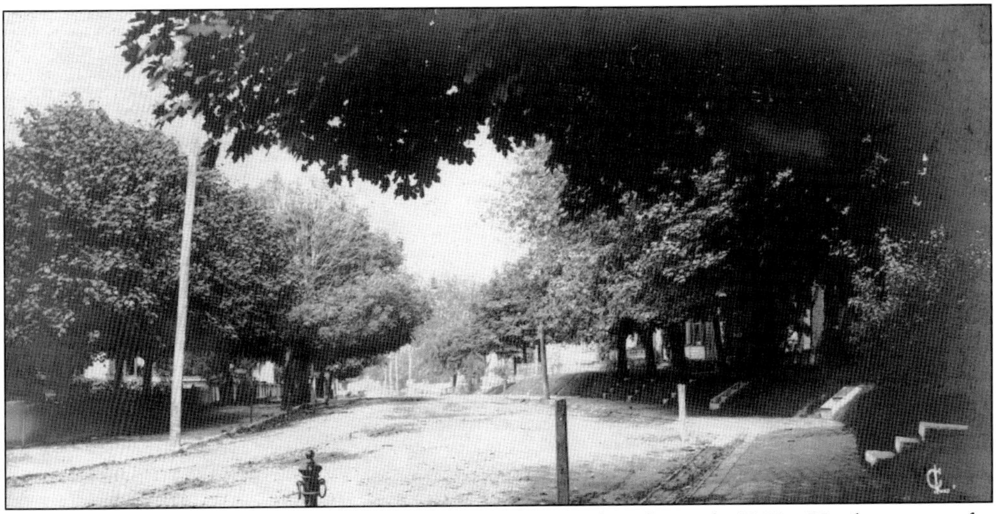

This is the 200 block of East Orange Street as in appeared in the early 1900s. Hitching posts for horses are visible on the right side of the street.

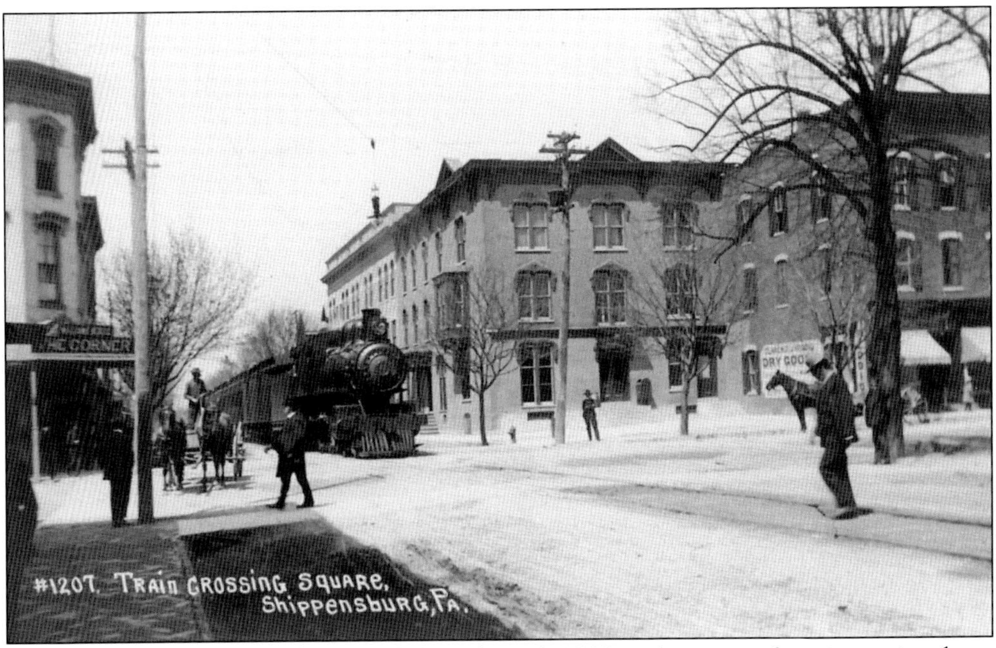

One of the most popular Laughlin cards from the early 1900s is this scene of a train coming down North Earl Street towards the square, the center of town, where North and South Earl Streets and East and West King Streets intersect. A store named The Corner stood on the northwest corner where the First National Bank would later be built. The northeast corner of the square had an open area beside a dry goods store.

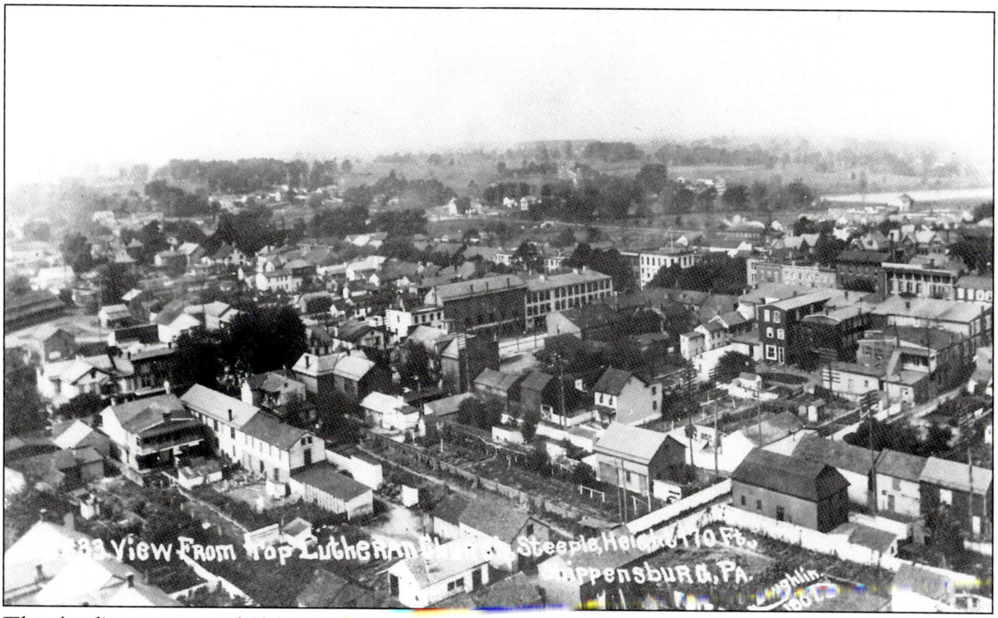

This bird's-eye view of Shippensburg was taken by Laughlin from the steeple of the Lutheran church located on the corner of East Orange and South Penn Streets.

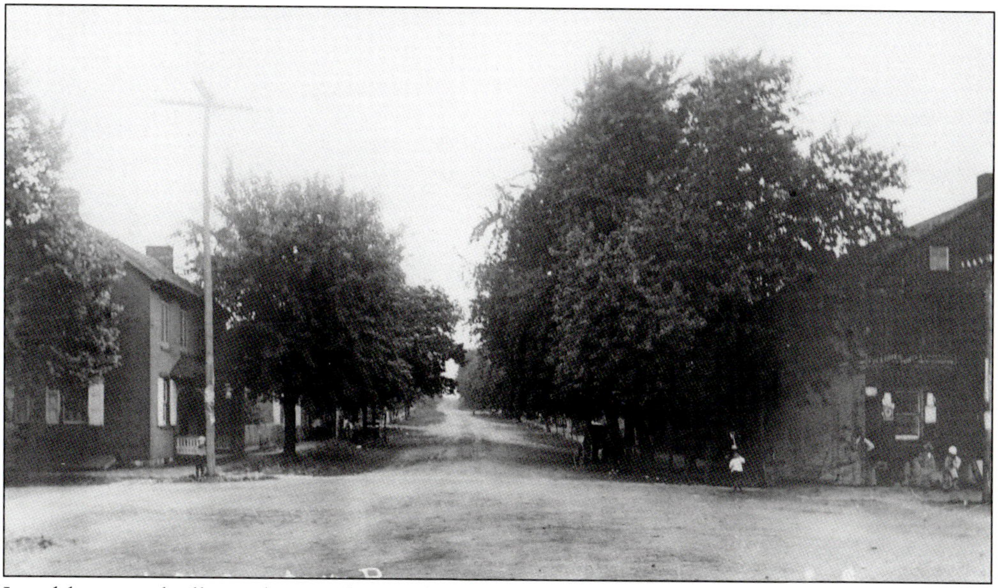

Laughlin visited villages close to Shippensburg to capture prominent features of these communities as well. This photograph from the early 1900s shows the main street of Orrstown. Founded in 1833, it was originally called Sporting Hill; the name was first changed to Southampton and later to Orrstown in honor of John and William Orr. By the time this picture was taken, the town had two general stores, a tannery, two blacksmiths, two wagon-repair shops, two tailors, two undertakers, and two hotels.

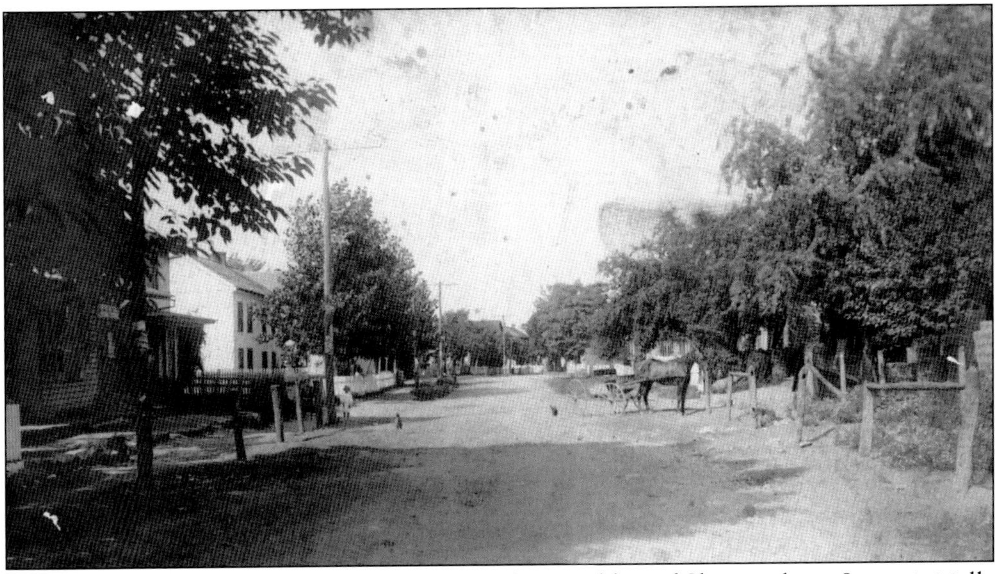

This is the main street of Walnut Bottom, another neighbor of Shippensburg. It was initially called Frystown after Peter Fry, an early resident. Before 1850, it was called Jacksonville after Pres. Andrew Jackson. In 1850, the name was changed to Walnut Bottom because of the many walnut trees in the area. The public school there was still called Jacksonville until it was closed in the 1970s.

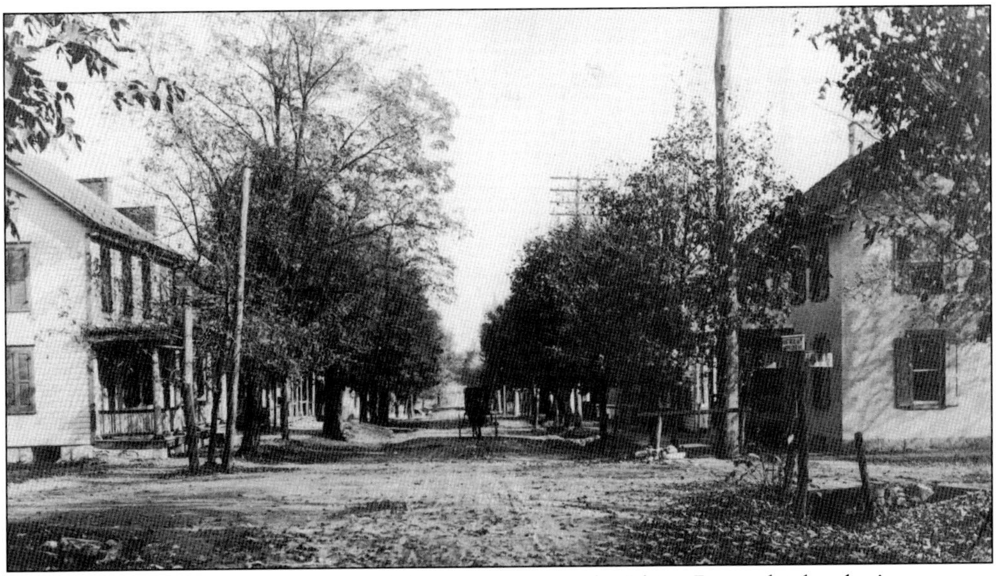

Originally called Strasburg in honor of the French city on the Rhine River, this locality's name was changed to Upper Strasburg in 1829 to avoid confusion with the Strasburg in Lancaster County. During the 19th century, country inns in and around Upper Strasburg provided food and lodging for travelers on the Three Mountain Road that ran from Shippensburg to Burnt Cabins.

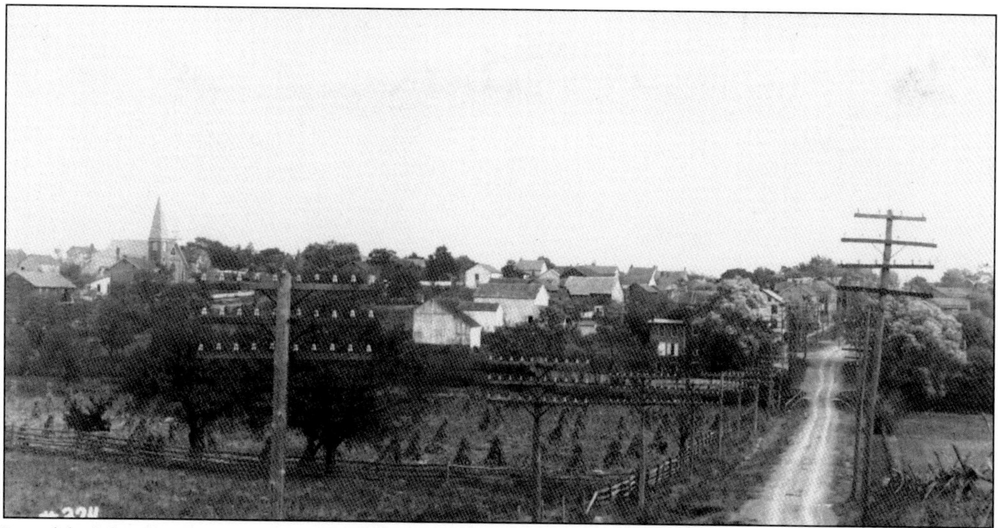

Laughlin's bird's-eye view of nearby Newburg shows the town around 1910. The road on the right side of the image—now Route 696—leads from Shippensburg to Newburg. When headed to Newburg from Shippensburg, it is the Newburg Road. When going in the other direction, it is called the Shippensburg Road. Newburg's economy supported a tannery, saddler shops, carriage shops, a tin shop, a brickyard, a cooper, several drugstores, a creamery, a cider press, two blacksmiths, two furniture factories, and two undertakers.

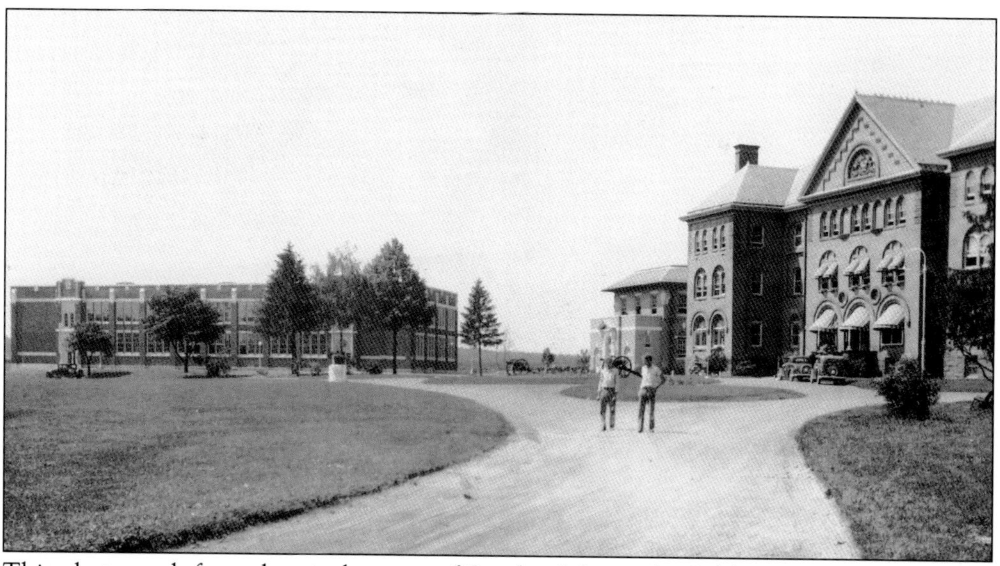

This photograph from the nearby town of Scotland shows the Soldiers' Orphans Industrial School, which opened in 1895. In 1951, the name was changed to Scotland School for Veterans' Children. Henceforth, the key requirements for admission were that a student was 16 years of age or younger and had a parent or grandparent who had served on active duty in the US military. In 2009, the school was closed following state budget cuts.

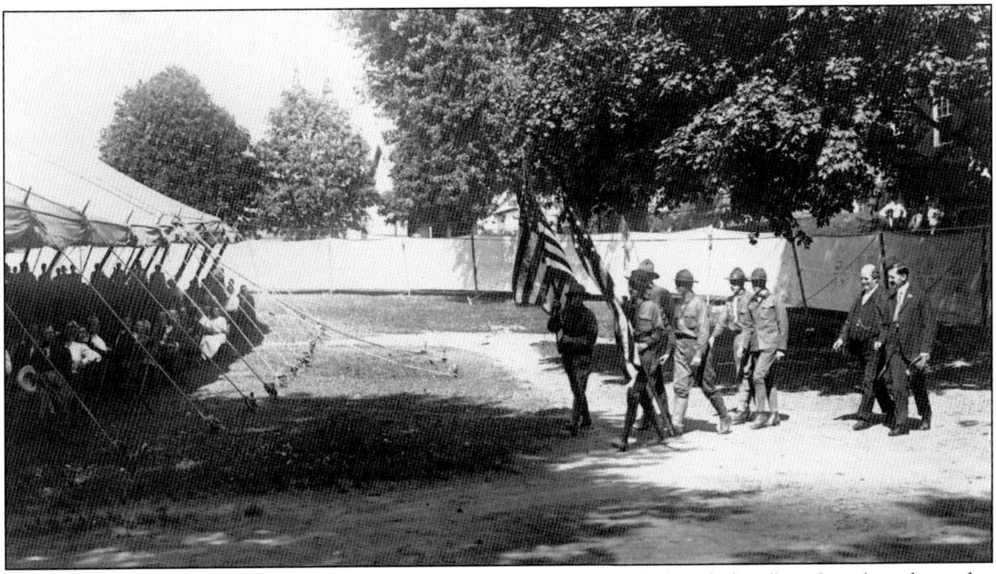

Three-time presidential candidate William Jennings Bryan (behind the flag detail and on the left), one of best known public lecturers of the time, came to Shippensburg in 1914 to speak at the Chautauqua tent program. Bryan is being escorted to the Chautauqua tent by J. Beattie Barbour of Shippensburg.

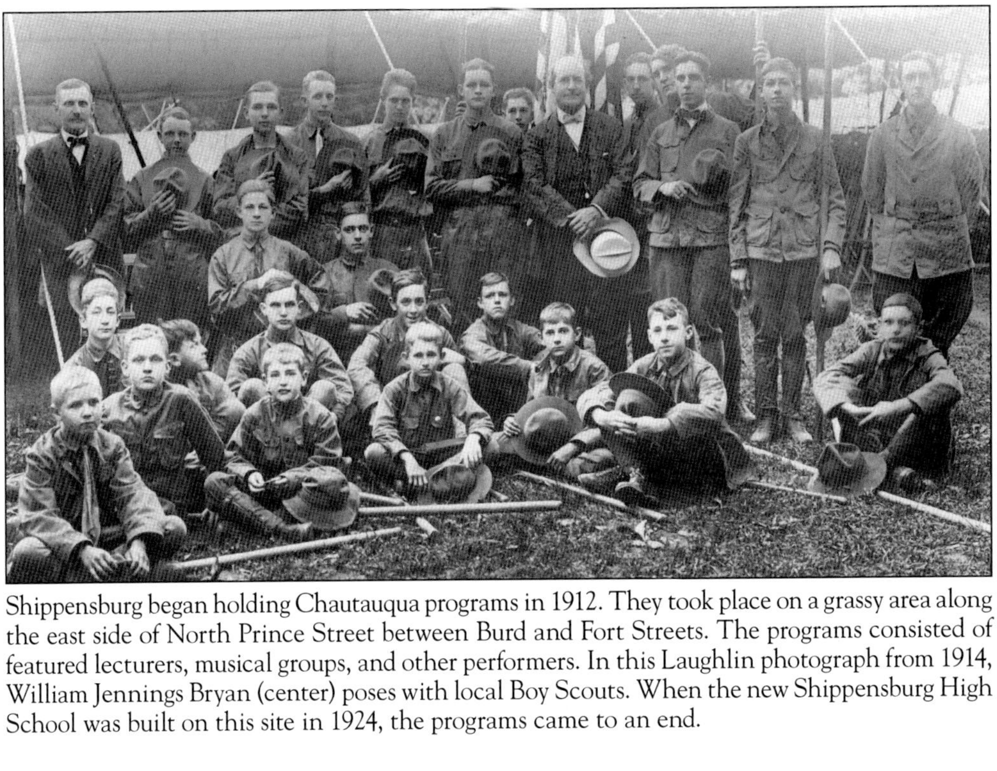

Shippensburg began holding Chautauqua programs in 1912. They took place on a grassy area along the east side of North Prince Street between Burd and Fort Streets. The programs consisted of featured lecturers, musical groups, and other performers. In this Laughlin photograph from 1914, William Jennings Bryan (center) poses with local Boy Scouts. When the new Shippensburg High School was built on this site in 1924, the programs came to an end.

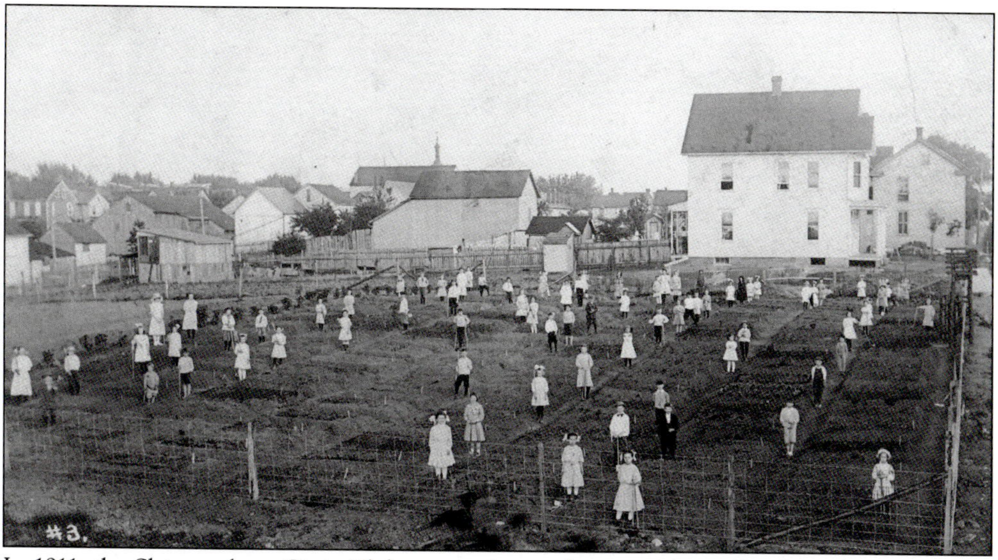

In 1911, the Shippensburg Civic Club acquired two adjoining lots on Burd Street, near Queen Street. After the land was plowed, it was divided into 170 numbered plots that were each six feet by eight feet in area. Volunteer gardeners pose for this Laughlin postcard photograph.

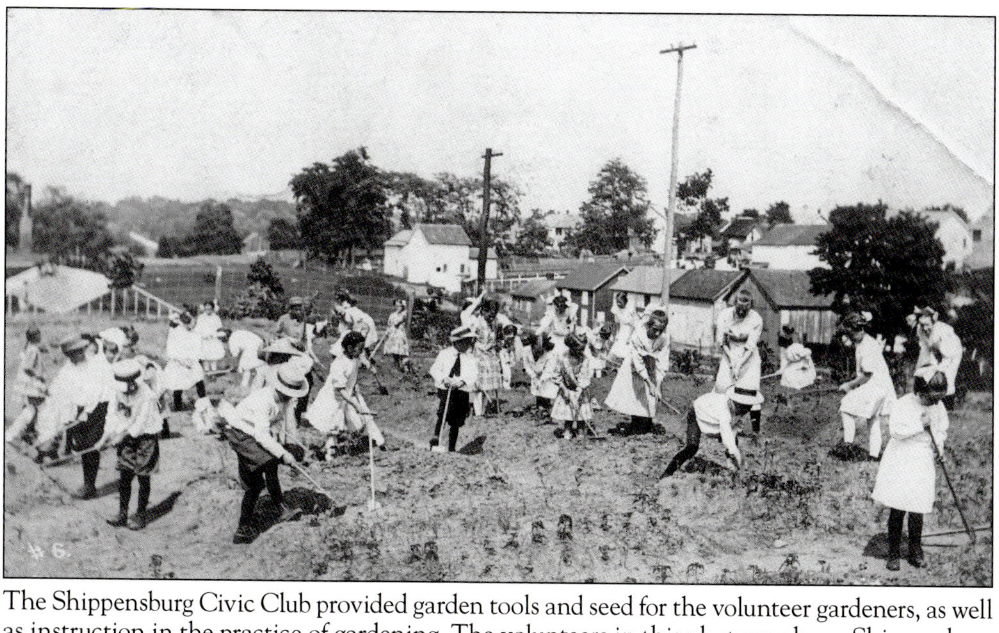

The Shippensburg Civic Club provided garden tools and seed for the volunteer gardeners, as well as instruction in the practice of gardening. The volunteers in this photograph are Shippensburg boys and girls.

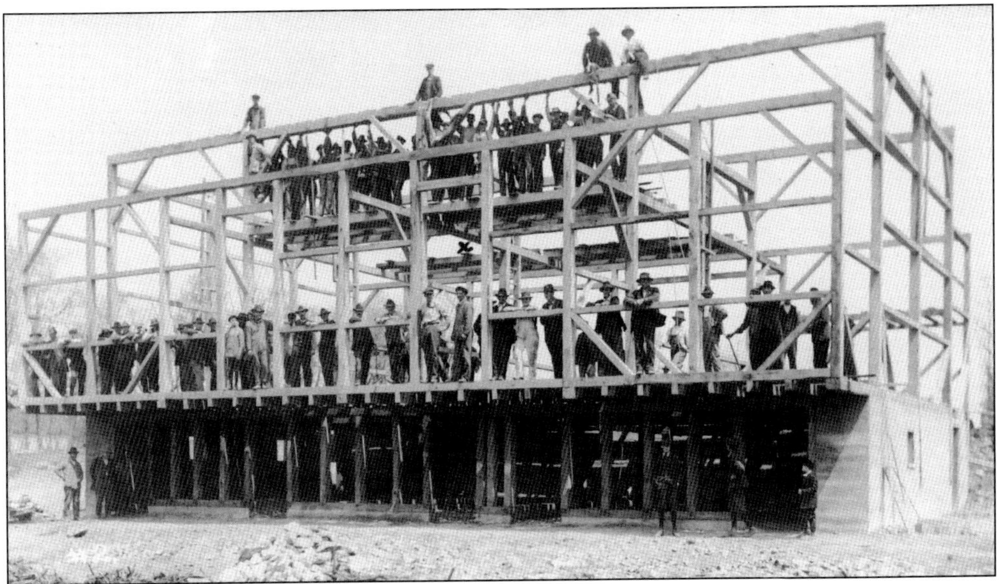

In this 1922 Laughlin photograph, local men are engaged in a barn raising. The barn they are working on was for Harry P. Keefer, whose farm was located just east of town along Route 11. R.F. Warren was the contractor.

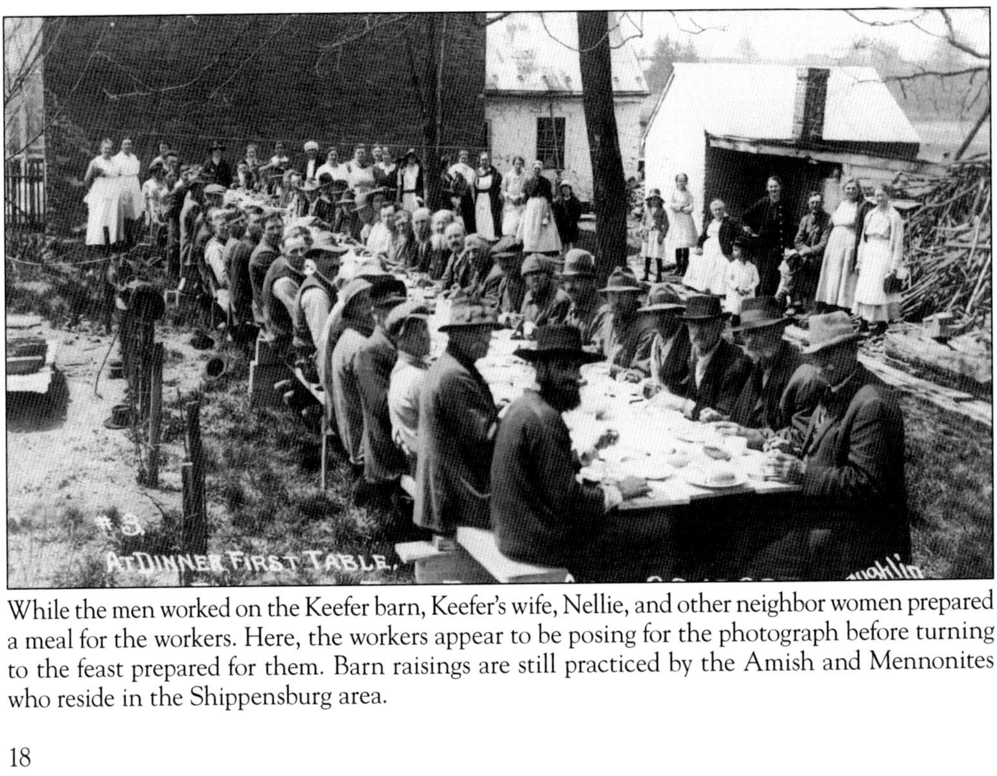

While the men worked on the Keefer barn, Keefer's wife, Nellie, and other neighbor women prepared a meal for the workers. Here, the workers appear to be posing for the photograph before turning to the feast prepared for them. Barn raisings are still practiced by the Amish and Mennonites who reside in the Shippensburg area.

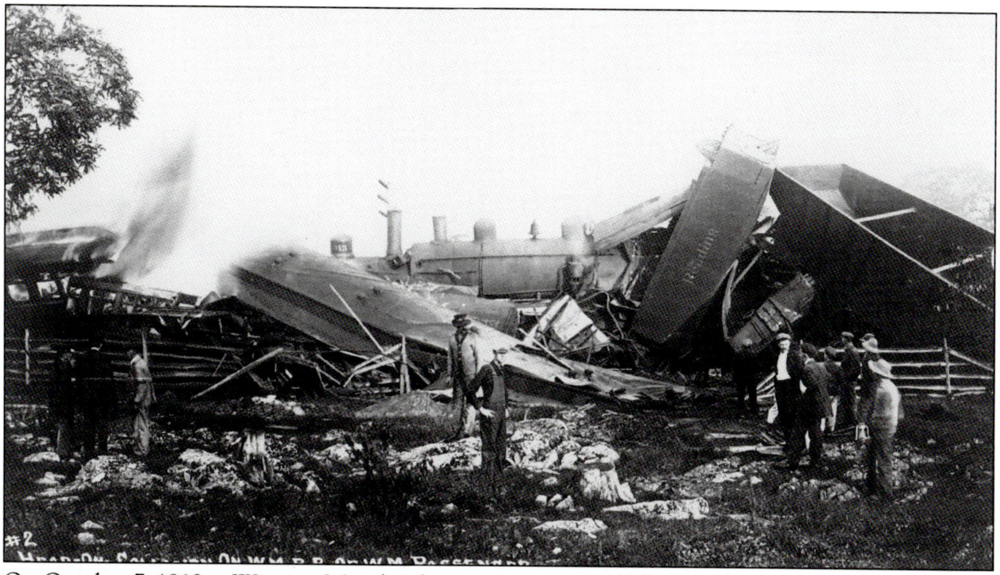

On October 7, 1912, a Western Maryland passenger train collided head on with a Reading freight train on the Western Maryland tracks west of Pinola. While there were no passengers aboard, four crewmen lost their lives in this unfortunate accident.

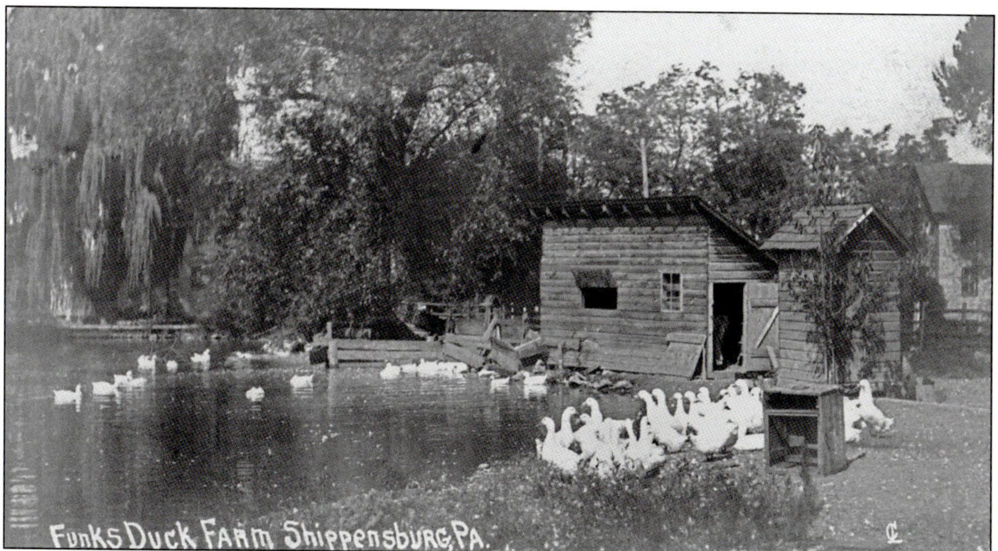

The Funk family of Shippensburg bought this mill located on the west side of Middle Spring Avenue. In addition to being millers, they raised ducks on the millpond shown here. The millpond was later drained, filled, and became the site of a complex of buildings built by Richard Textiles.

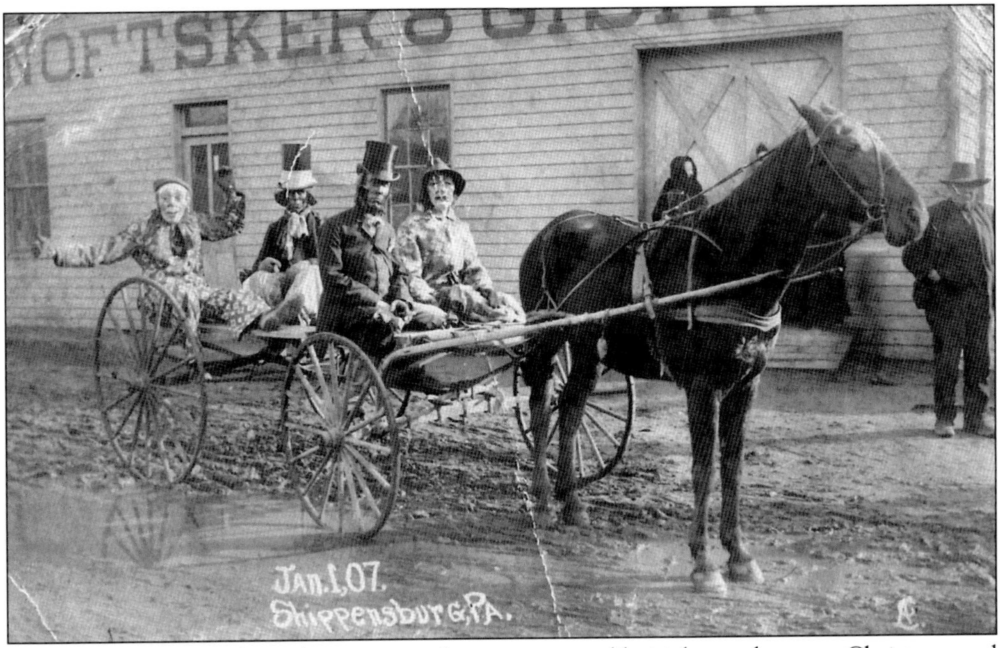

"Belsnickling" parties dressed in masquerade costumes would visit homes between Christmas and New Year's Day. The Belsnicklers would sing songs, and the residents of the homes they visited would try to identify the performers. This custom died out in the late 1920s. These Belsnicklers are performing on New Year's Day 1907 in front of the Noftsker and Gish carriage factory at the southeast corner of West Orange and South Fayette Streets.

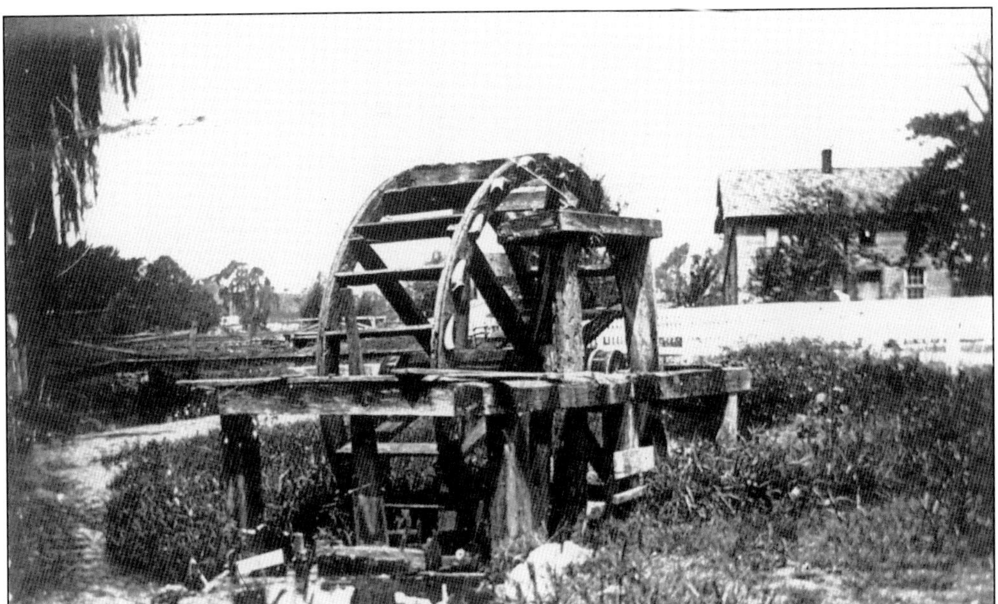

Located in a narrow channel of water along the east side of Branch Creek between King and Burd Streets, this waterwheel lifted water that was poured into a trough and carried to the Angle Tannery. Since the wheel was not used after 1890, this 1910 photograph shows it standing in ruin.

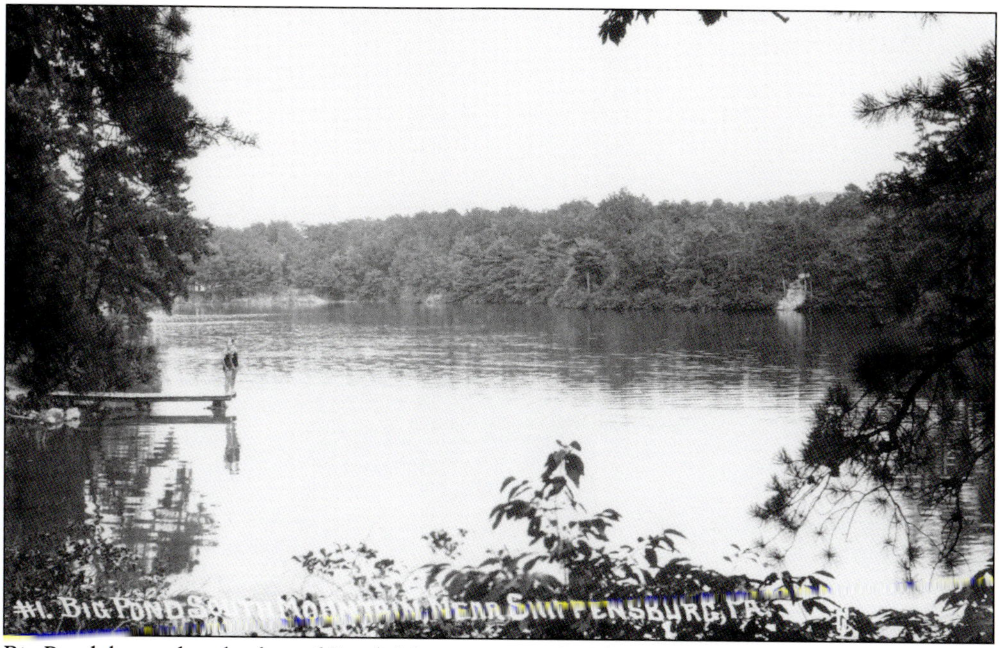

Big Pond, located at the foot of South Mountain near Leesburg, was a popular recreation spot for Shippensburg-area residents for many decades. It was once the ore hole for an iron furnace that was erected nearby in the 1830s. The land surrounding the pond is now privately owned and is not open to the public.

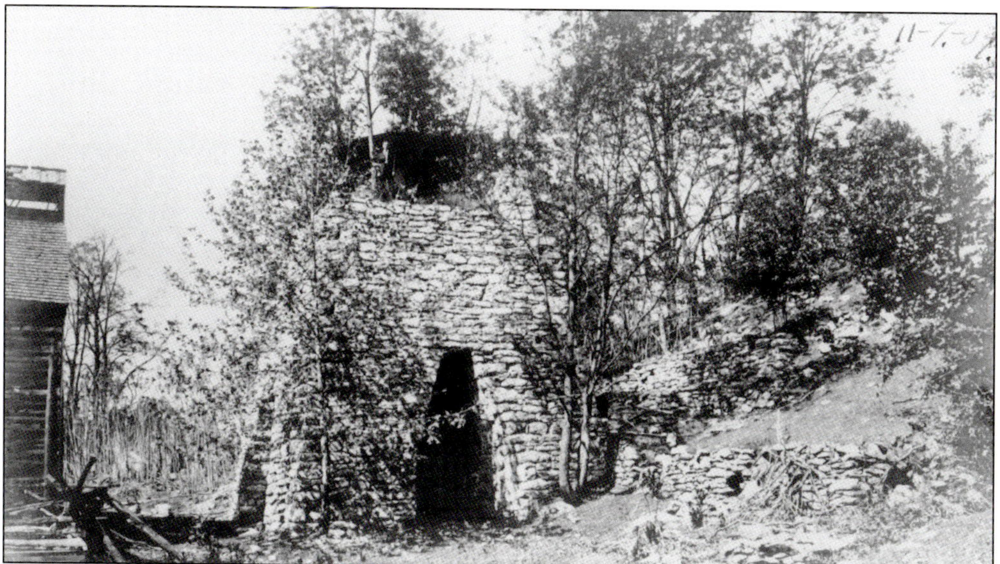

This Big Pond iron furnace was built during the 1830s. After being abandoned in 1873, it was remodeled and resumed operations in 1880. That year, a fire broke out, and buildings at the site were destroyed, including the engine house, which contained a pair of stationary blowers that supplied blast to the furnace. The blowers were destroyed, and the furnace was never used again.

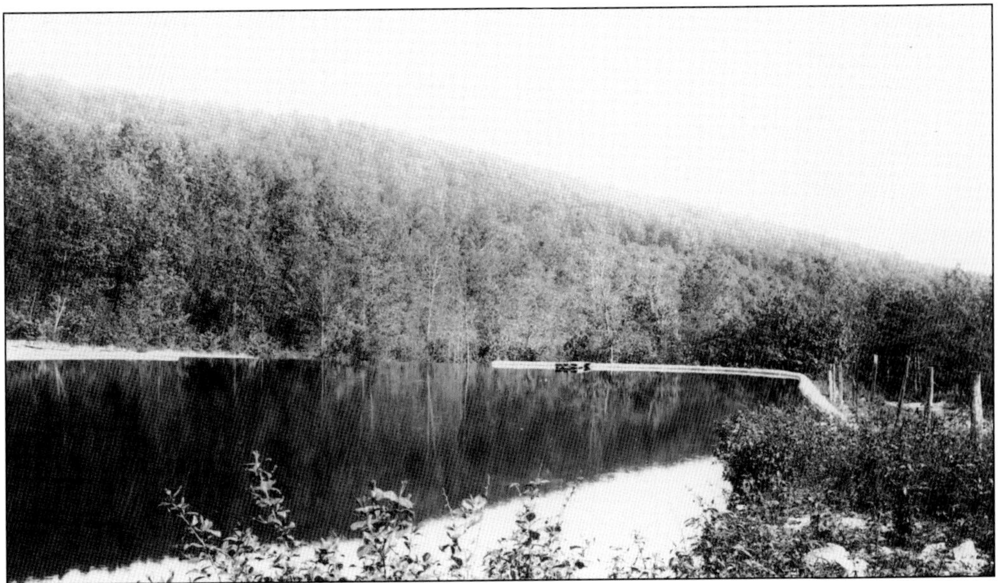

In 1892, Shippensburg Borough leased a tract of land near Cleversburg and built a dam on Milesburn Run. Although the dam no longer exists, it was a partial source of Shippensburg's water supply for many years.

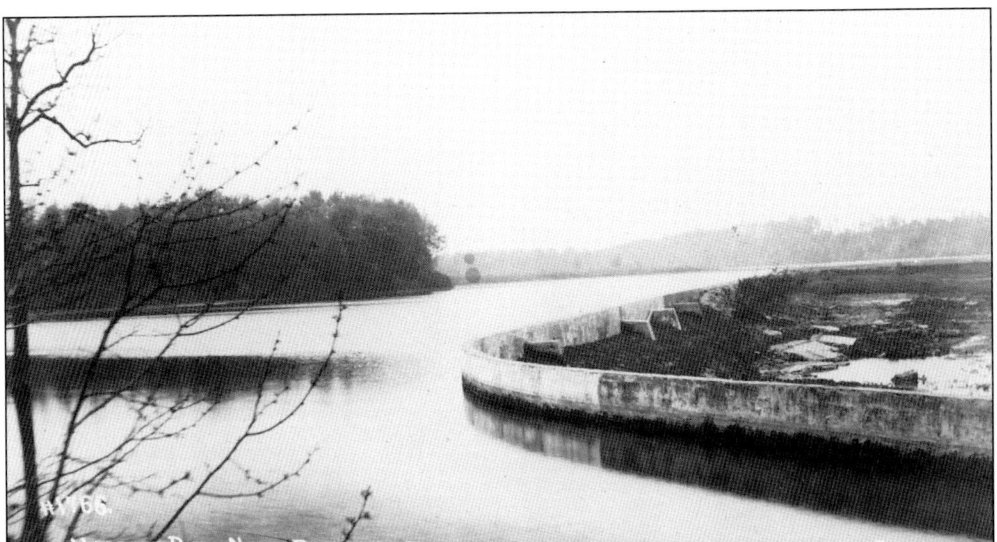

This is the Hosfeld Dam near Roxbury. It was built by the Shippensburg Gas and Electric Company, which was owned by the Hosfeld family. It was one of two dams at Roxbury that captured water from Conodoguinet Creek and a source of the water and electricity supplied to Shippensburg.

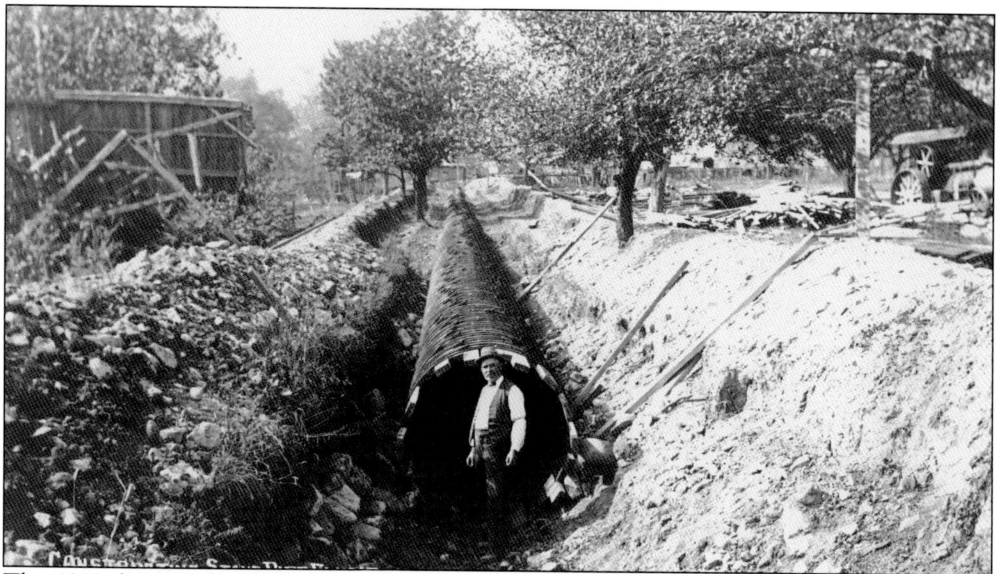

This 1914 photograph shows a stave pipe flume being constructed to carry water from the Roxbury Dam to a power plant that would supply electricity to the Shippensburg Gas and Electric Company. The plant no longer exists.

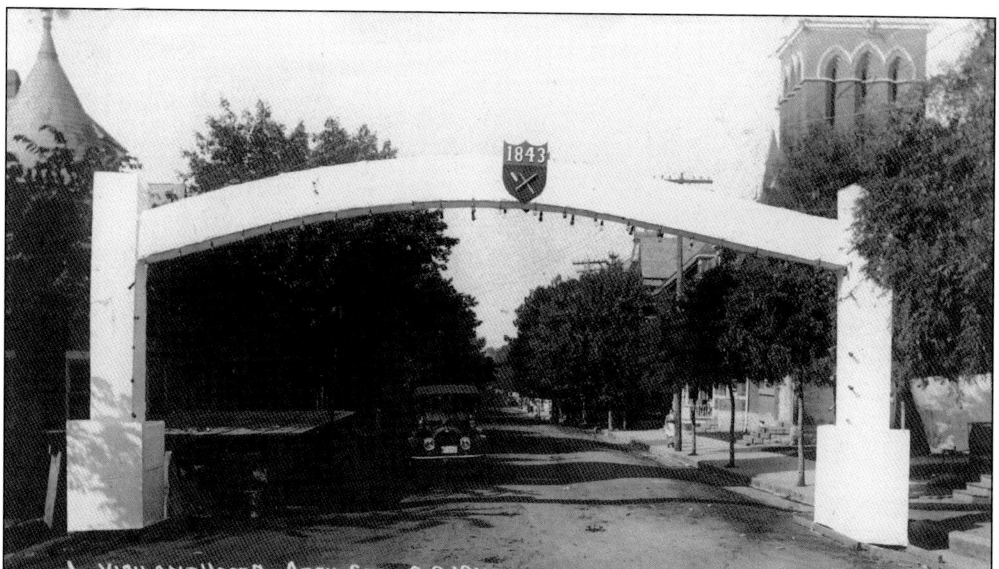

The Vigilant Hose Company Arch was built to welcome visitors to the 1915 Firemen's Convention. Hosted by the Vigilant Hose Company, the event lasted for two days and gave visiting firemen from nearby areas an opportunity to show off their pumps and other firefighting equipment.

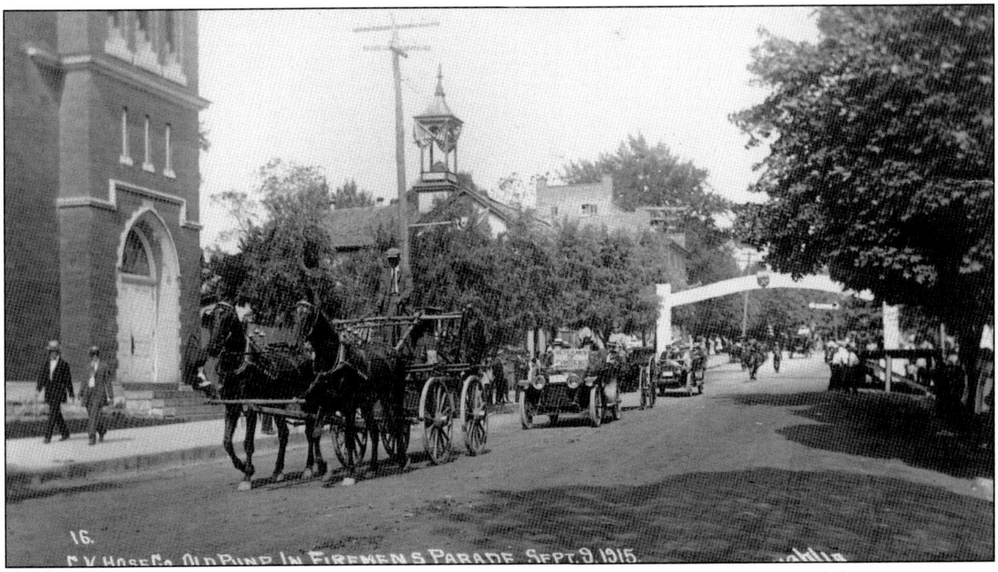

The highlight of the convention was the firemen's parade on the second day of the convention. The Cumberland Valley Hose Company's old horse-drawn pump leads the parade through the welcome arch. The building in the left foreground is the Church of God.

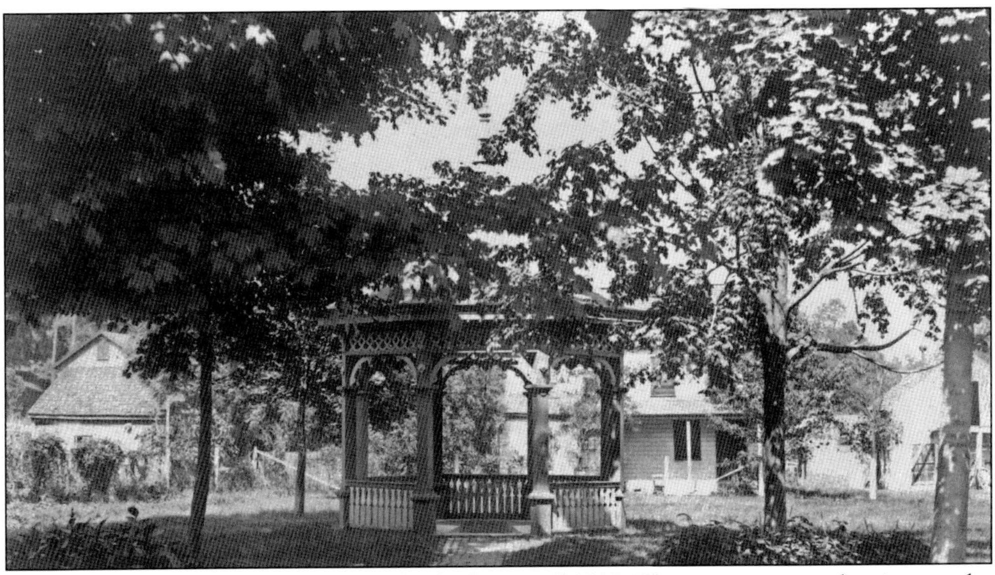

The gazebo on the "Old Spring Lot" was built around 1900. There was a natural spring on the lot, but townspeople were reluctant to drink the water because of a rumor that the water came from below Spring Hill Cemetery. In 1919, the borough placed a public drinking fountain at the gazebo. The Corn Festival Committee renovated the gazebo in 1990. Weddings are occasionally held at this site.

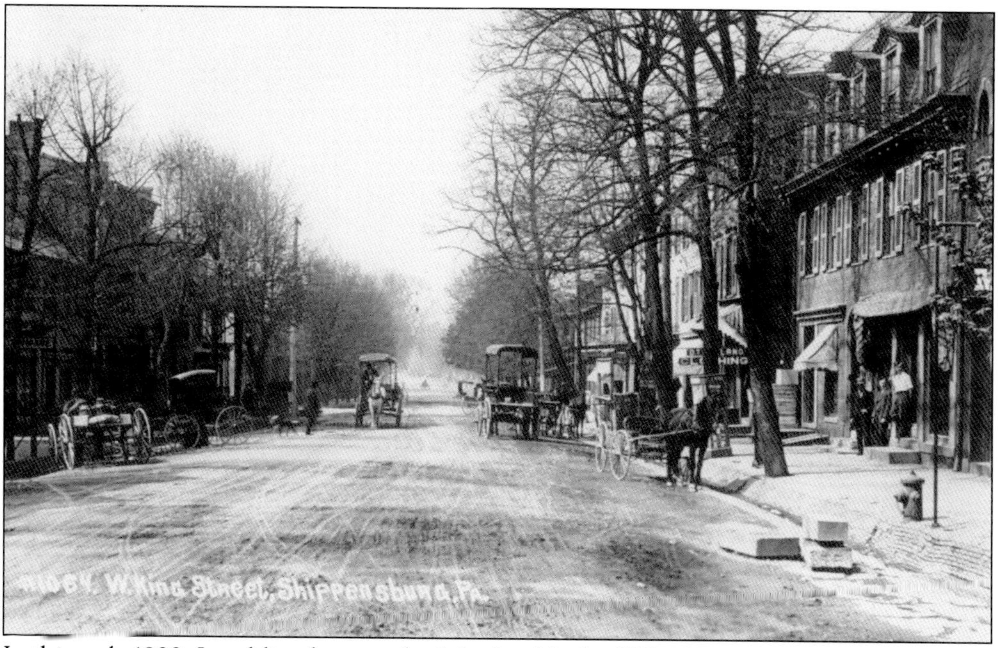

In this early-1900s Laughlin photograph of the first block of West King Street, the brick curbing is visible on the right side. Someone has apparently stacked materials in the street in front of a fire hydrant, an action that would likely result in a fine in the present day.

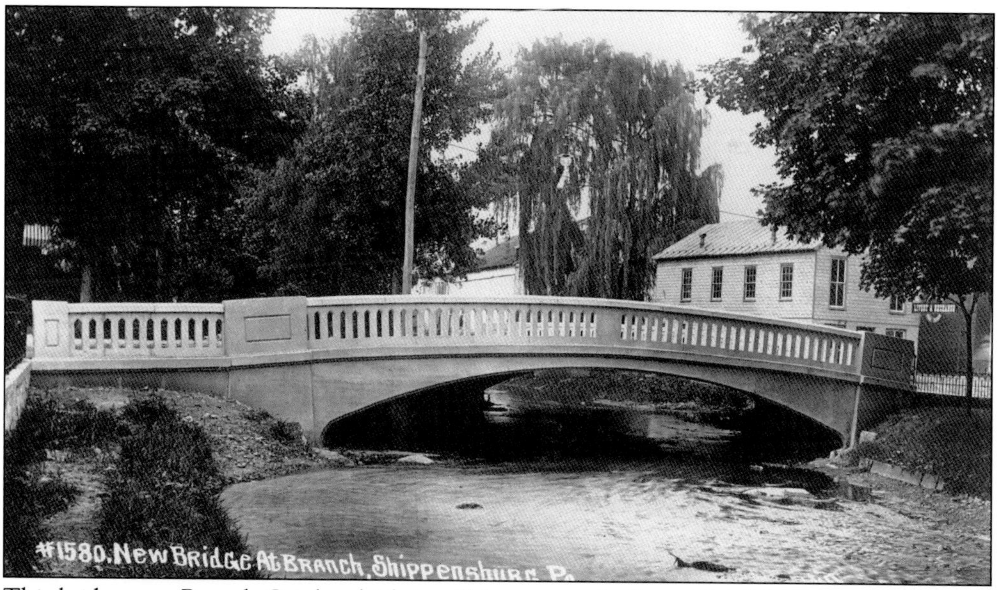

This bridge over Branch Creek, which is still in use, was built in 1911. There is an image of an Indian's head on the cement side rail of the bridge; it was originally called the Indian Head Bridge because the stream flowing under the bridge comes from Dykeman Spring, which was originally called Indian Head Spring.

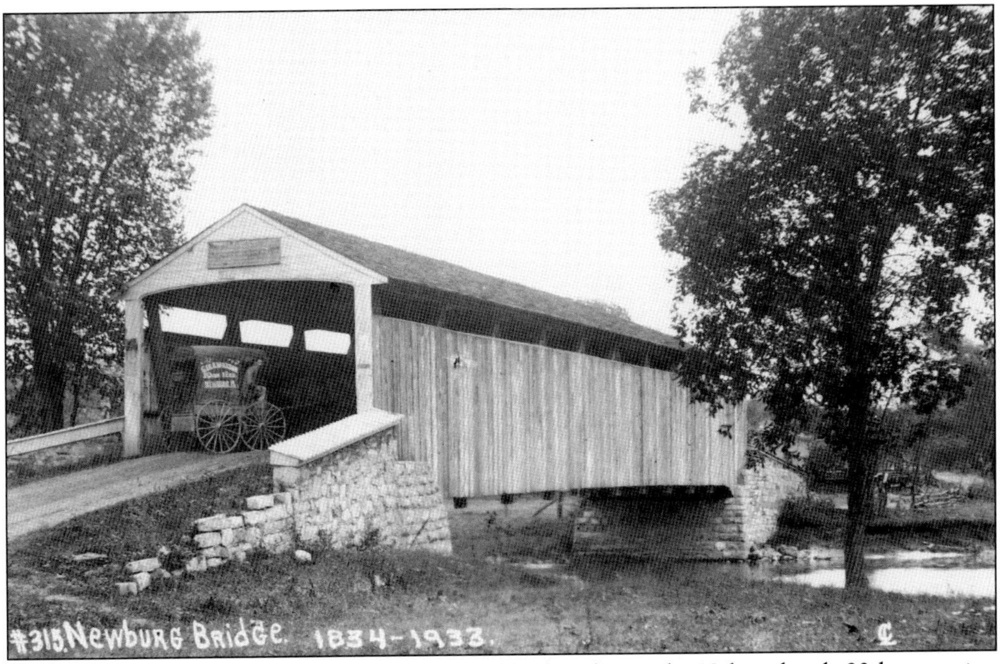

Shippensburg travelers frequently crossed covered bridges during the 19th and early 20th centuries. Only one such bridge remains in Cumberland County, but at one time there were more than 50. This one—the Newburg, or "Kats Cabin," Bridge—was built over the Conodoguinet Creek, midway between Newburg and Shippensburg. It was dismantled in 1938 and replaced with a steel span.

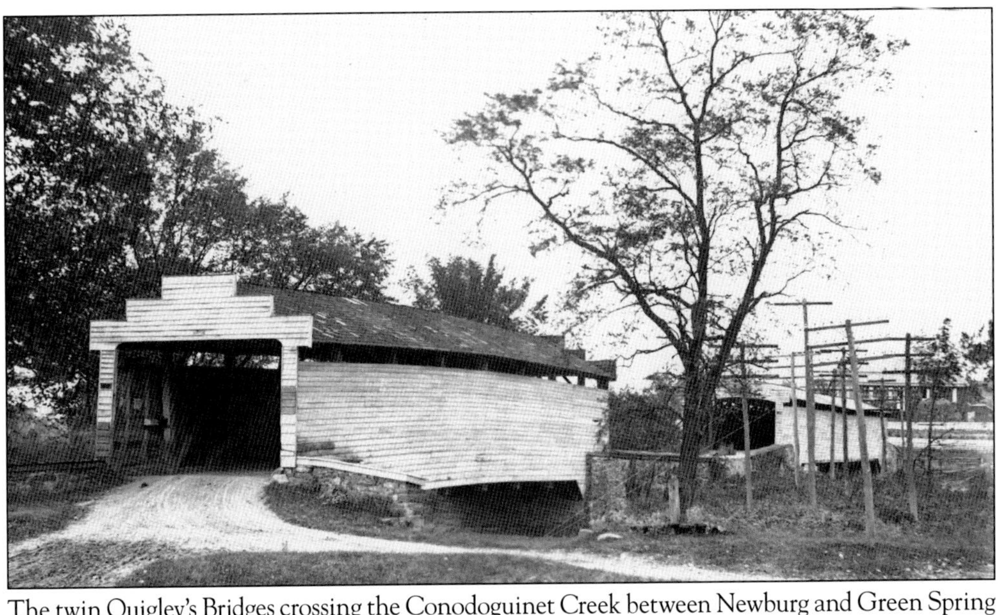

The twin Quigley's Bridges crossing the Conodoguinet Creek between Newburg and Green Spring in Hopewell Township were unique among covered bridges in the Shippensburg area. Surviving until 1947, they were replaced with two steel bridges, which are still in place. The first photograph Clyde Laughlin ever took was of these bridges.

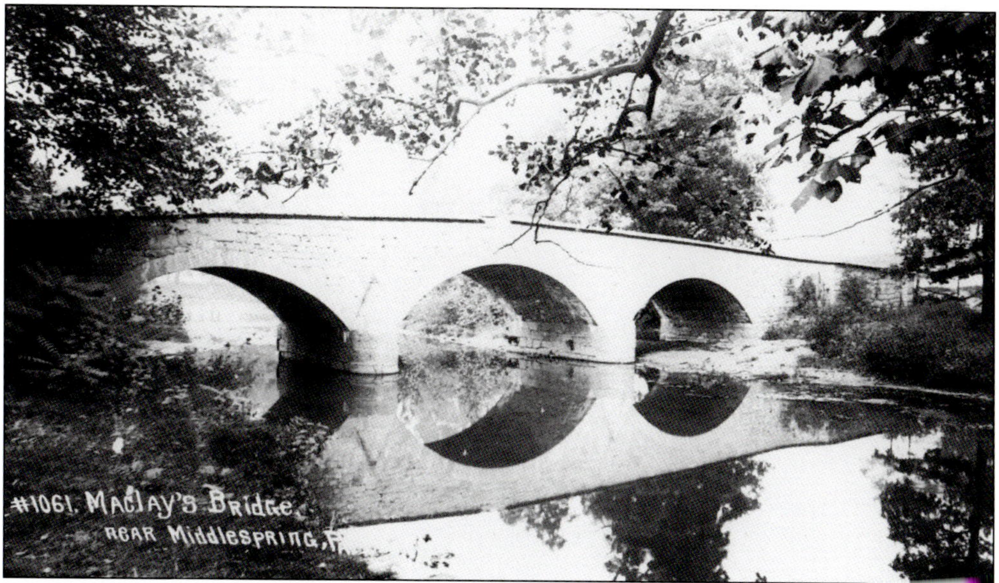

Maclay's Bridge is one of two stone-arch bridges that span Conodoguinet Creek near Middle Spring. The bridges, built in 1827 by Silas Harry, were named for the Maclay family, who operated a mill along the creek. Extensive repairs were made to this span in 2009.

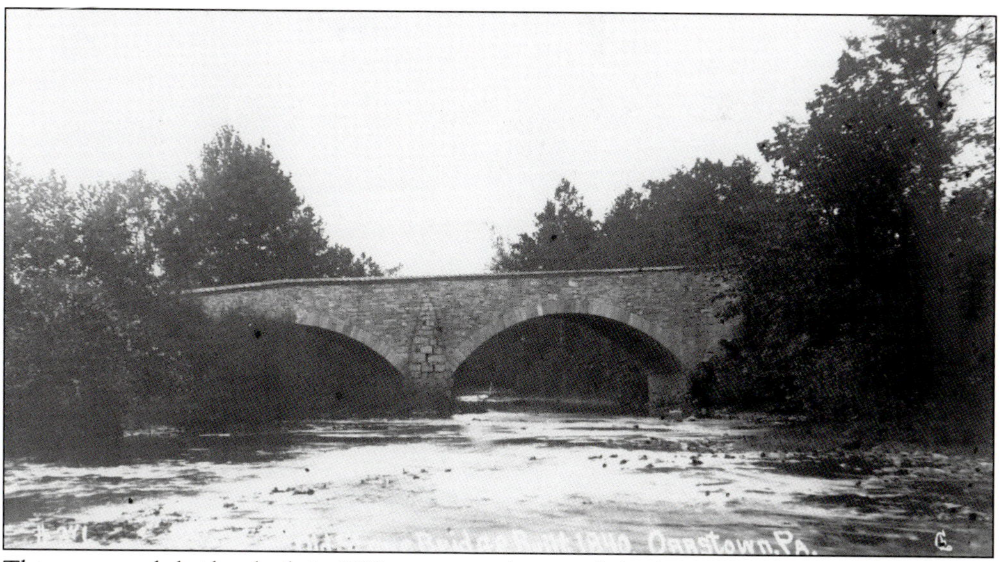

This stone-arch bridge, built in 1838, was one of two such bridges near Orrstown. One crossed Conodoguinet Creek on the road from Shippensburg to Roxbury, and the other crossed Herrons Run on the road to Shippensburg. They were both replaced in 1940 with bridges made of steel and concrete.

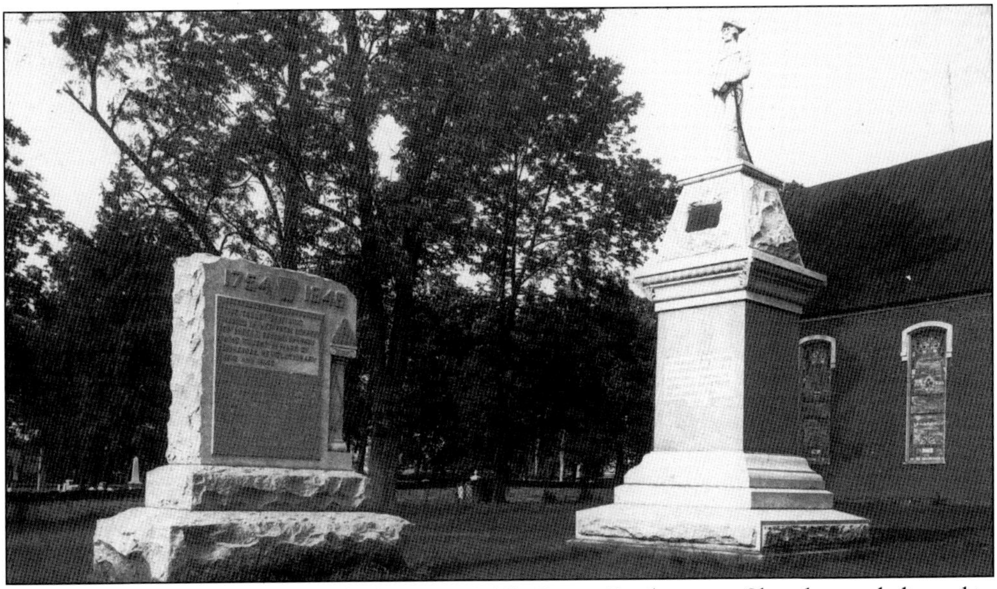

The Soldiers Monument, outside the historic Middle Spring Presbyterian Church, was dedicated in 1905 and commemorates veterans from the Middle Spring area who participated in wars between 1754 and 1846. The tablet to the left of the monument, erected in 1910, is inscribed with the names of 141 soldiers who served in the conflicts.

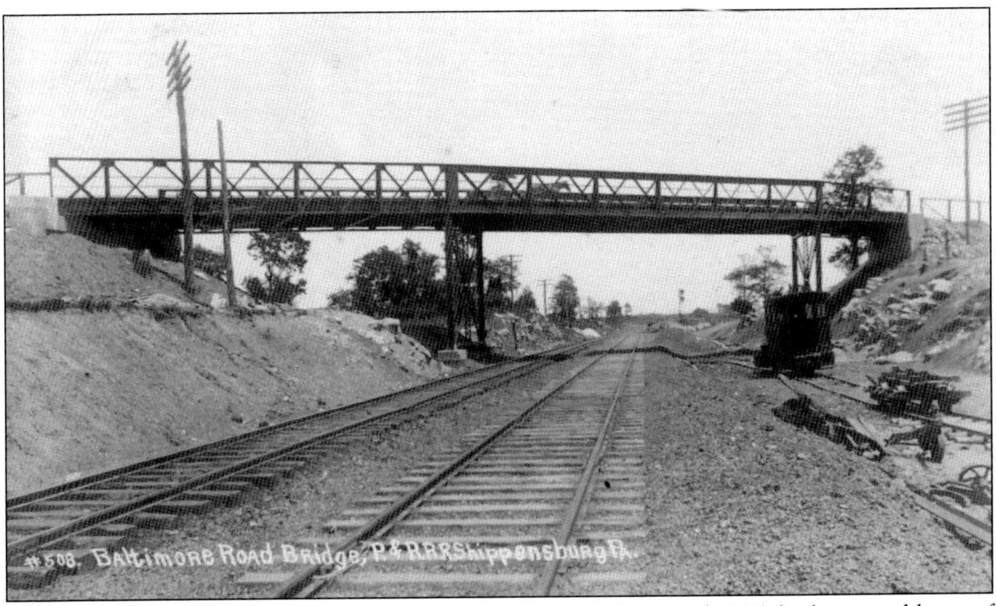

This wood-and-steel bridge over the Reading Railroad, built around 1905, had a posted limit of 12 tons, which posed a problem for modern fire trucks and other vehicles—which tend to weigh 20 tons or more—needing to cross. It was replaced in 1986 by a wider, stronger bridge made of reinforced concrete.

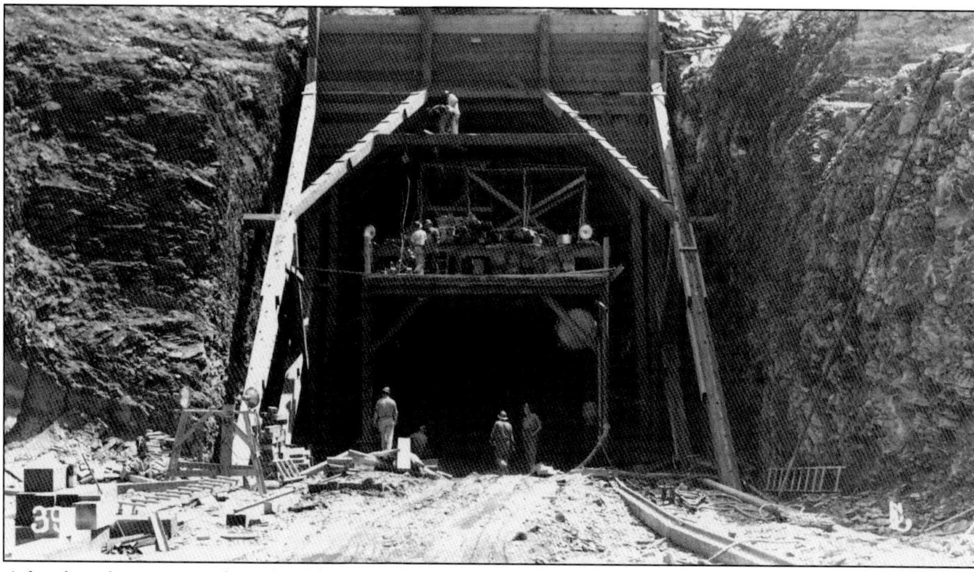

After breaking ground on October 27, 1938, work began to convert an unfinished railroad project, known as "Vanderbilt's Folly," into the Pennsylvania Turnpike. This Laughlin postcard, entitled "Work on Pa. Turnpike in Günter's Valley," shows work being done on the tunnel. Shippensburg was home to one of four field offices set up for the construction of the turnpike.

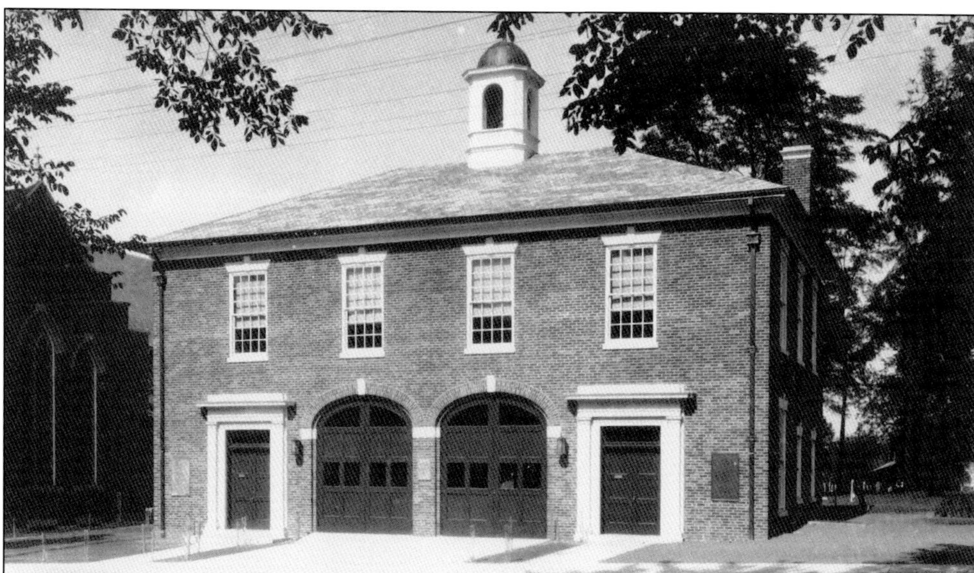

The Shippensburg Municipal Building was constructed in 1928. It originally housed borough offices, municipal police, and the Vigilant Hose Company. After the departure of the offices and the police, it became the home to only the Vigilant Hose Company, which provided the community with extensive and lovely Christmas decorations each year. In 2011, the fire company began building a new and much larger fire station along Walnut Bottom Road.

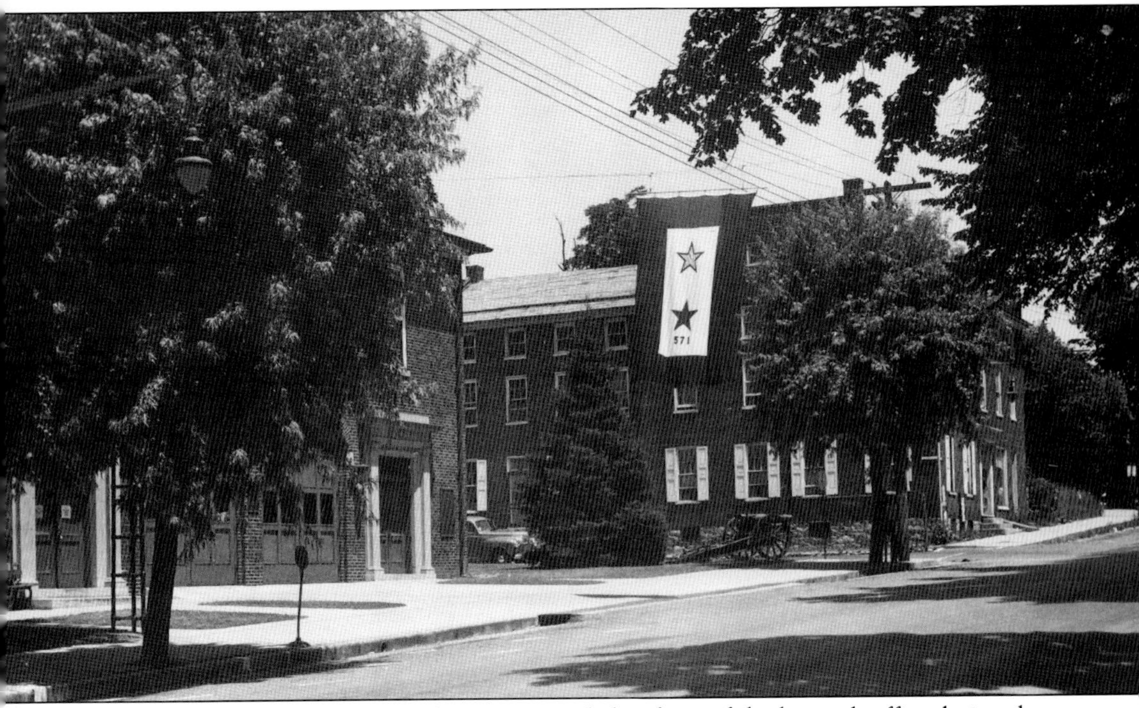

The World War Two Service Flag was suspended in front of the borough office during the war. The number 571 on the flag represents the number of men and women from the Shippensburg area who were serving in the armed forces at the time. A 150-millimeter German howitzer from World War I is visible in the center of the photograph at the corner of North Prince and East King Streets. The Martin Building is behind the howitzer.

Two

BUSINESSES, MANUFACTURING, AND TRANSPORTATION

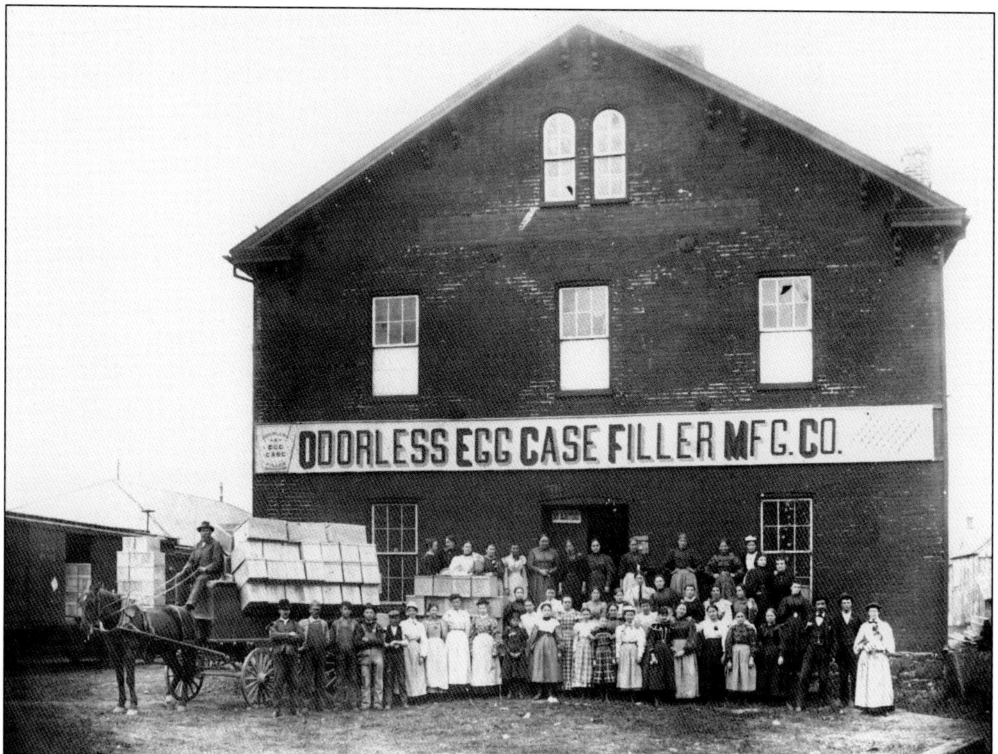

This 1898 photograph by D.C. Moll depicts the Odorless Egg Case Filler Manufacturing Company, which was located on South Earl Street. Workers assembled "fillers"—inside packing of firm strawboard placed in empty crates in preparation for shipping eggs. In 1906, the business was destroyed by fire, leaving "scores of female help" without employment, according to the February 13, 1906, *Shippensburg News*.

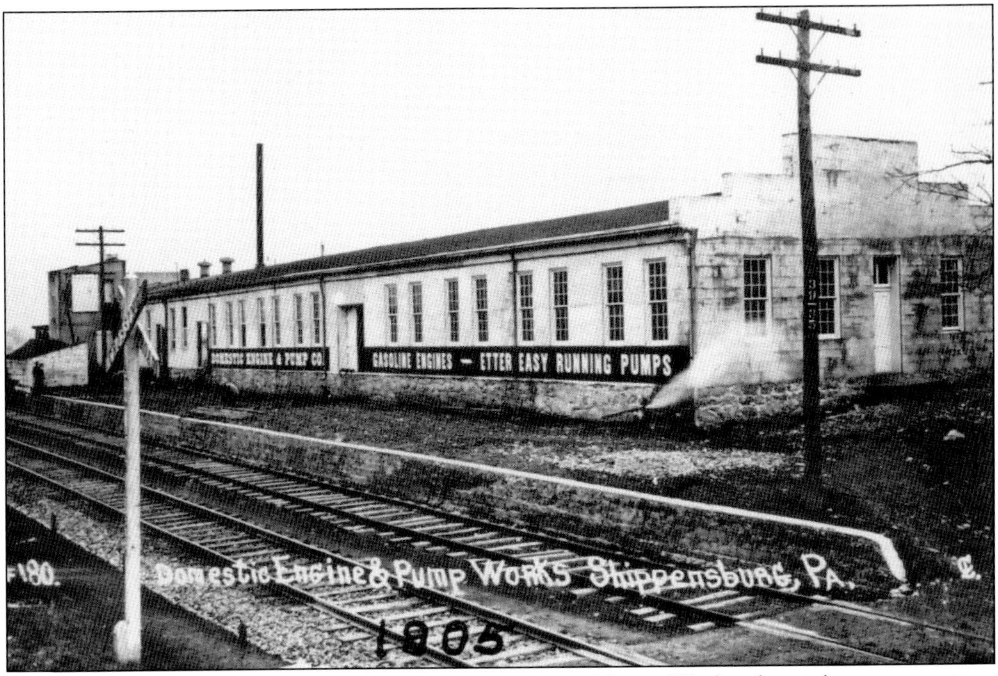

This Laughlin photograph shows the Domestic Engine and Pump Works when it began operations in 1905. The Pennsylvania Railroad passed by the plant. The Cumberland Valley State Normal School (now Shippensburg University) campus was west of this plant. In 1966, the Domestic Pump and Manufacturing Company, as it was then known, employed nearly 200 workers in the manufacturing of domestic and industrial pumps.

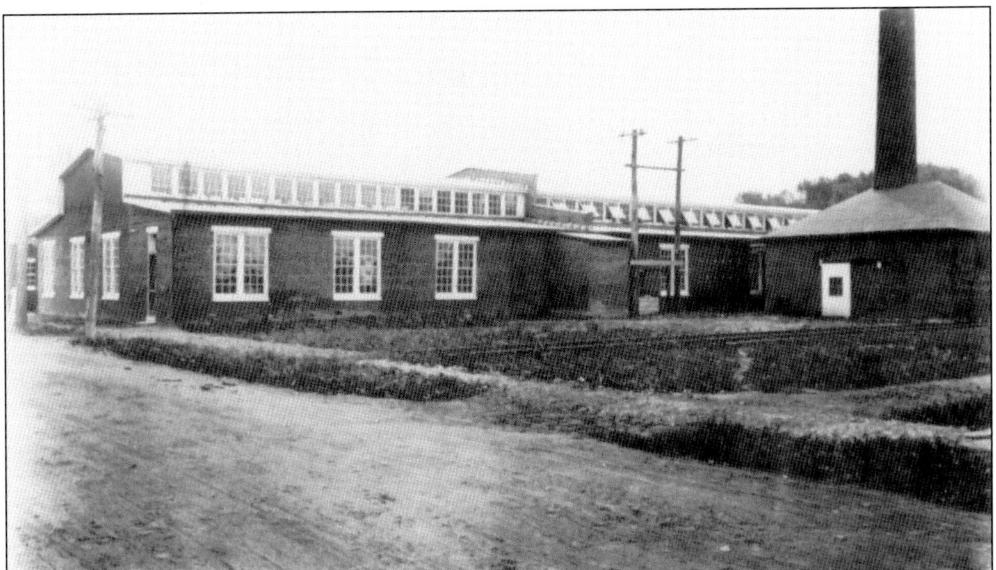

This 1922 photograph shows the Piedmont Silk Plant on North Seneca Street. It was shut down in the early 1930s because of the Great Depression. The Richard Textile plant later occupied this site.

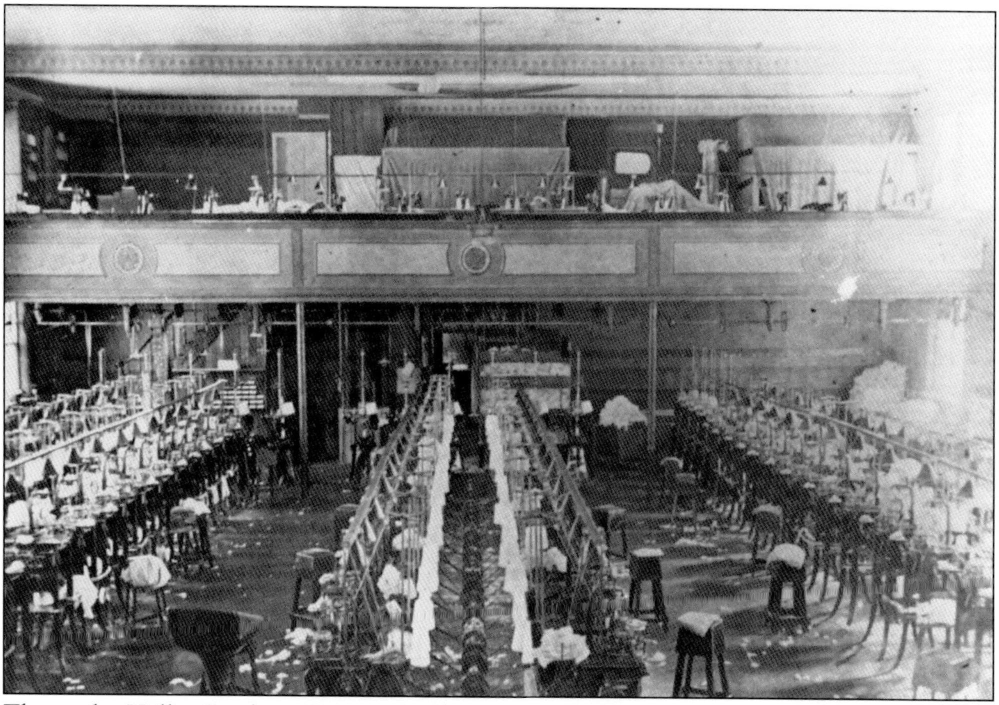

This is the Hollar Stocking Knitting Mill around 1914. It was on the second floor of the Old Opera House at 63 East King Street. Frank Hollar Sr. ran it from before 1900 until 1918. Among other items, it produced men's white socks that were shipped to Reading to be dyed black.

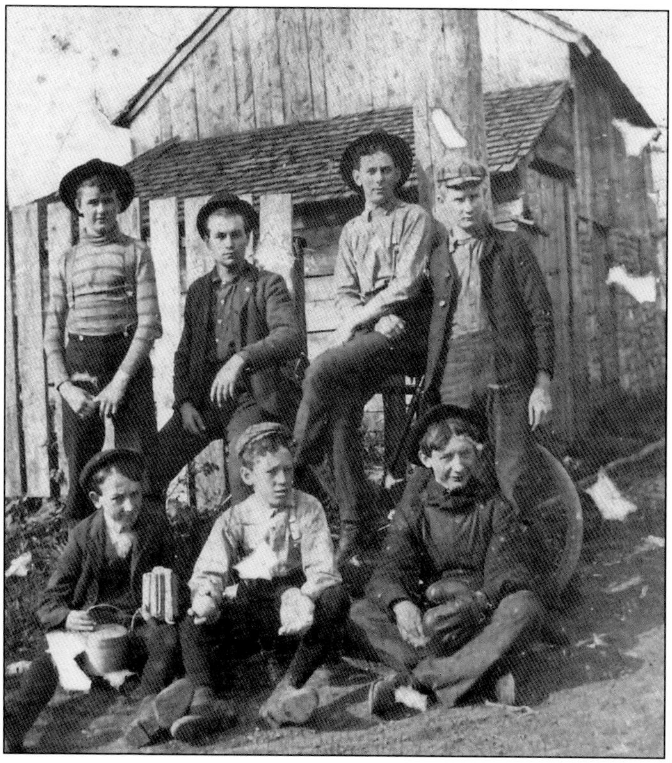

The young men in this 1902 photograph were responsible for packing the white stockings into crates for shipment to Reading. The firm dyeing the stockings sent them back wet to Shippensburg. These same "packing boys" unloaded the bags of wet stockings and stretched them over thin boards. After drying and "fancy stitching" by young girls, the stockings were loaded into crates by these same boys for shipment.

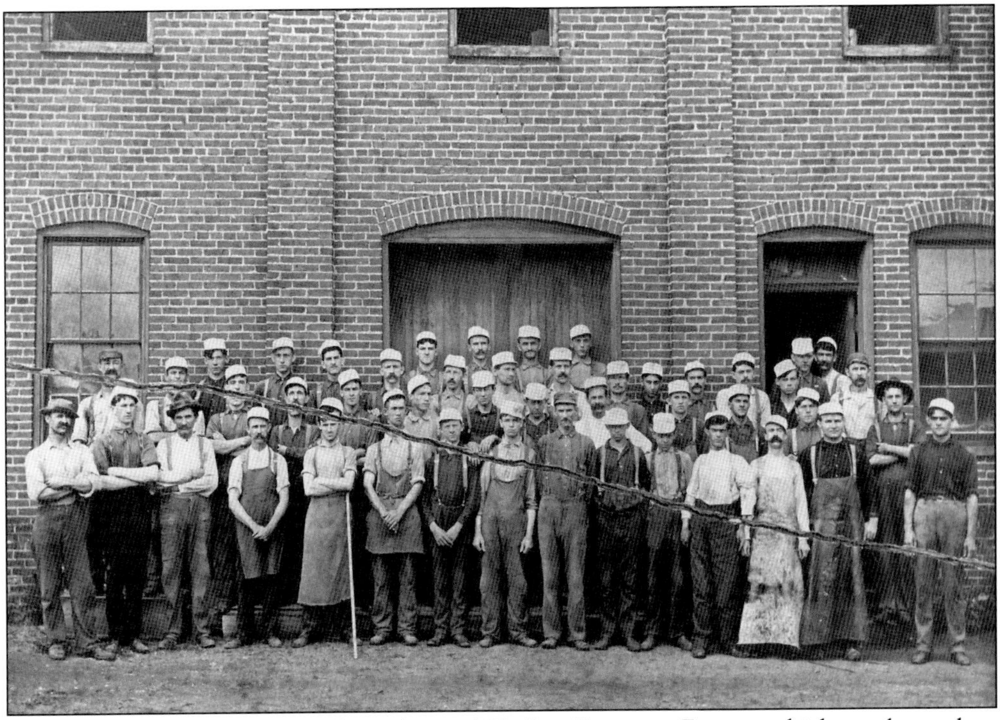

This is the 1904 workforce for the Boher and Phillips Furniture Factory, which was located on the east side of South Earl Street, beyond Orange Street. John E. Boher and Clifford Phillips set up the factory where these men worked. The plant went out of operation in 1923 and was torn down. Many of the skilled workers laid off because of this closing found work with the Peerless Furniture Factory on Lurgan Avenue.

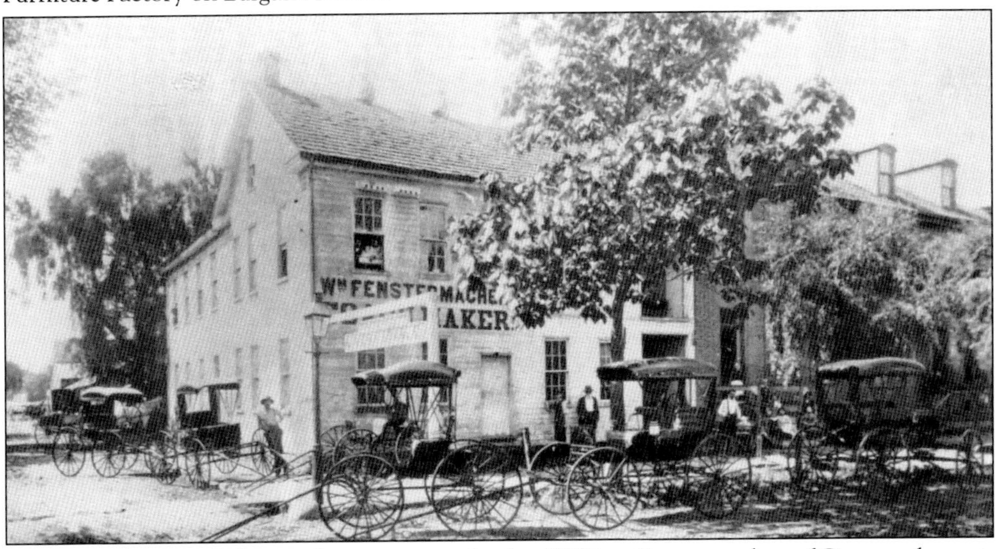

This 1884 photograph depicts the carriage works that William Fenstermacher, of German descent, established in 1867 on the southwest corner of West King and Fayette Streets. The man at left, leaning on a buggy, is a Mr. Knoder, the blacksmith at the shop. Wearing a hat and sporting a beard, Fenstermacher, who ran the shop, is pictured between the two buggies on the right. He fathered 13 children, four of whom grew to maturity.

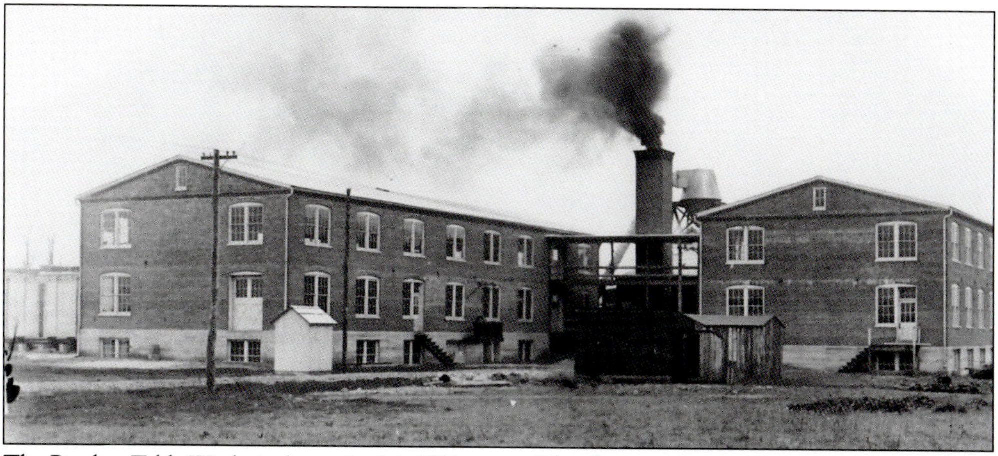

The Peerless Table Works is shown in this 1911 image. The plant was located between Lurgan Avenue and the Reading Railroad tracks, about a block north of West King Street. The plant produced household furniture, but not the stuffed or upholstered type. In July 1966, Affiliated Industries Inc., makers of counters and showcases, bought the plant and set up its business there.

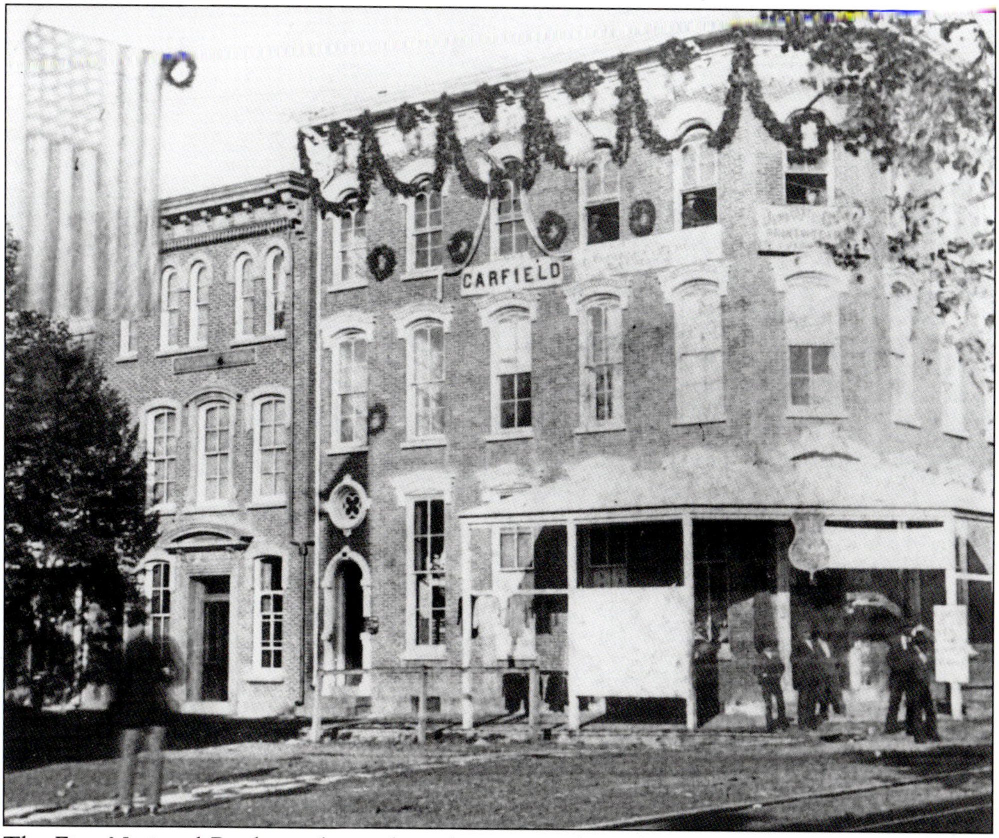

The First National Bank was located on the corner of North Earl and West King Streets. At the time of this photograph (1881), it was draped in mourning for Pres. James A. Garfield, who had been assassinated by madman Charles J. Guiteau. In 1920, the bank consolidated the two buildings. In 2011, this building was occupied by Liberty Tax Service on the lower floor and other tenants on the upper floors.

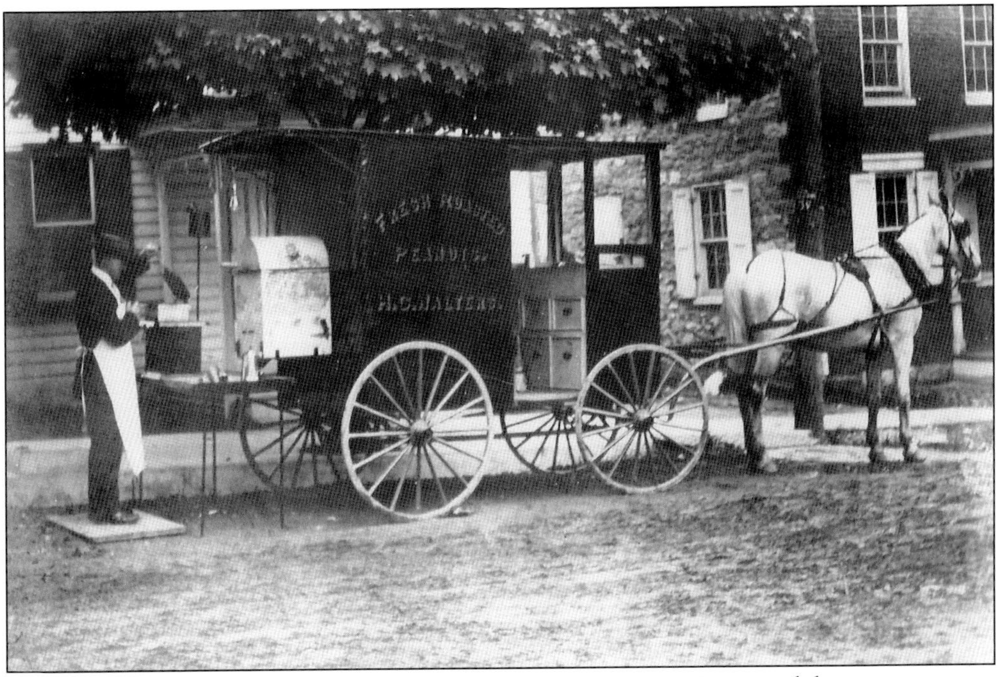

Harry "Had" C. Walters stands in front of his home at 337 East King Street with his peanut wagon. He roasted the peanuts with the shells on as he drove from one spot to another on King Street on summer evenings. Walters operated the peanut wagon from about 1910 until the 1930s.

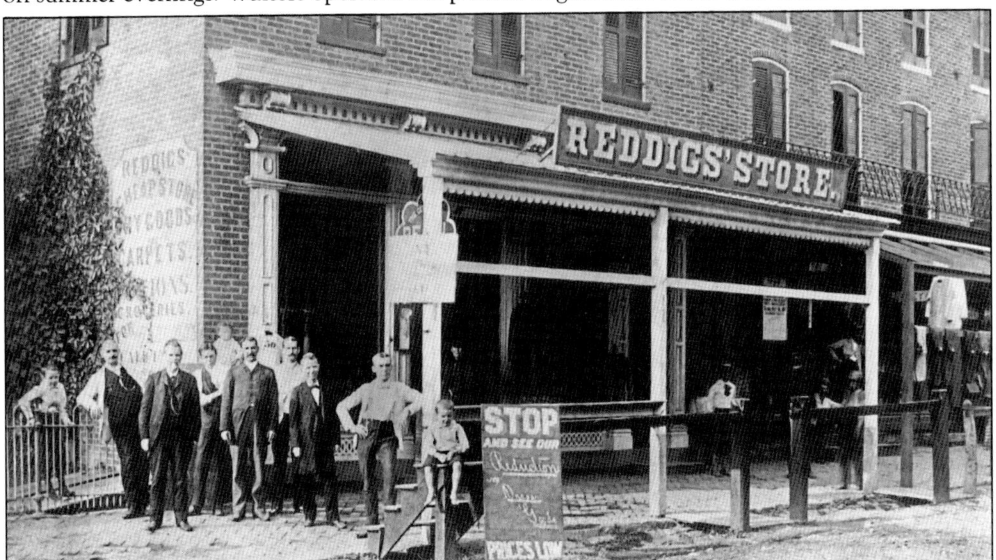

This is an 1890 photograph of Reddig's Store, located on the northeast corner of East King and North Earl Streets. The store was opened by Joseph Nevin. In 1851, he offered Jeremiah Reddig and his brother, Jacob, a partnership in his dry goods business. The brothers accepted and bought out Nevin's interest six years later. In 1928, G.C. Murphy purchased the building. After the closing of Murphy's, the building was occupied for a time by Dollar General; it is now the home of the Cumberland Valley Animal Shelter Thrift Store. All of those pictured are members of the extended Reddig family.

J.L. Hockersmith and Son Grocery, located at 14 West King Street, specialized in groceries and Queensware, a brand of tin ware used for cooking. Inside the door on the left was the Ben Washington Barber Shop. In the early 1900s, a third story was added to this building. The Hockersmith Grocery continued to do business until September 28, 1974, when "Ted" Hockersmith, grandson of the founder, closed the store and retired.

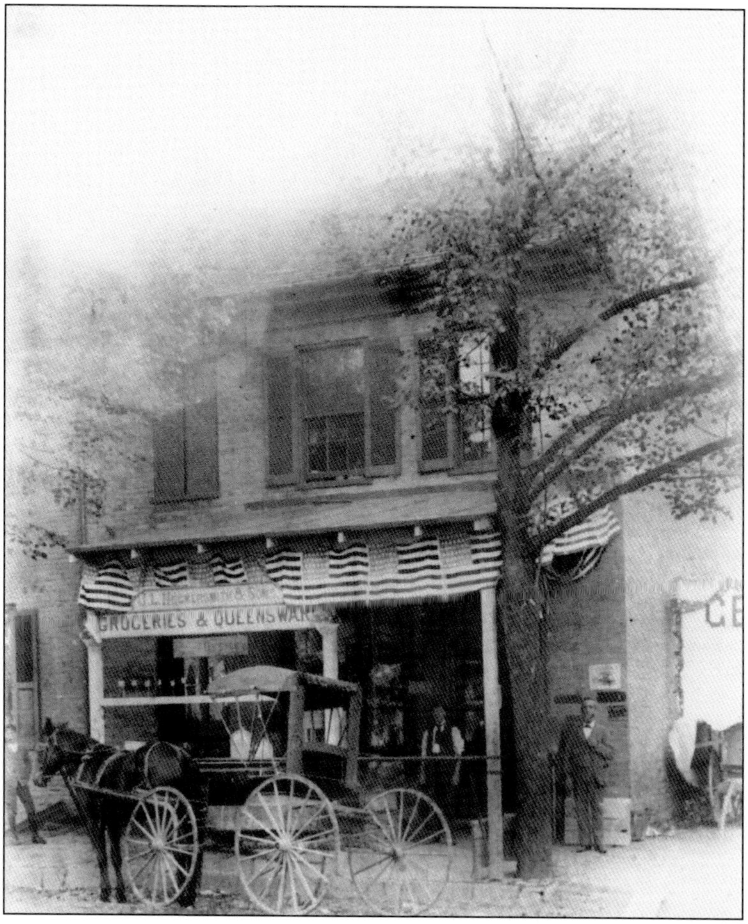

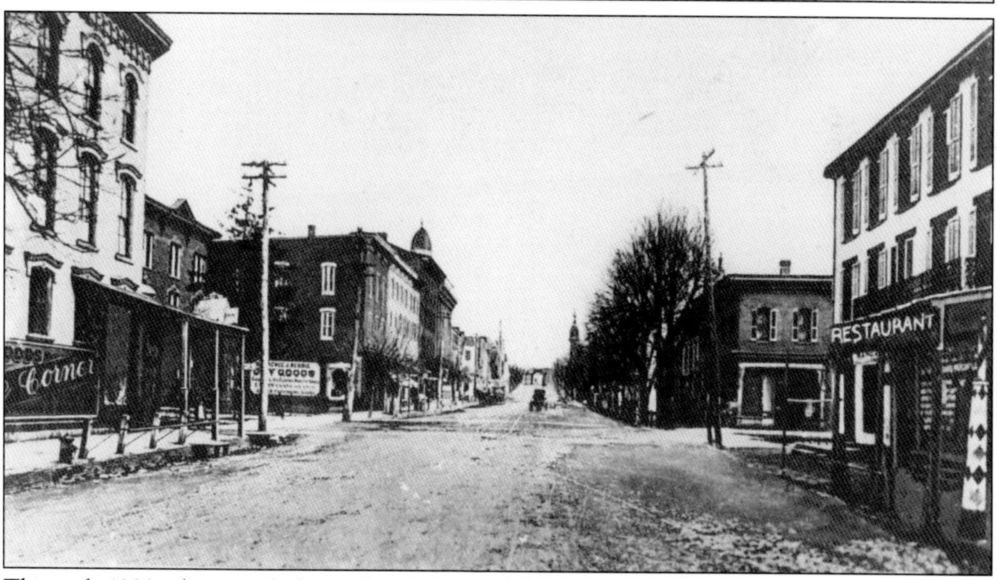

This early-1900s photograph shows King Street and the public square facing east. The church steeple at left belongs to the Methodist church, while the one at right is on the Presbyterian church.

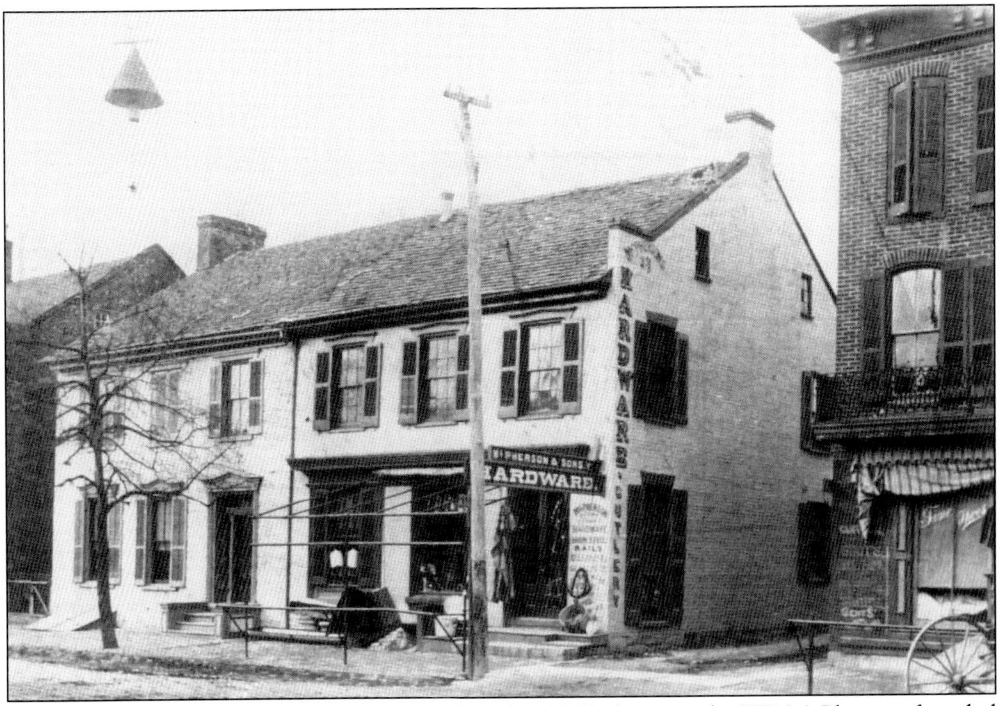

The McPherson Hardware Store is featured in this 1905 photograph. J.W. McPherson founded the store at this location, 35 West King Street, in 1856. While the front remains the same, the store has expanded to the rear, to the site of the former Benders' Tavern. The store now operates as Pague & Fegan Hardware. It may be the oldest hardware store still operating in the state of Pennsylvania.

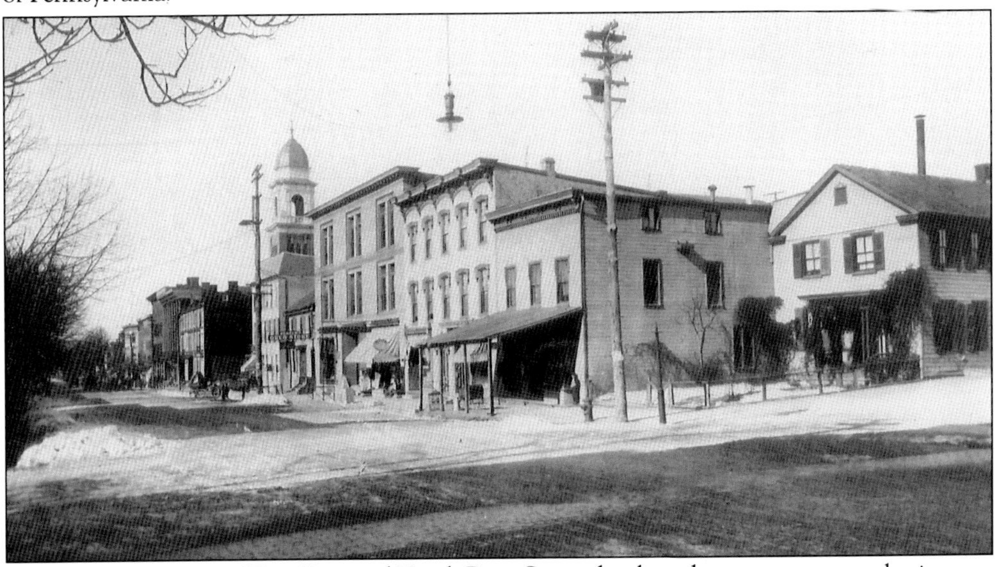

The northwest corner of East King and North Penn Streets has been home to numerous businesses. In the early 1900s, around the time of this photograph, it was called Duke's Corner; the Duke family lived in the house set back from the corner. In 1916, Frank Hollar bought and restructured the entire corner, but he sold the building to make way for the post office in 1927. Orrstown Bank now occupies the site.

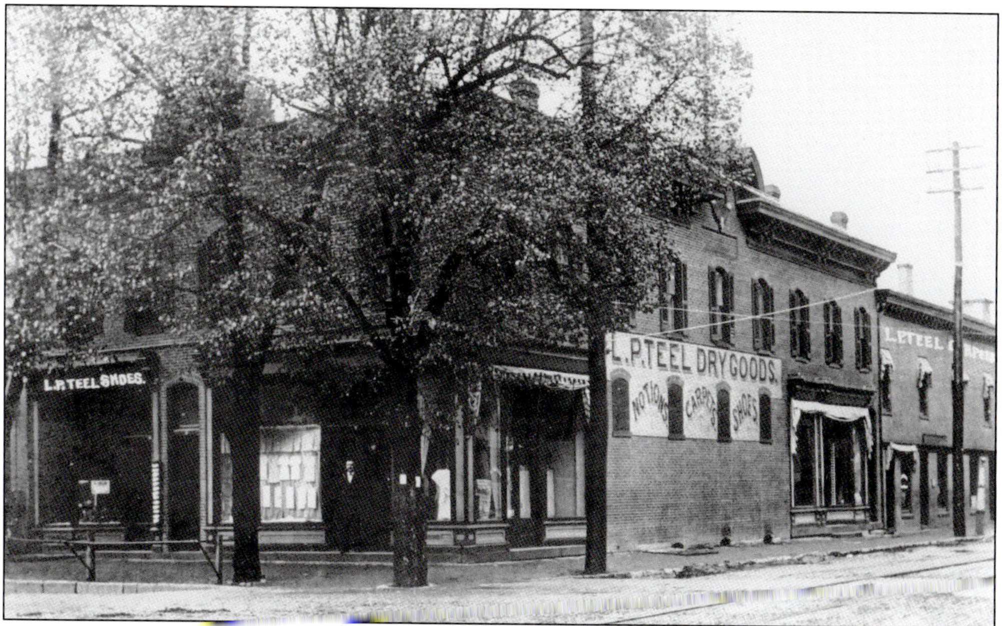

This 1913 photograph shows that the southeast corner of the square was occupied by three stores, all of which were owned by L.P. Teel: a shoe store, a dry goods store, and a carpet store. Teel is standing left of center in the photograph.

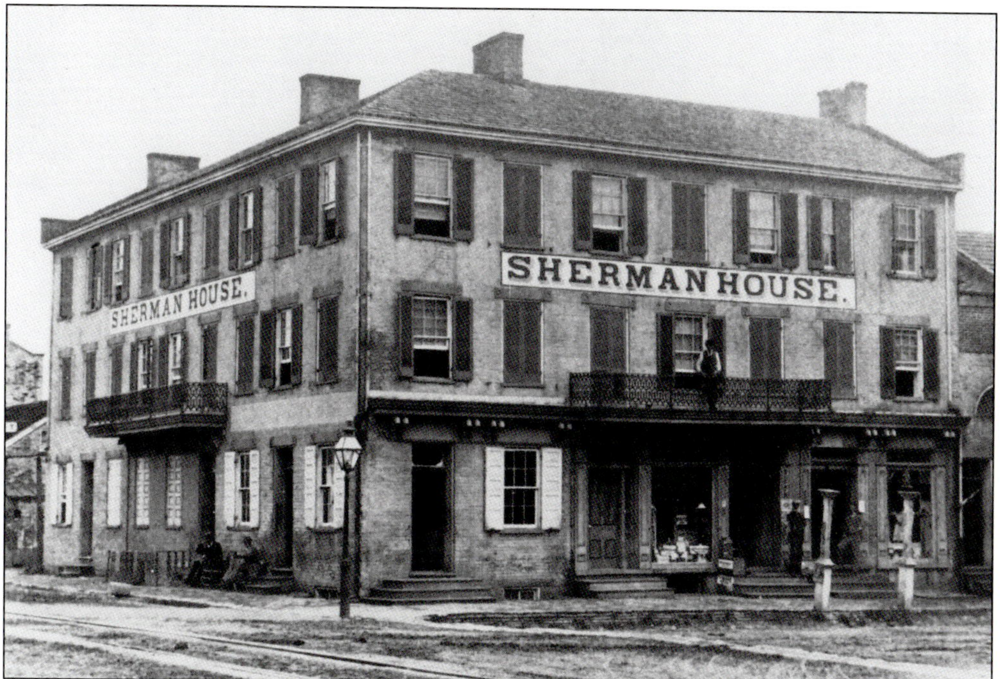

The Hotel Sherman, or the Sherman House, was located on the corner of South Earl and West King Streets. Built in 1839, it was first called the Union Hotel. In late June 1863, upon hearing of the Confederate advance towards Shippensburg, volunteer citizens hurriedly painted over "Union" and renamed it Sherman to avoid antagonizing the invaders. Fortunately, General Sherman's marches had not yet happened—or the name change might have made things worse!

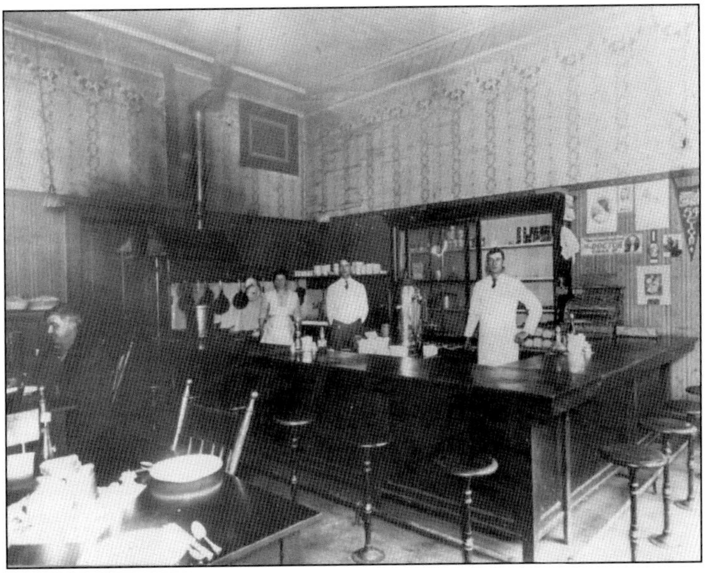

This c. 1920 photograph shows the inside of the Sherman Hotel Restaurant. To the left of the restaurant was the dining room, where fancy banquets were held for as many as 60 people. Also on the ground level was the lobby, where salesmen displayed their wares for Shippensburg's retailers.

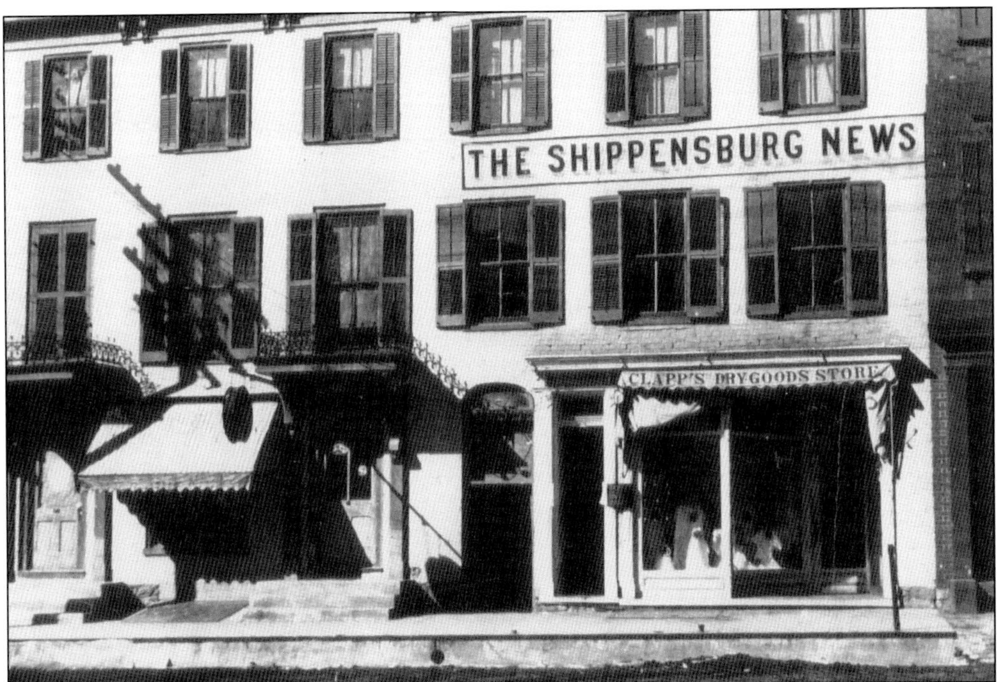

The *Weekly News* was founded on April 26, 1844, and became the *Shippensburg News* (the organization's building is pictured) in 1850. In 1927, it was purchased by Ralph T. and Elmer Wolfrom. Later that year, they bought the *Shippensburg Chronicle*, a rival newspaper located on South Earl Street, and merged the two papers into the *News-Chronicle*. The office and plant were moved several miles north along Route 11, but recently the office was returned to Shippensburg. The paper is still published twice weekly.

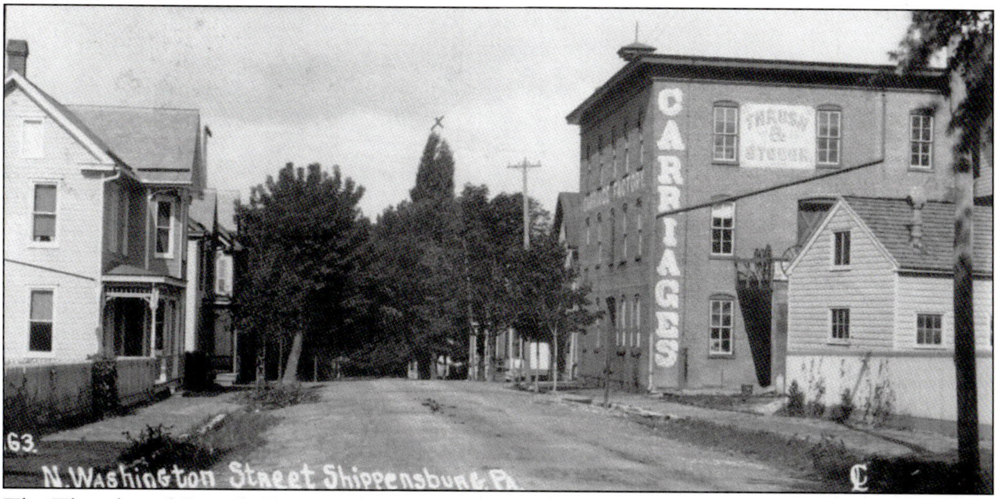

The Thrush and Stough Carriage factory was located at 11–13 North Washington Street. When the business first opened in 1854, it was known as Walburn and Thrush. The building, erected in 1875, was called the "Brick Shop"—in 1889, it became Thrush and Stough. All kinds of carriages, from simple to luxury models, were manufactured here. The business closed in 1918, but the first floor now houses the Wash Tub Laundromat.

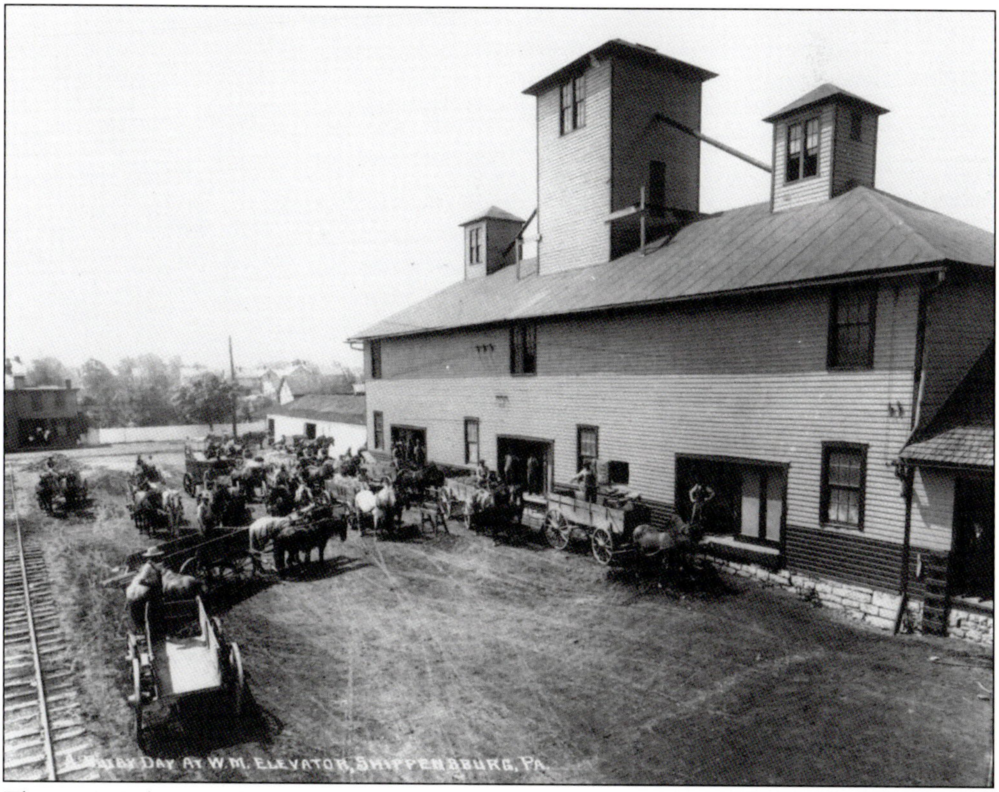

This c. 1900 photograph shows the Western Maryland Railroad Elevator and Warehouse on North Earl and Fort Streets. Farmers are bringing in wagonloads of corn and grain in canvas bags to be weighed. This became the People's Warehouse in 1935, and it closed in 1968. It burned down on the morning of July 8, 1974.

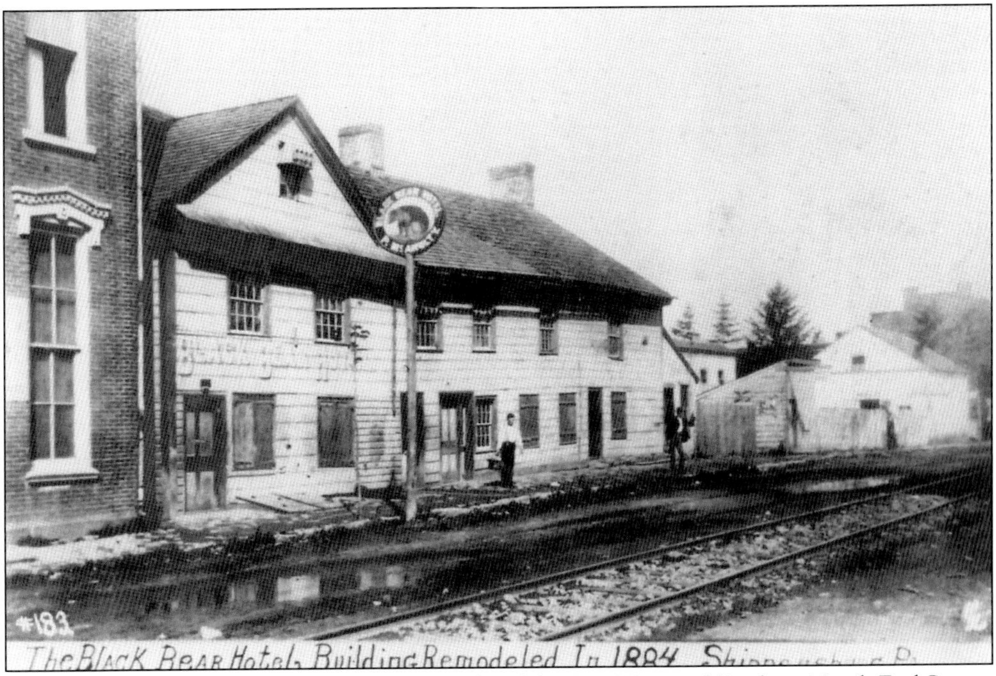

This is the Black Bear Hotel, located to the right of the First National Bank on North Earl Street, as it appeared in 1884. It had a reputation for attracting a very rowdy clientele. The building was torn down in 1961, and the First National Bank built its drive-up annex and parking lot on the same location in the following year.

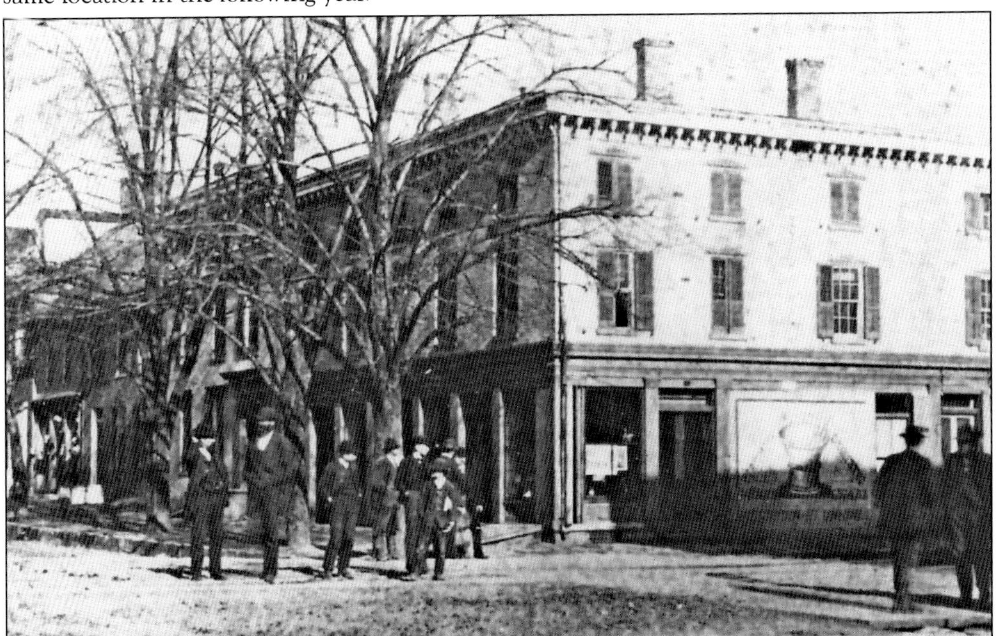

This 1884 photograph by H. Frank Beidel shows the southeast corner of the square. The log structure formerly in this space was torn down in 1884 to make way for the building pictured here. W.T.S. Jamison built the Bazaar, which occupied this location until the early 1900s. It is currently the location of an ATM owned by the Pennsylvania State Employees' Credit Union (PSECU).

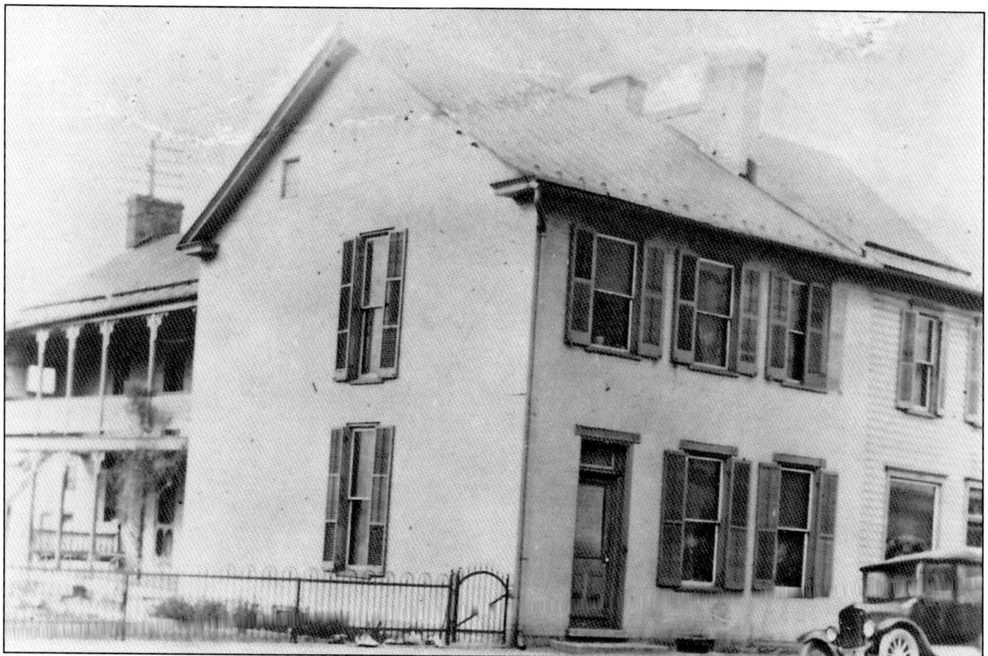

Known as the Mansion House, this building was the residence of widow Claronna Catherine Stumbaugh in the late 1920s, around the time this picture was taken. In earlier times, the Mansion House provided lodging and served meals. Before Prohibition, it also served alcoholic beverages. It was torn down in 1935 to make way for the Hub City Club at 42 South Earl Street.

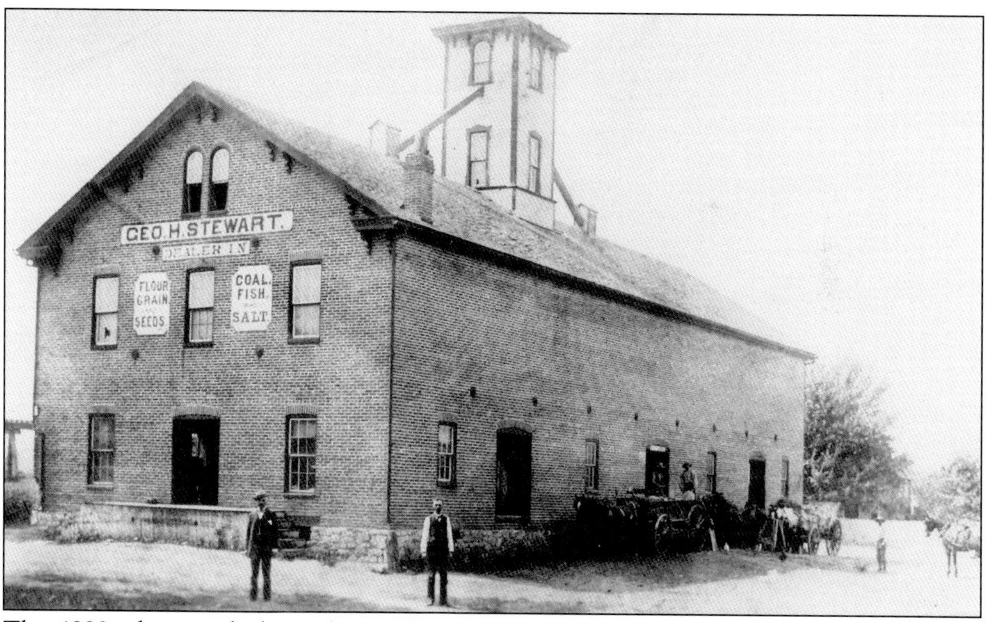

This 1880s photograph shows the warehouse of George H. Stewart. He is listed as a dealer in flour, grain, seeds, coal, fish, and salt. Its east end faced the Cumberland Valley Railroad tracks, while its west end fronted Seneca Street. It was later converted into the Odorless Egg Crate Filler Manufacturing Company. Stewart is pictured at left, W.A. Nickles is in the center, and Andrew Gross is in the Conestoga wagon. The man at far right is unidentified.

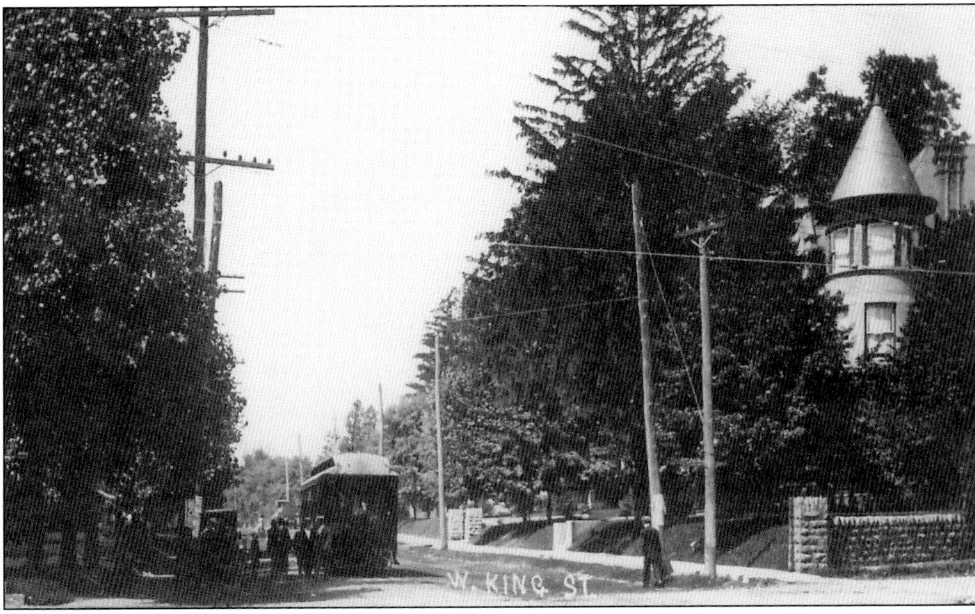

In this 1920 image, car No. 30 of the Chambersburg-Shippensburg Railroad is halted at its terminal on West King Street at the Morris Street intersection. Service to Shippensburg was added in June 1914 and continued until November 1925, when the line went out of business.

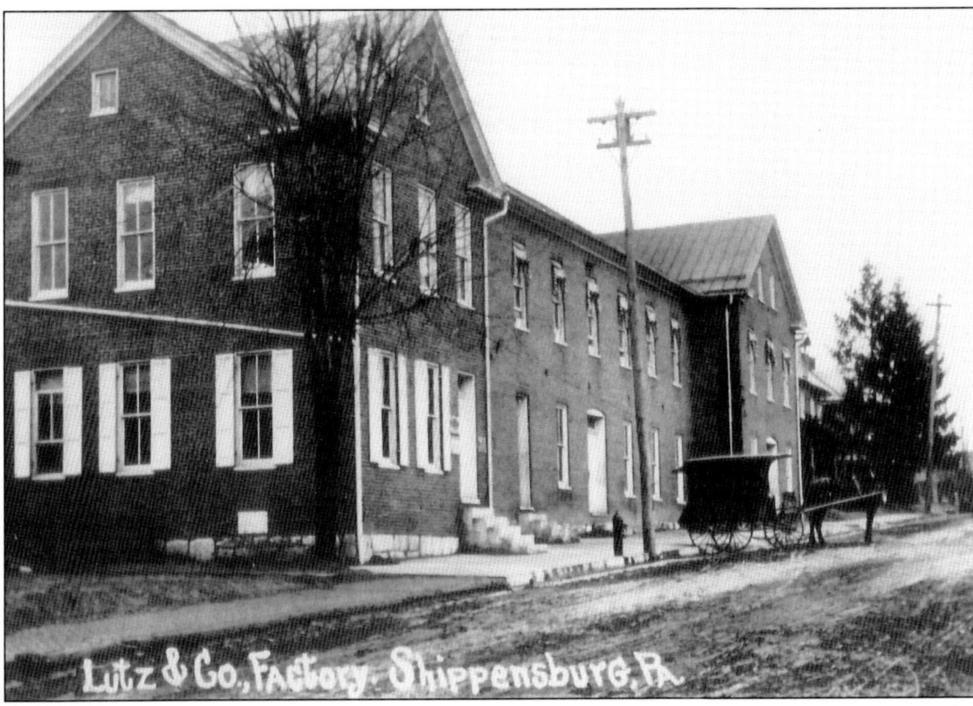

Lutz & Co., makers of men's pants and overalls, was located at 105 South Prince Street in this photograph from about 1907. It farmed out work to peoples' homes, and this photograph seems to be showing piecework being either loaded onto or unloaded from the wagon. By 1923, the company was known as Penn Pants Company. After the pants factory moved in 1937, John Hosfeld bought the building and converted it into apartments.

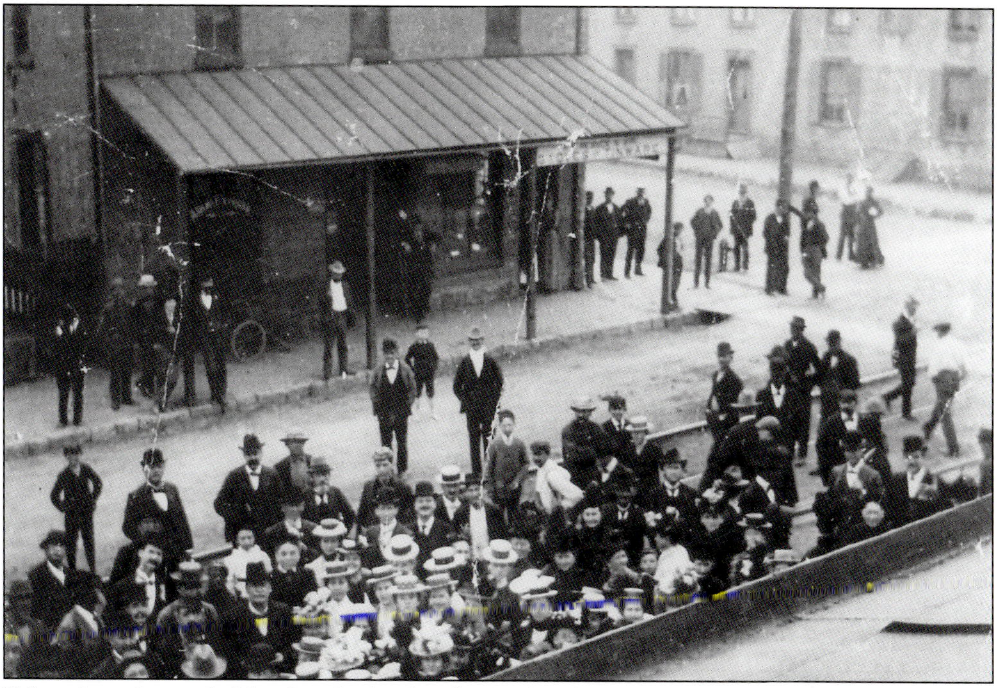

Taken from the roof of the Cumberland Valley Railroad passenger station, this 1896 photograph shows passengers waiting for the train. The station was located at the intersection of South Earl Street and West Orange Street. The building with the roofed front was occupied by Earl Rebuck's Tin Shop and the Adams Express Agency. Around 1904, it housed the Bijou Theatre on the second floor and a billiard hall on the street level; it is now occupied by Shippen Cleaners.

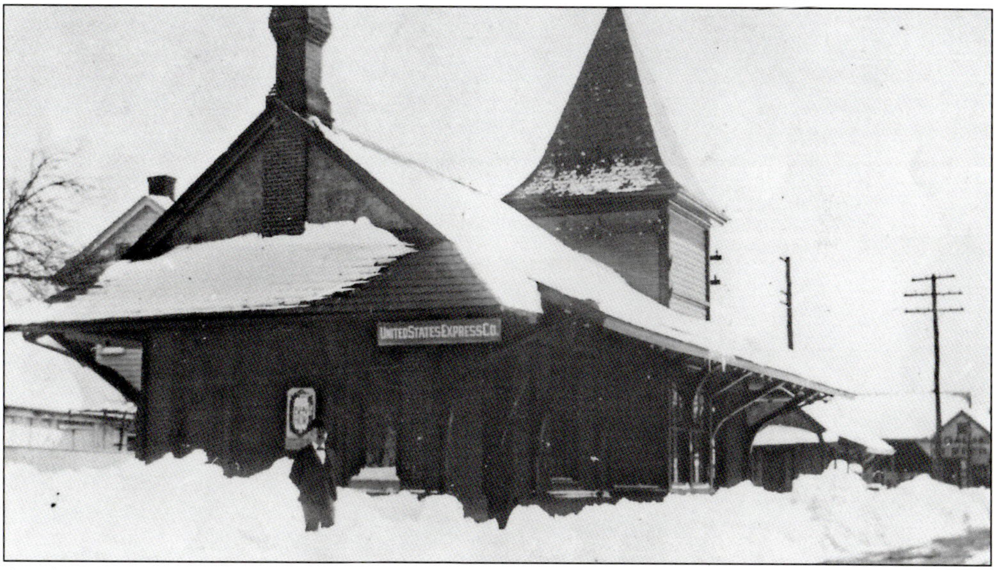

On the south side of West King Street, at the intersection with North Fayette Street, the Western Maryland Railroad built this passenger station in 1886. Shortly thereafter, the Philadelphia & Reading Railway extended its tracks to this station from its South Penn Street terminal, and both railroads used the station. This photograph dates from 1901. The Shippensburg Public Library moved into this building in 1937, paying a rent of $10 per month. It was torn down in 1958.

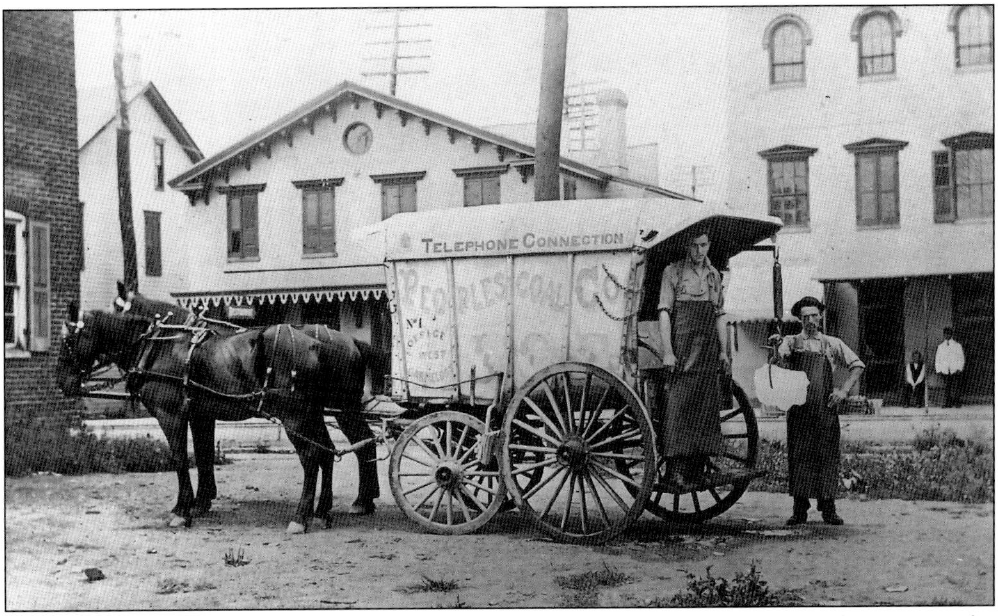

The Peoples' Coal and Ice Company wagon is shown in this photograph from about 1917. The location is South Earl Street. The building with the round window was the Cumberland Valley Railroad's passenger station until 1886, when it was replaced by a new structure at South Earl and West Orange Streets. The man standing on the wagon is W. Albert "Baldy" Clark, and the man holding the block of ice is believed to be Herbert Pechart.

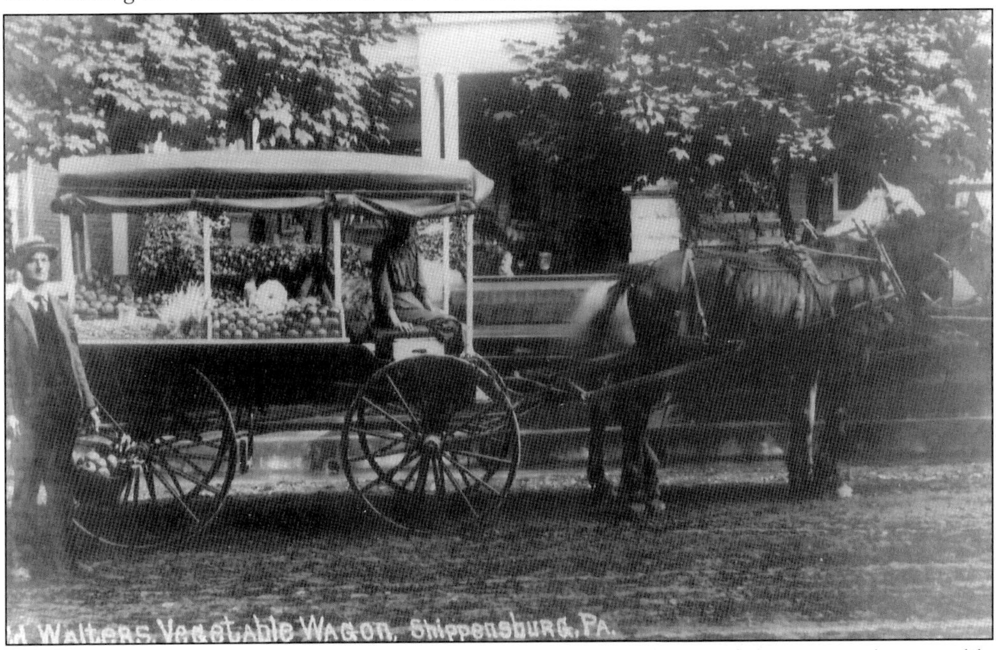

This 1910 photograph by Clyde Laughlin shows Edward D. Walters with his two-mule vegetable vending wagon in front of the Frank Hollar Mansion (now an apartment house) on East King Street. Walters hired young boys to help man his wagon, paying them 10¢ an hour for evenings and 50¢ for all day on Saturday. A number of students at the Normal School worked for Walters to help earn money to pay for their expenses.

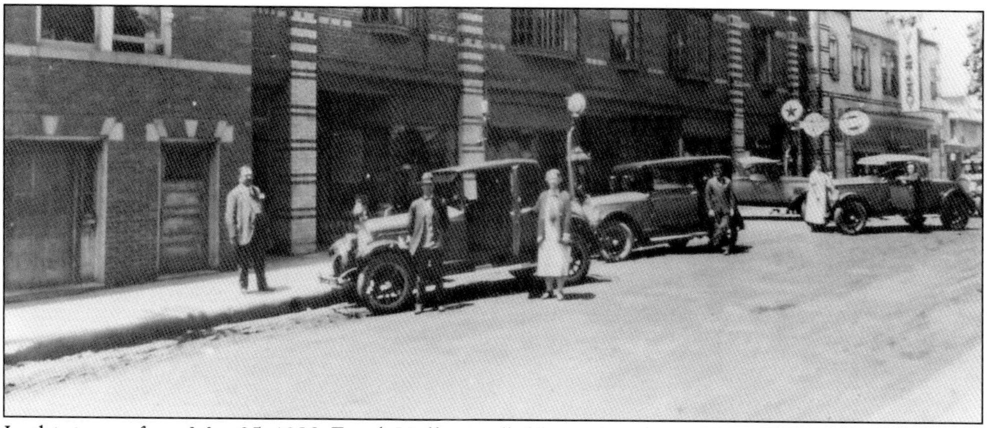

In this image from May 25, 1928, Frank Hollar Sr. (left) stands in front of the Hollar Garage at 6–10 North Penn Street. Farther up the street is the Victory Theatre, which Hollar built in 1920.

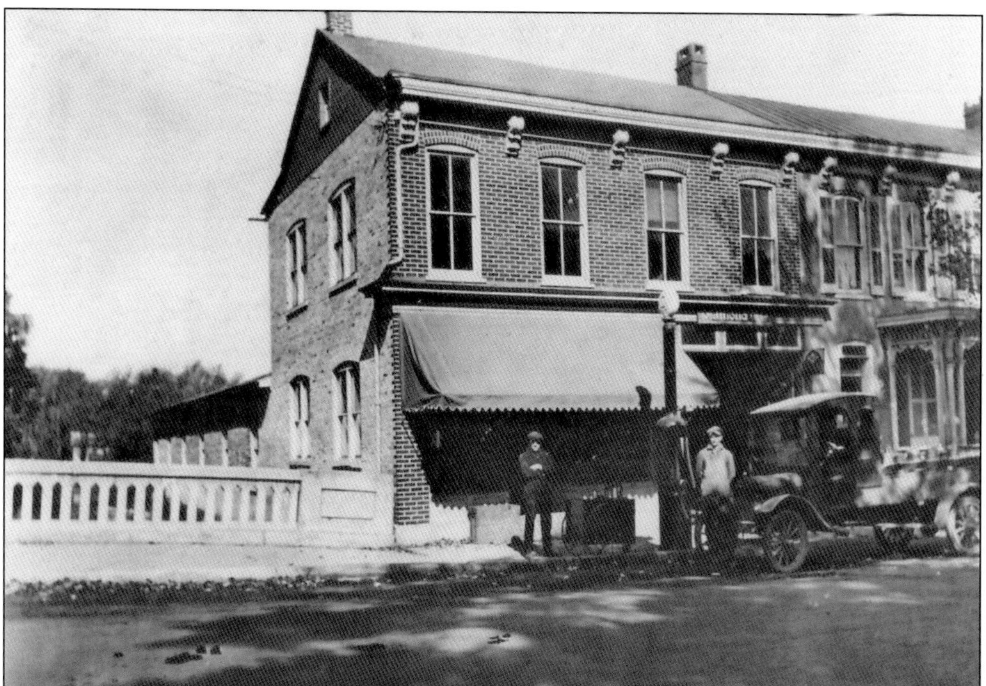

This 1930 photograph shows Hall's Garage, located at 69–71 West King Street, next to the Branch Creek Bridge. Prior to this date, it was the location of Goodhart's Livery Stable .The man on the left is believed to be the owner, Arthur Frank Hall. The truck in front is a 1925 Model T Ford.

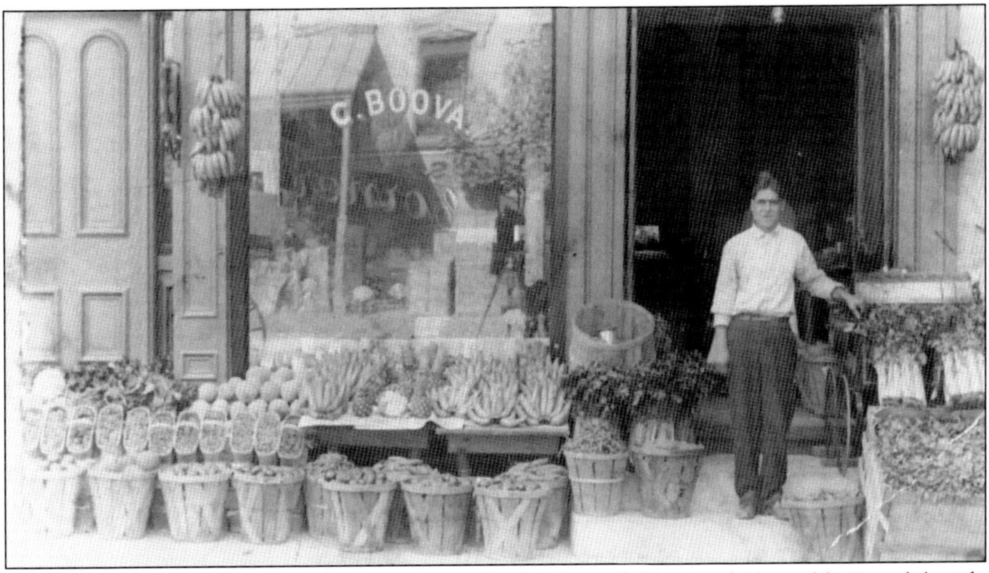

A common fixture on West King Street was Charley Boova's Fruit and Vegetable Stand, beside the Hotel Sherman. This c. 1913 photograph was taken by A.S. Goodhart.

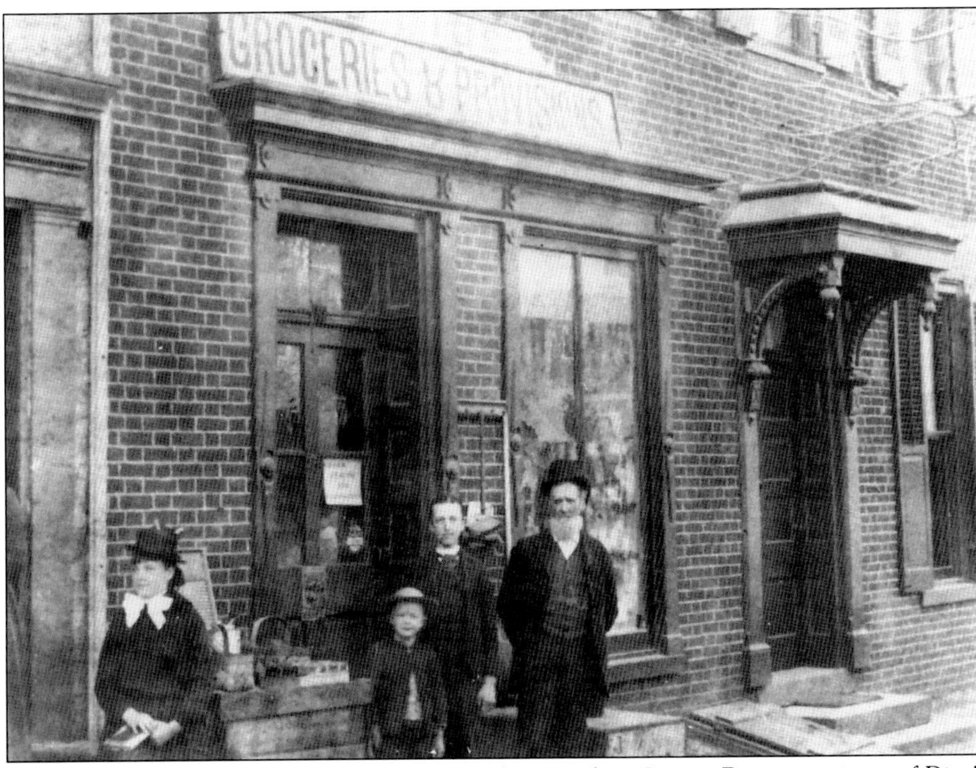

The bearded gentleman at right in this 1890 photograph is George Dice, proprietor of Dice's Grocery and Provision Store at 69 East King Street. The building was torn down sometime after 1900 to make way for a large brick dwelling for Frank Hollar Sr.

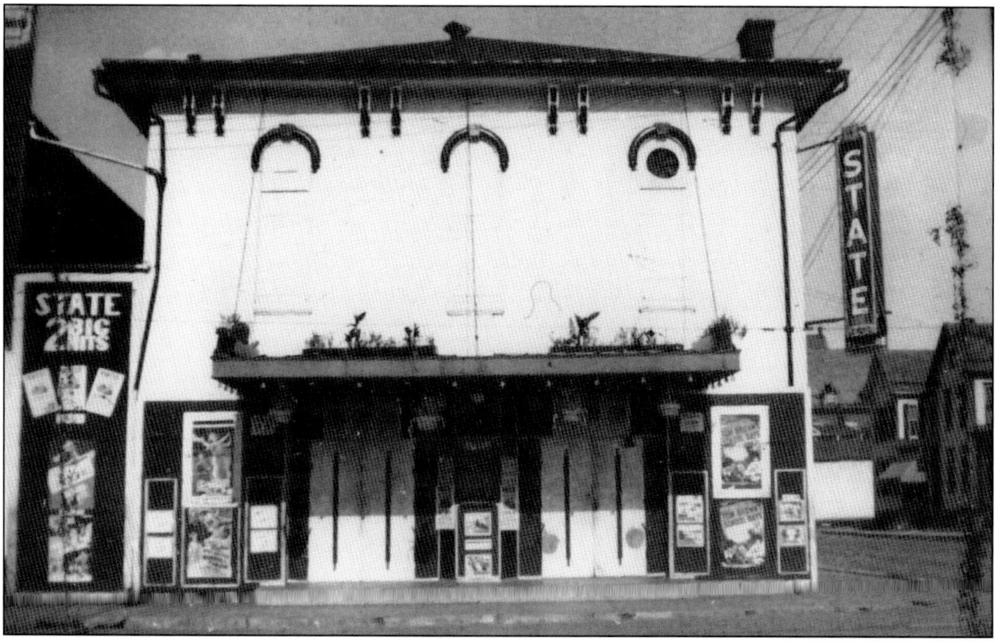

The State Theatre was located on the northeast corner of South Earl and East Orange Streets. Previously known as the Bijou and later the Lyric Theatre, it became the State Theatre in 1930. It was heavily damaged by fire in 1954, but was reopened in May 1955 as the Cumberland Valley Theatre. It closed down permanently after the last show on January 19, 1958. The site is now occupied by Shippen Cleaners.

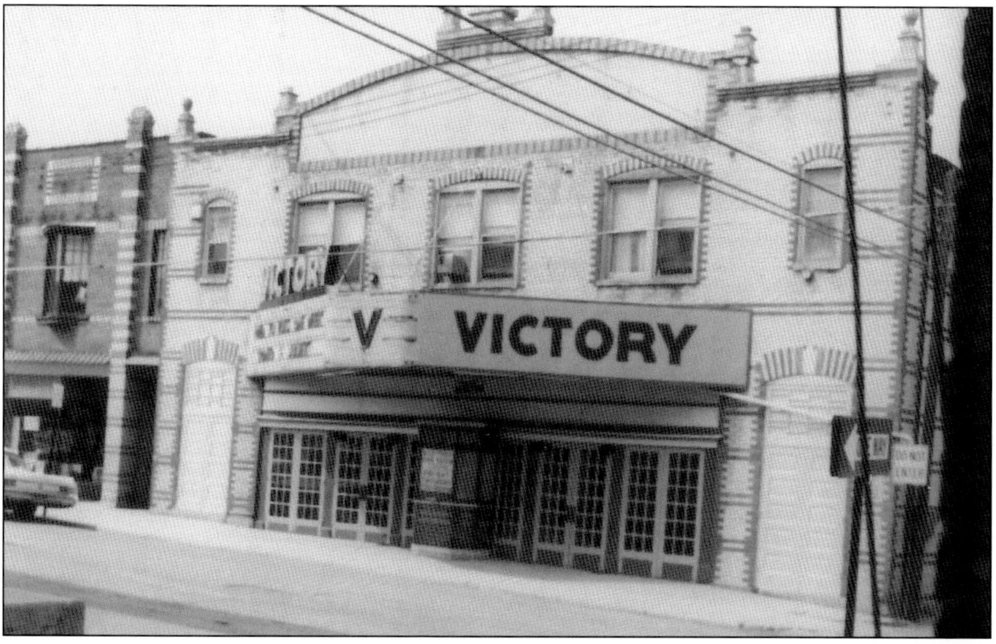

The Victory Theatre, pictured here in the 1960s, was opened in 1921 by Frank Hollar Sr., who initially called it the Victory Playhouse. The building changed hands in 1971 and, after extensive renovations, reopened as the College Cinema. When the theater was destroyed by a fire in 1990, the site became the drive-through for Orrstown Bank.

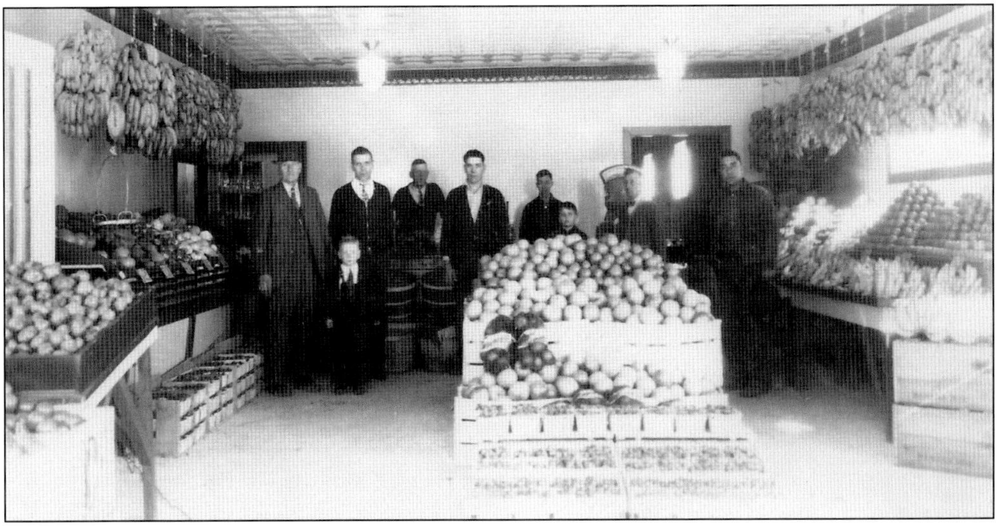

Frank S. Cressler, at left, and his crew pose for this 1936 photograph of Cressler's Fruit Market, located at 209 West King Street. After World War II, Cressler expanded the store and it became the major supermarket in Shippensburg during the 1970s and 1980s (others included Acme and the A&P). In 1990, it was sold to the Weis chain by the Cresslers and relocated to a Route 11 South location; locals still refer to it as Cressler's.

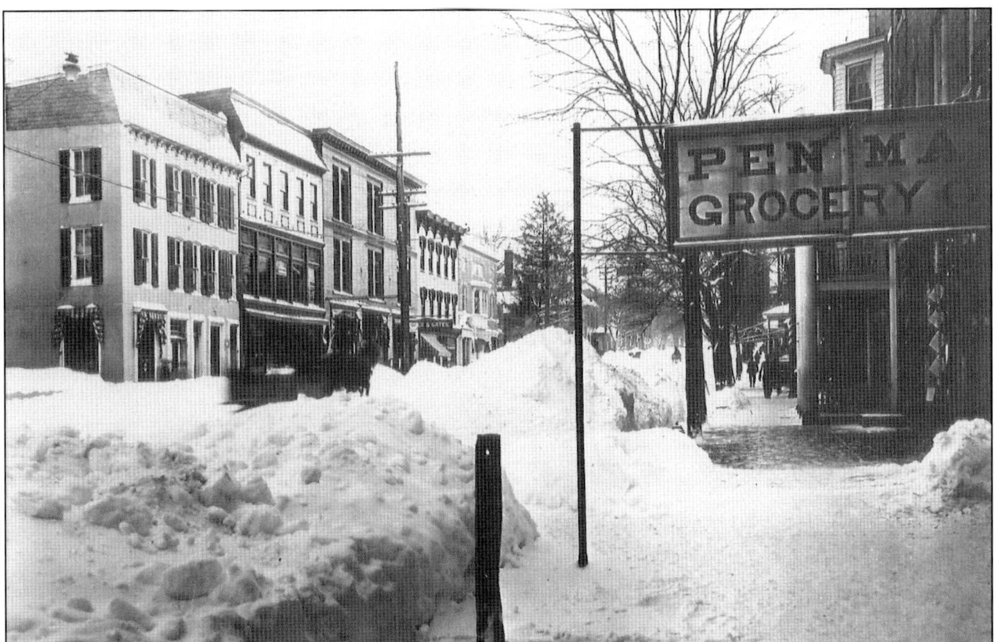

This photograph from 1920 shows the north side of East King Street after a snowstorm. The Old Opera House is the third building up on the left side. The Pen Mar Grocery is on the west side of Apple Avenue, at right in the image.

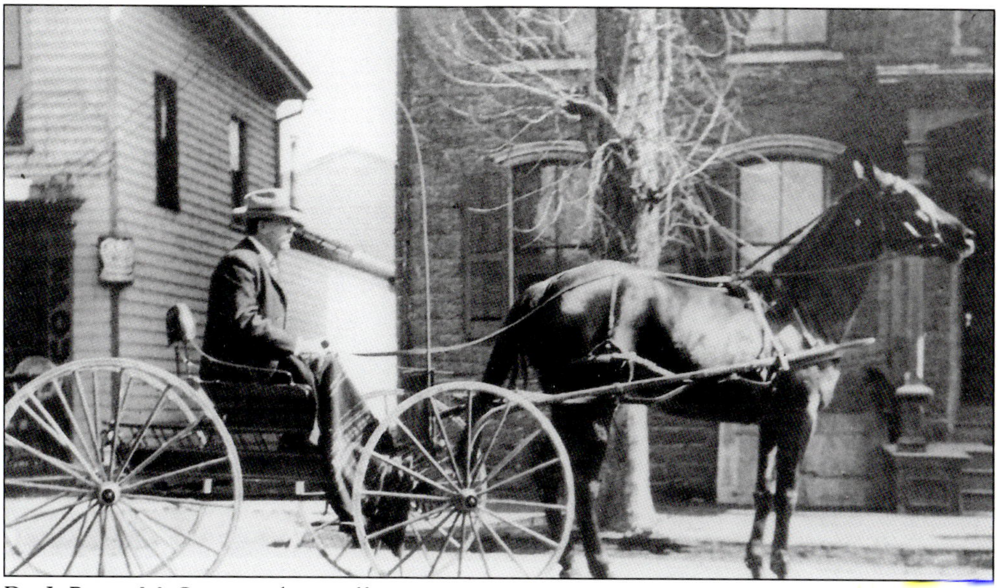

Dr. J. Bruce McCreary, whose office was at 47 West King Street, is shown making a house call in this 1914 photograph. He is beside McGowan's tin shop (left), now the site of the post office, and the Dr. Alexander Stewart stone house (right), now the home of the Shippensburg Historical Society.

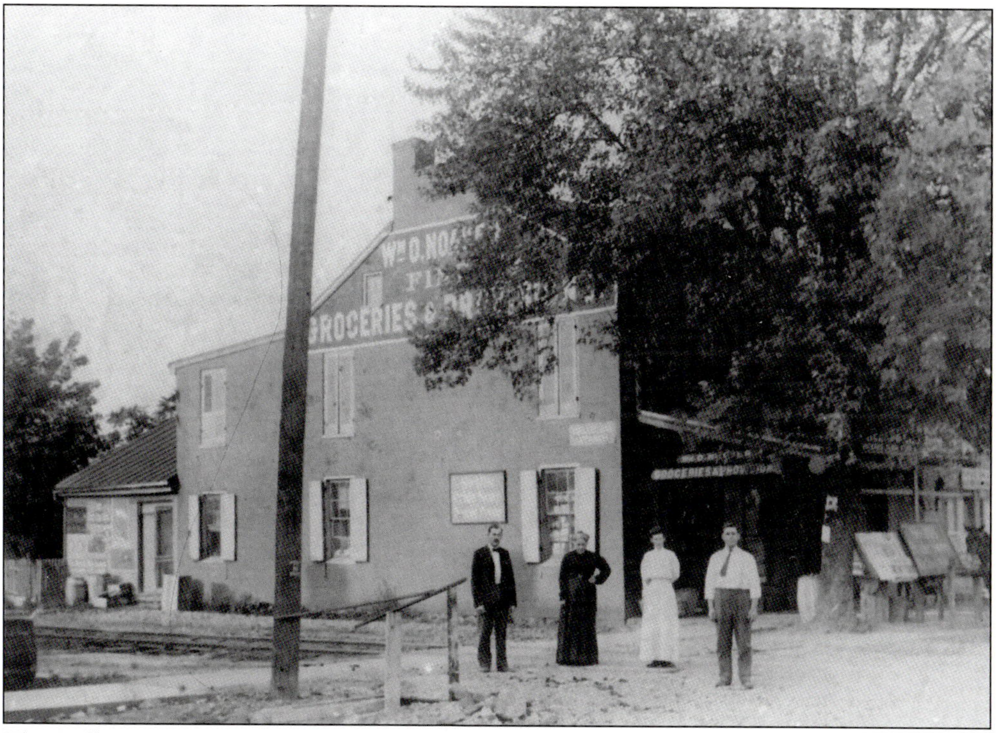

The William O. Noaker Grocery and Dry Goods store was located at the northeastern corner of King and North Fayette Streets at 85 West King Street. Pictured here are, from left to right, William Noaker, Mary Noaker, Florence Noaker, and Roy Gensler. The photograph was taken around 1910.

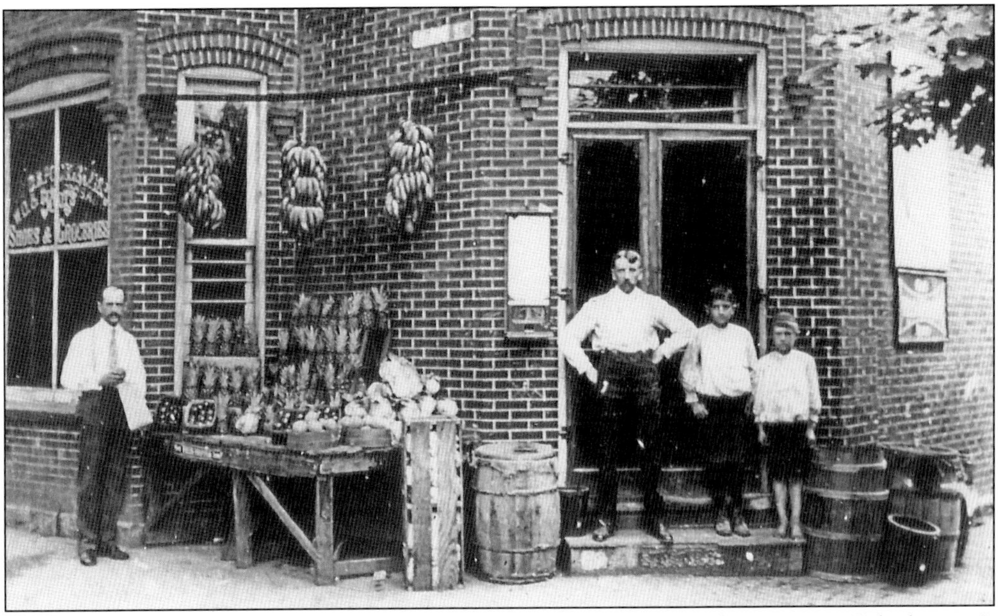

Brothers David (left) and William (left, standing in doorway) Fogelsanger, ran Folgelsanger's Grocery Store as partners at the time of this photograph in 1908. The boy on the far right in the doorway is Lincoln S. "Link" Fogelsanger, age 8, who as a young man took over this business and operated it until about 1948. The building is now occupied by Farner's Billiard Room.

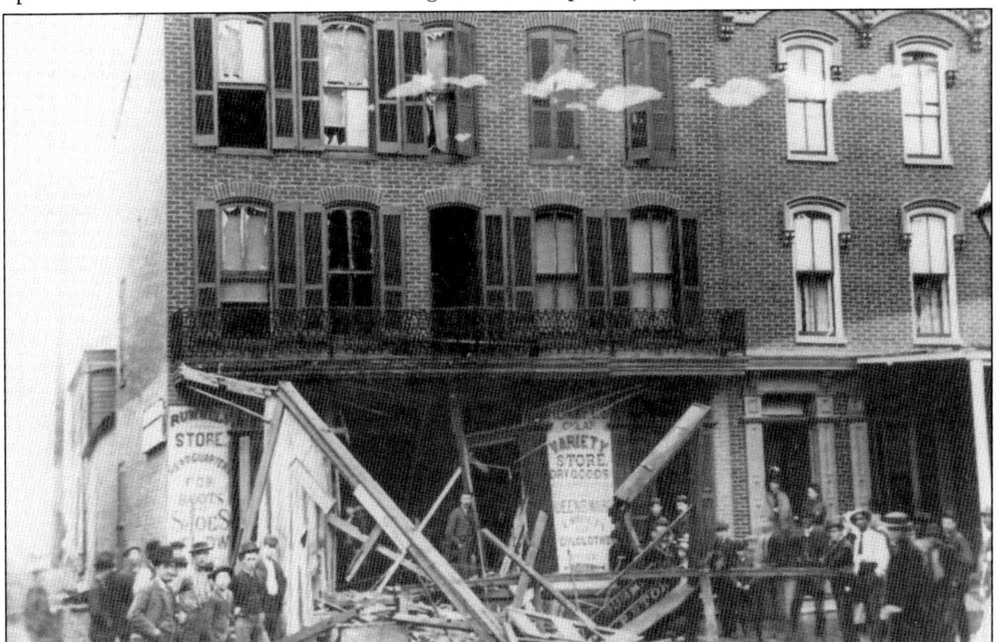

J. Calvin Rummel operated the J.C. Rummel's Variety Store at 33 West King Street, selling a variety of household goods. Rummel was an ardent supporter of the Prohibition Party, angering the anti-prohibition element in Shippensburg, who tried to send him a message by dynamiting the front of his store—the aftermath is shown in this 1888 photograph. The damage was repaired, but Rummel soon sold this store and founded the Shippensburg Manufacturing Company.

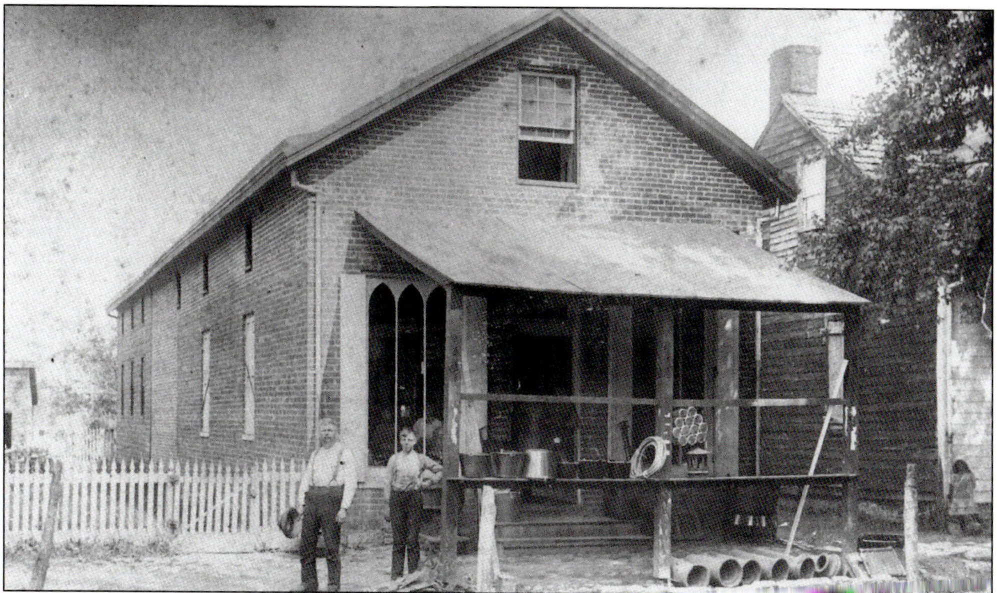

Edgar A. Walters (left), a Civil War veteran, ran this hardware store until he died in 1877. His son Brady, pictured at right, continued to operate the store until the 1930s. The store was located on the north side of the first block of West King Street.

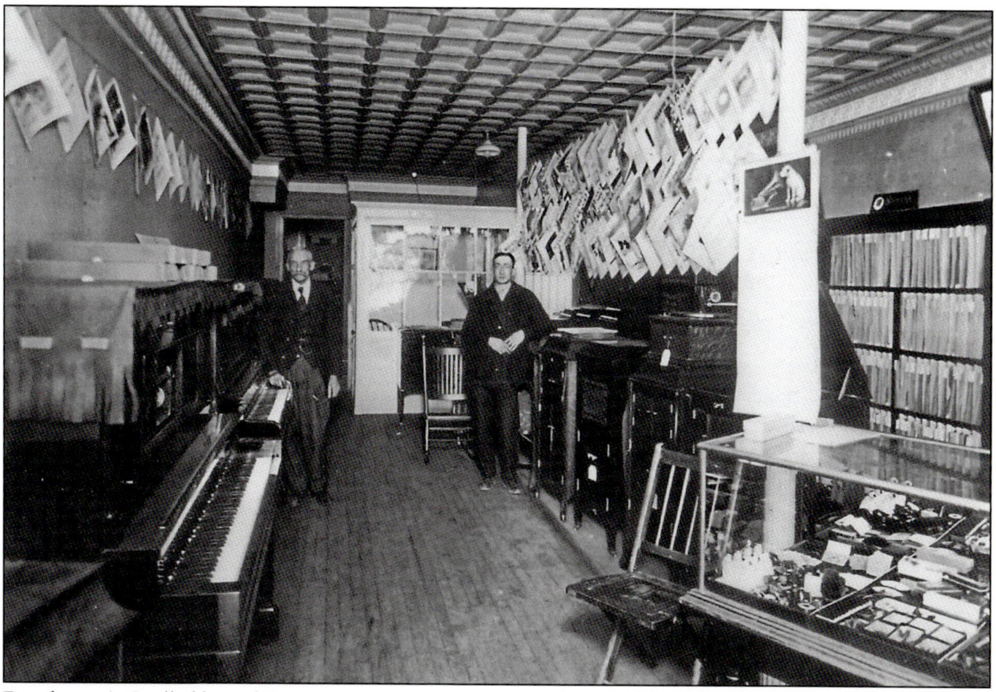

Brothers A.C. (left) and Frank R. Squires operated this music store at 43 East King Street at the time this photograph was taken in 1921. Earlier, around 1910, A.C. had run a jewelry store at 23 East King Street. By 1933, the Squires family began to sell large household items. The main Squires showroom is now south of Shippensburg on Route 11, between Shippensburg and Chambersburg.

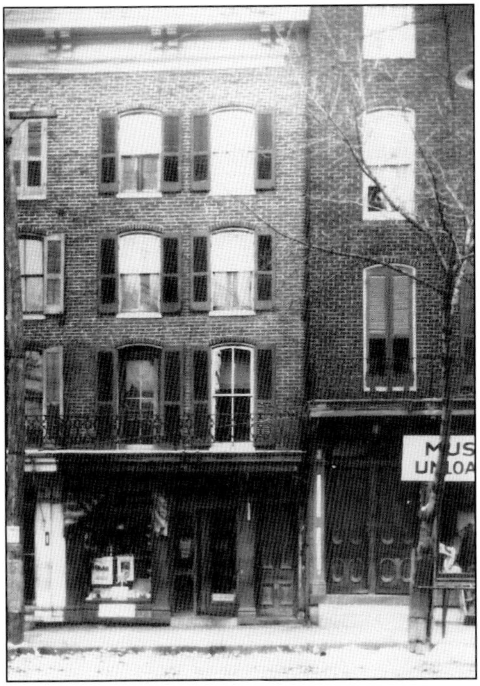

The building on the right in this 1908 photograph, at 19 East King Street, was owned by Charles Viener, a Lithuanian of Jewish extraction, and was next to Arthur Burkhart's Restaurant on the left. Viener came to Shippensburg as a peddler with a pack on his back in 1903. After leasing several buildings in town, he rented the first floor of the structure, and in 1920 he bought the building and continued to operate his clothing store there until the late 1940s. It was called Charlie Viener's Underselling Store.

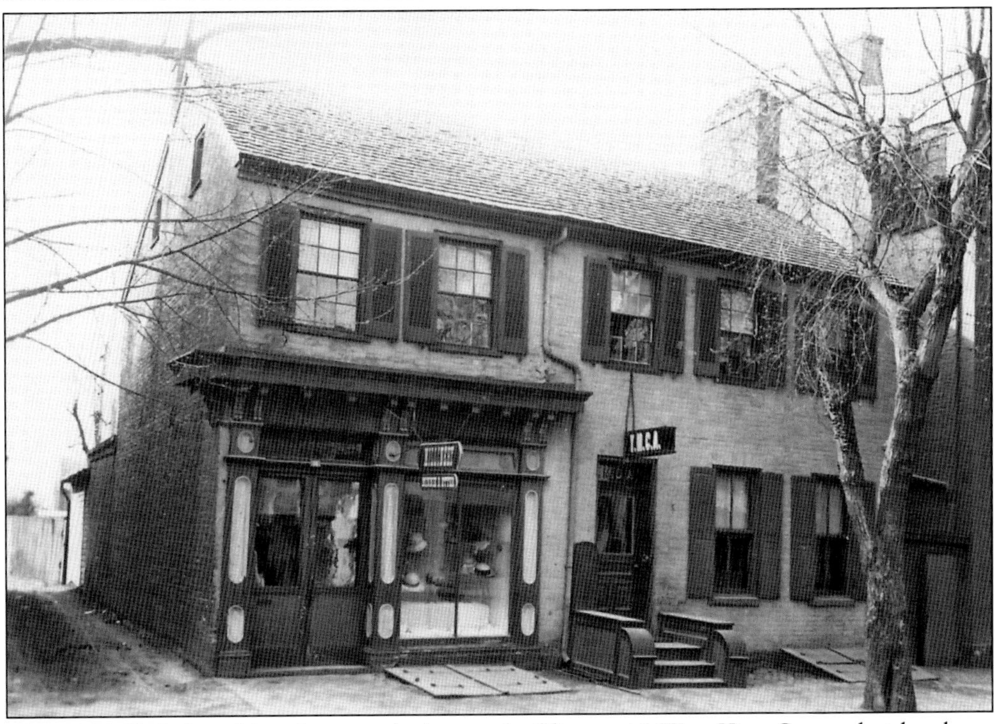

This 1906 Clyde Laughlin photograph shows a building at 16 West King Street that has been called the Benjamin Cole House. At the time this picture was taken, however, it housed a millinery store and a YMCA. In 1920, Eber Neff bought the property and used the left side for Neff's Bakery. The Valley Baking Company bought the property in 1920 and began operating a snack bar out of the right side in 1968.

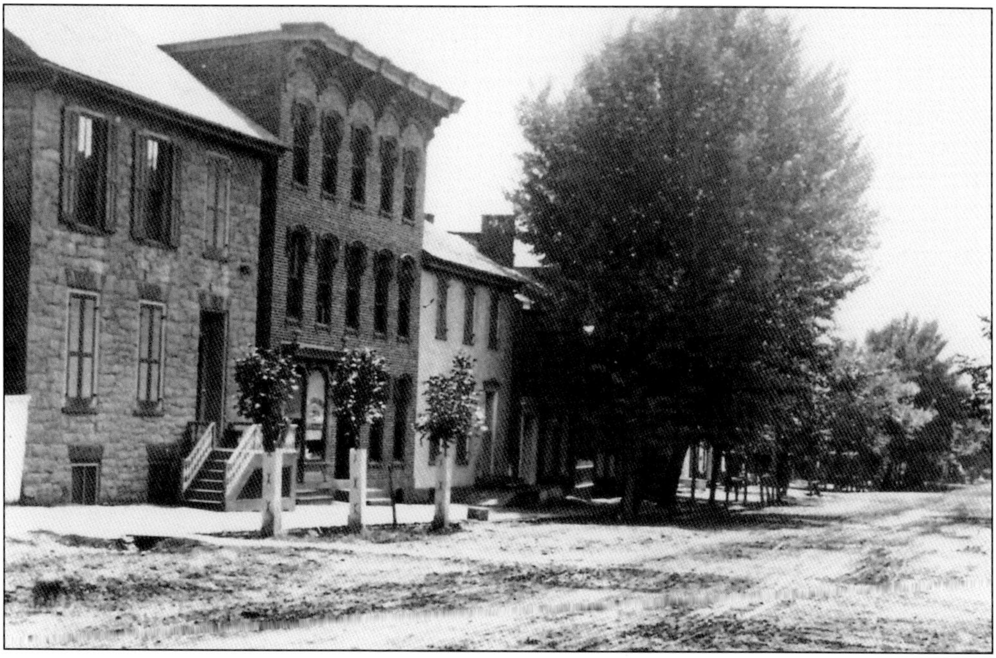

Shown in this 1893 H. Frank Beidel photograph, the second building from the left (64–66 East King Street) housed Klink's Bakery on the first floor; the second and third stories were used for apartments. Since 1930, the first floor has been occupied by insurance agencies.

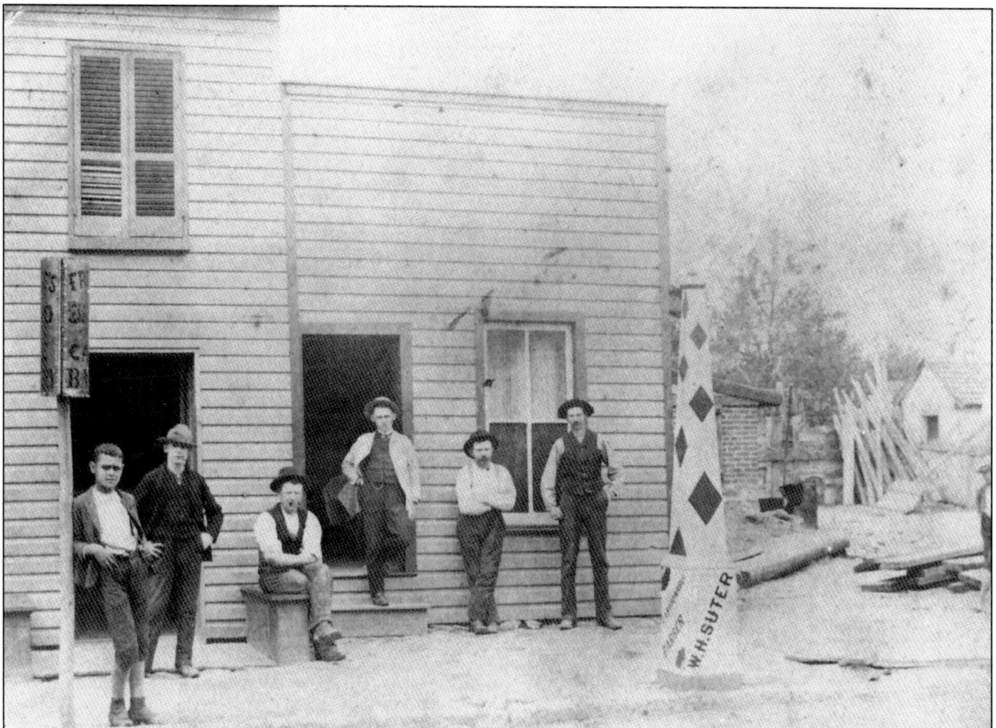

The W.H. Suter Barbershop was located on the north end of the Black Bear Hotel on North Earl Street, as shown in this 1880s photograph. One could have a beer while waiting for a haircut.

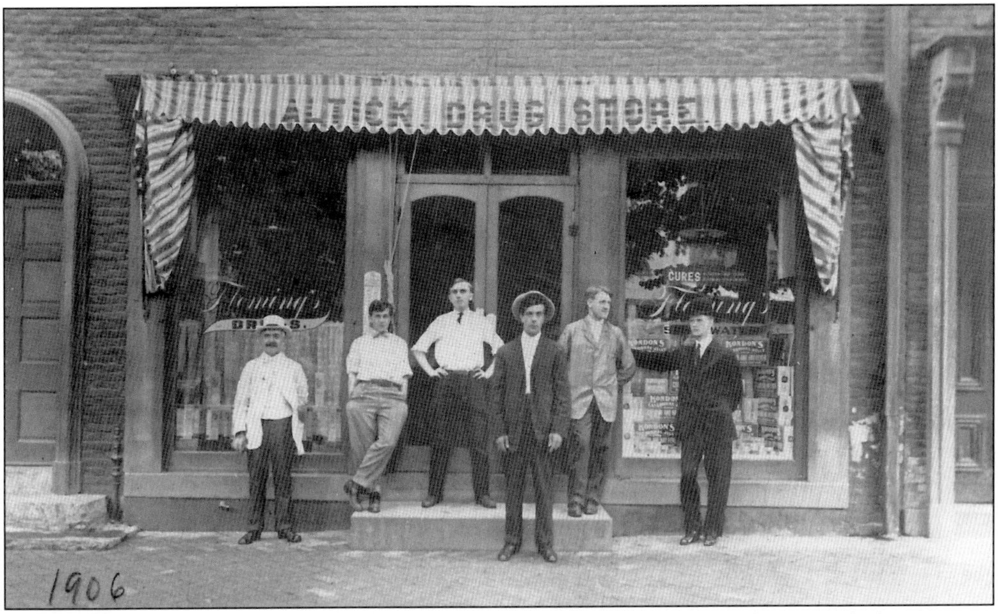

This 1906 photograph shows Fleming's Drug Store, located on the north side of West King Street next to what was then the First National Bank. Frank Fleming Sr. is on the far left. The name *Fleming* is on the window, but *Altick*, the name of the former owners, is still on the awning. Dr. Harry B. Etter is on the far right.

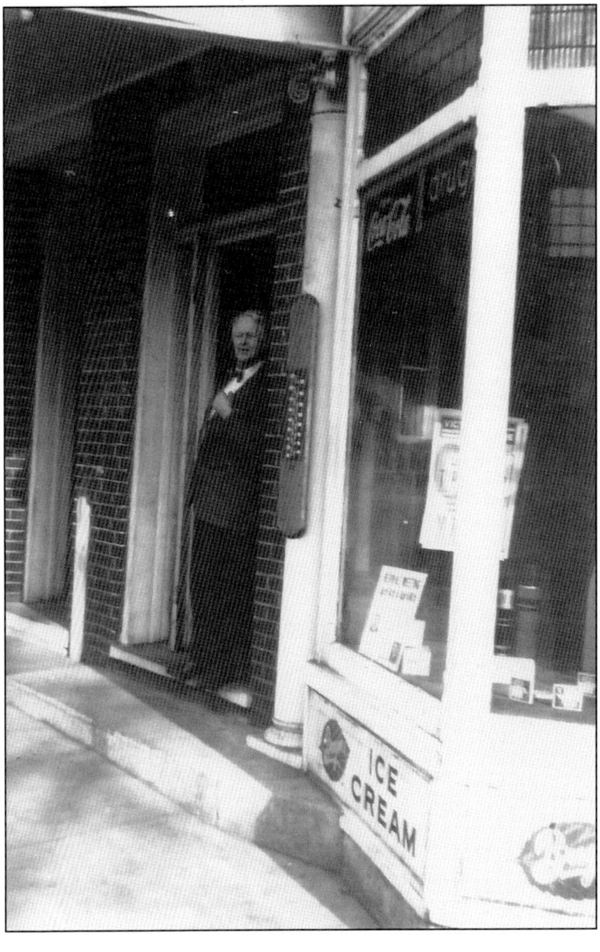

In this 1920s image, Roy E. "Doc" Martin stands in the doorway of his pharmacy at 100 East King Street, on the southeast corner of East King and South Penn Streets. Doc Martin was well known for his little green pills ("greenies"), which could supposedly cure a wide range of female maladies.

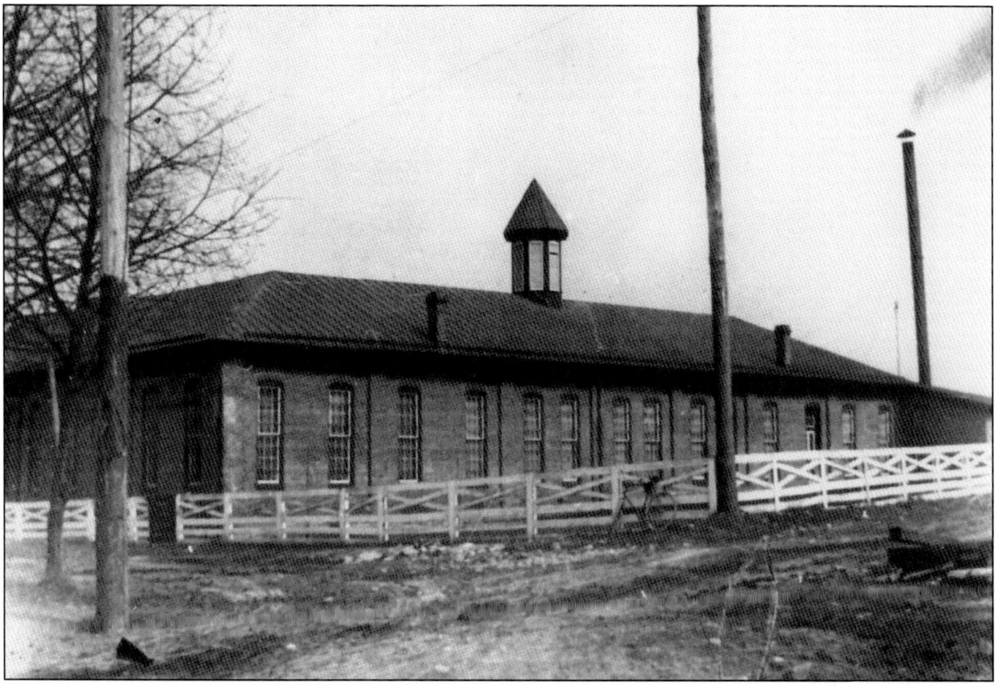

From 1817, a mill stood at this location on the corner of West Garfield and South Fayette Streets, but it burned down in 1889. In the spring of that year, the Metcalfe Engine Works was built on the site, as shown in this 1894 picture. In 1895, however, this plant also burned down. The site was then taken over by the Shippensburg Manufacturing Company, which erected a plant to produce pants. In 1913, this plant became known as Rummel Himes and Company.

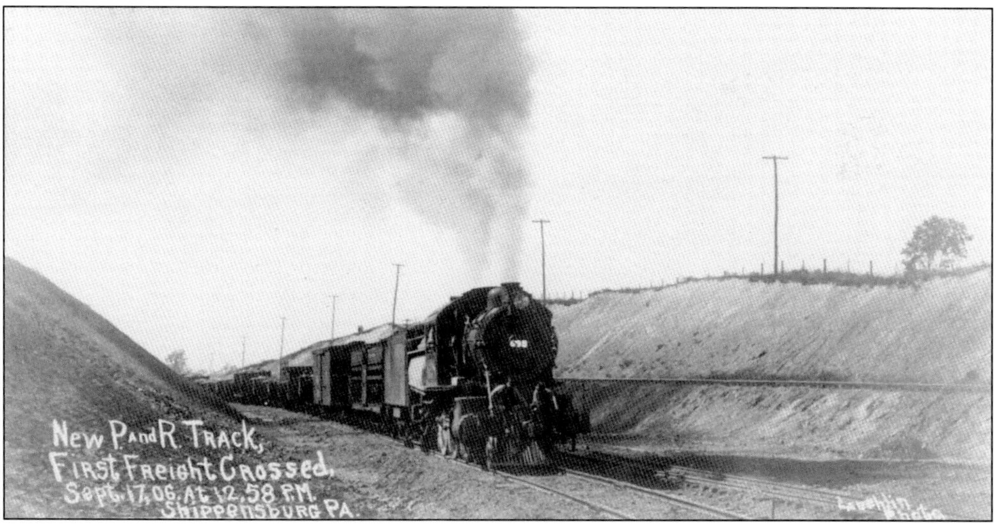

As he did in so many of his postcards, Clyde Laughlin captured the precise time when an important event occurred. In this photograph, he documents the first freight train to travel on the track built by the Philadelphia & Reading Railway that led into Shippensburg. The historic event occurred at 12:58 p.m. on September 17, 1906.

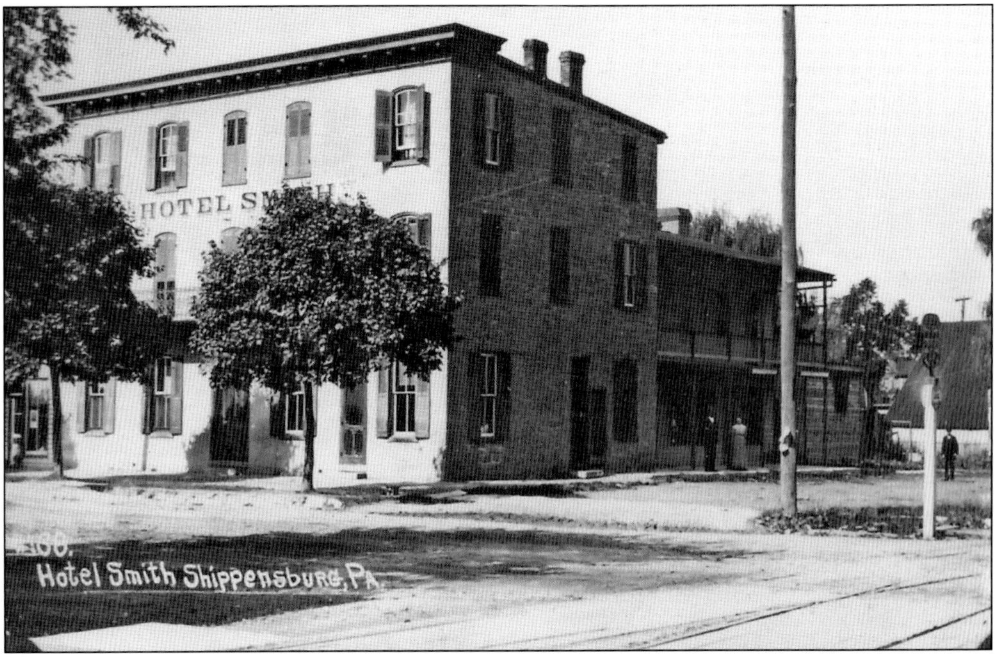

This location at 105 West King Street has been the home of a number of hotels. From 1850 until about 1880, it was known as the Madison House; from 1880 until 1890, it was the National Hotel. This 1910 photograph shows the building as the Hotel Smith.

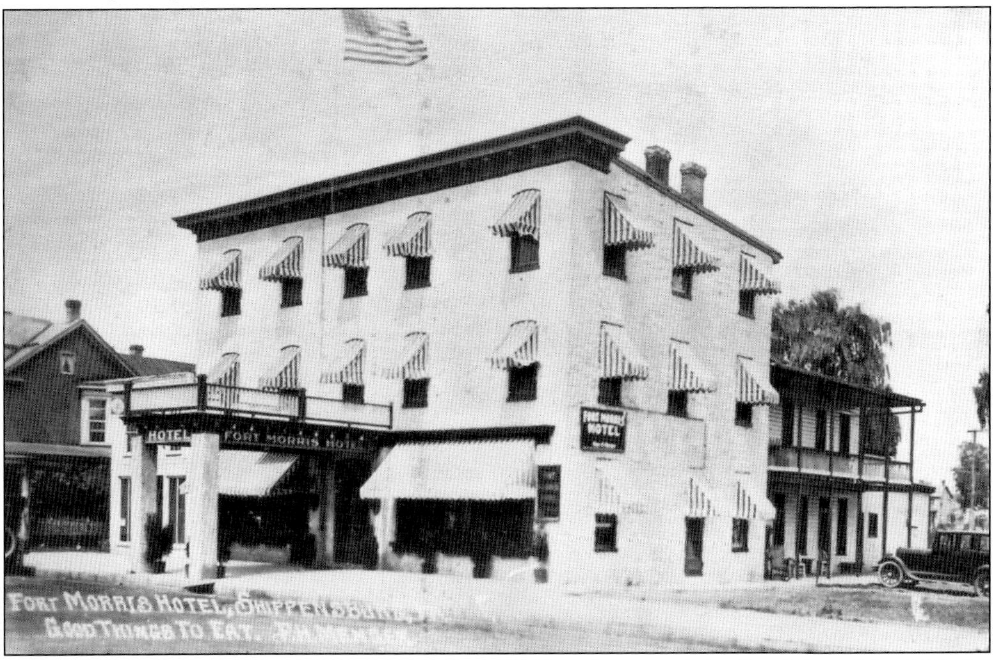

The building pictured above was restyled in about 1923 and renamed the Fort Morris Hotel. Under this title it became a favored watering hole for many of the faculty and students at Shippensburg State Teachers' College (now Shippensburg University) during the 1950s, 1960s, and 1970s. In recent years, it has had a number of owners and name changes; it is currently known as the Shipwreck Pub and Inn.

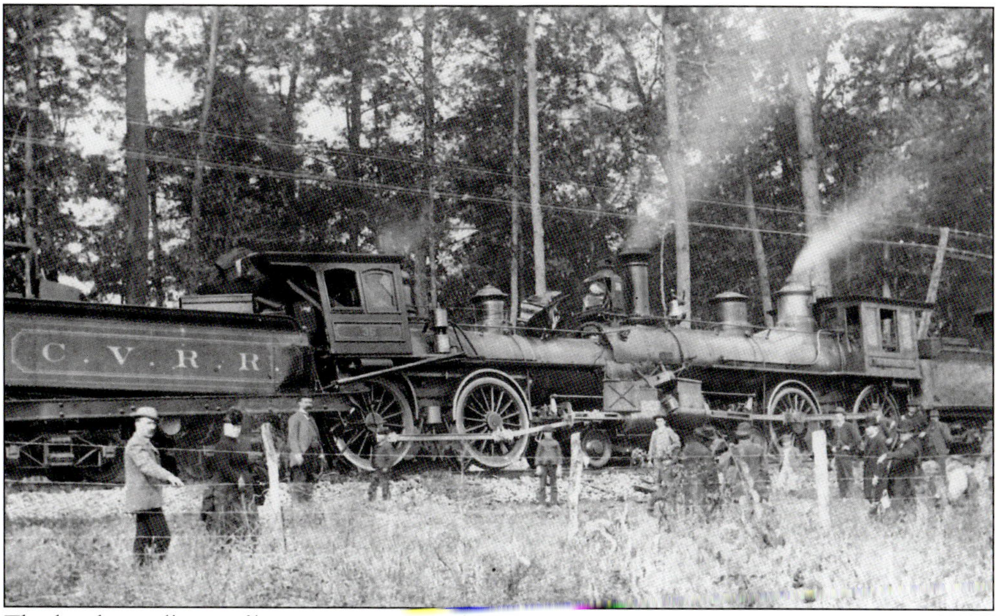

This head on collision of locomotives occurred on October 18, 1888, on the single-track Cumberland Valley Railroad. The accident happened as the trains were passing through Britton's Woods, about a mile northeast of Shippensburg.

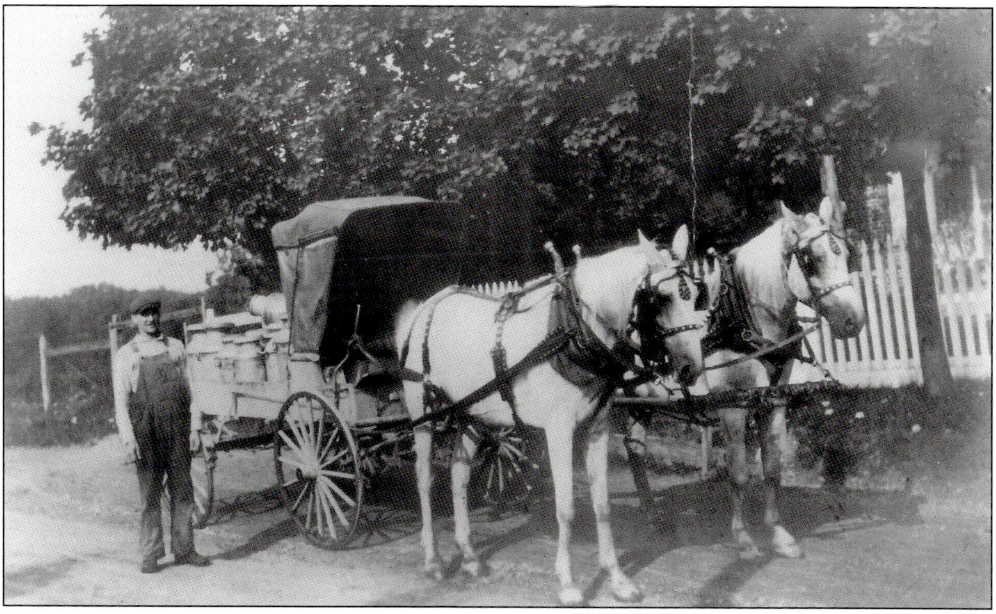

G. Raymond "Shorty" Fogelsonger, a well-known local businessman, poses with his first dray wagon in the early 1900s. The horses are Pierce and Colt. Fogelsonger, who hauled milk in the mornings and "anything" in the afternoons, is pictured somewhere on Ridge Road.

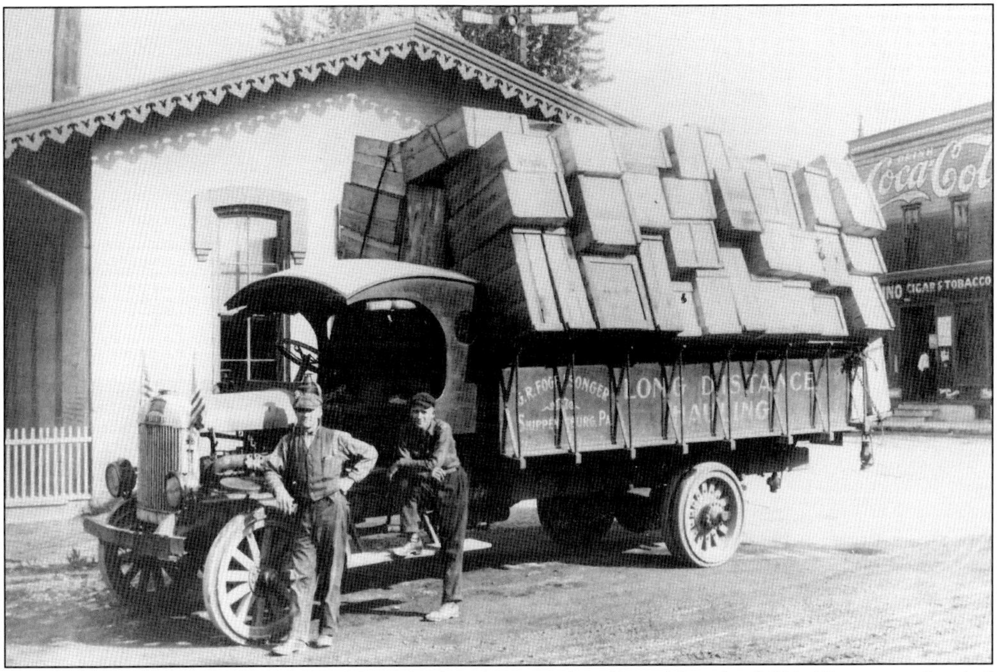

In 1910, Shorty Fogelsonger (left) bought his first truck, a Republic, for $550. Here, it is loaded with empty wooden packing boxes and headed for the Beistle Company on East Burd Street. The fancy building behind the truck is the Cumberland Valley Railroad passenger station on South Earl Street. To the right of Shorty is John "Slats" McCune, who would serve in World War I.

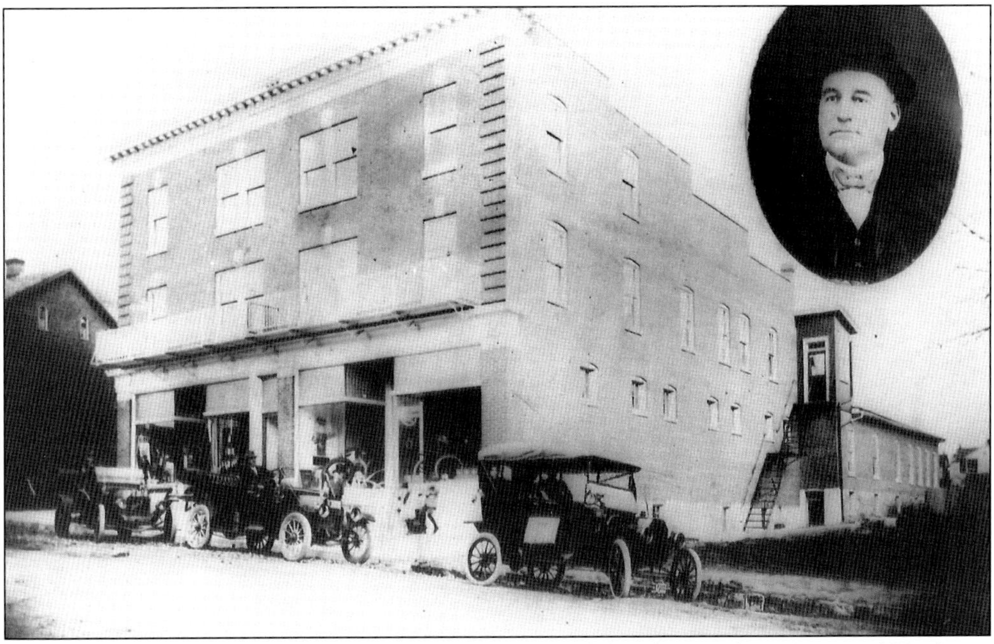
When Joseph L. Miller and H.K. Latshaw (inset) acquired the Shippensburg Auto and Hardware Company in 1913, Miller bought the automobile business, while Latshaw purchased the hardware business. Miller had erected the building in 1910 at 204 East King Street, and he opened a Ford agency in the right front, while Latshaw opened his hardware business in the left front.

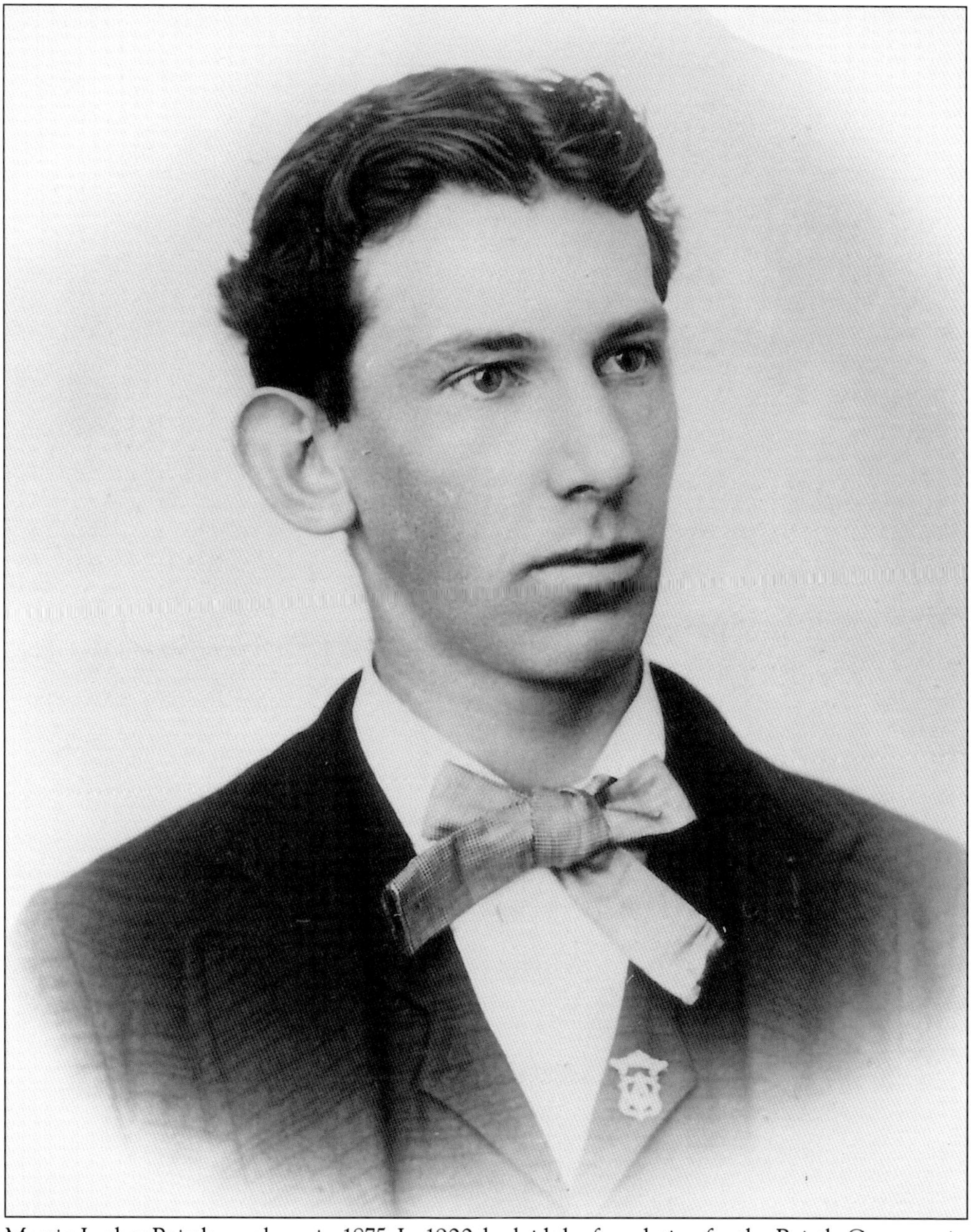

Martin Luther Beistle was born in 1875. In 1900, he laid the foundation for the Beistle Company in the basement of his Pennsylvania home, making artificial flowers and wooden products, primarily for hotel lobby décor. In 1907, he settled in Shippensburg and worked in a second-story stable loft. In 1910, he brought the technology for producing honeycomb tissues to the United States. Previously, such products were only available from Europe (particularly Germany) and Asia. World War I greatly stimulated demand for his products, since Germany was no longer a source. Beistle acquired numerous patents, which greatly added to the company's success. Beistle died in 1935, leaving the company in the hands of his son-in-law Henry E. Luhrs; the Luhrs family has led the business since. Both Beistle and the Luhrs family have been generous financial contributors to the town and various university programs.

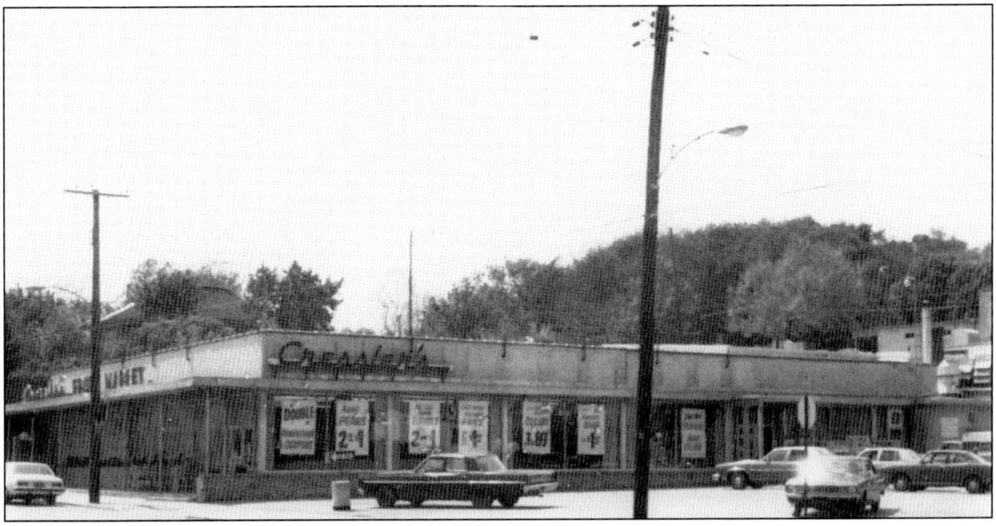

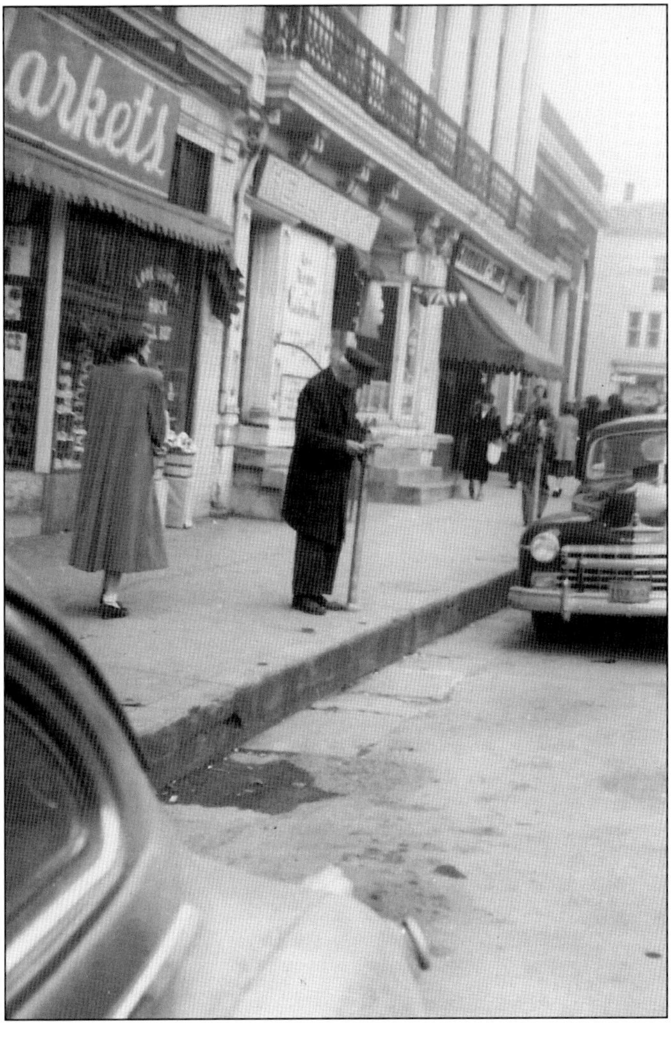

Frank S. Cressler and his wife, Anna Mary, went into the fruit and vegetable business on Spring Street in 1932. In 1936 or 1937, Frank built a grocery store on the corner of West King and North Fayette Streets. In 1948, he built Cressler's Fruit Market, shown in this 1960s picture. During the 1990s, Cressler's store left this location and moved out of town to Route 11 South.

In this 1949 photograph, Robert L. Britton checks meters in front of the Acme Market, located in the old Viener Building at 19 East King Street. Britton had operated a harness shop on West King Street until 1948, but closed his business because of the shrunken market for harnesses.

Ray Weaver, proprietor of Weaver's Cut Rate Drug Store at 16 East King Street, and saleslady Mabel Cressler wear costumes to celebrate Old-Fashioned Days in 1957. Shippensburg was celebrating the completion of the sewer project and the repaving of the streets, which had been dug up since 1953.

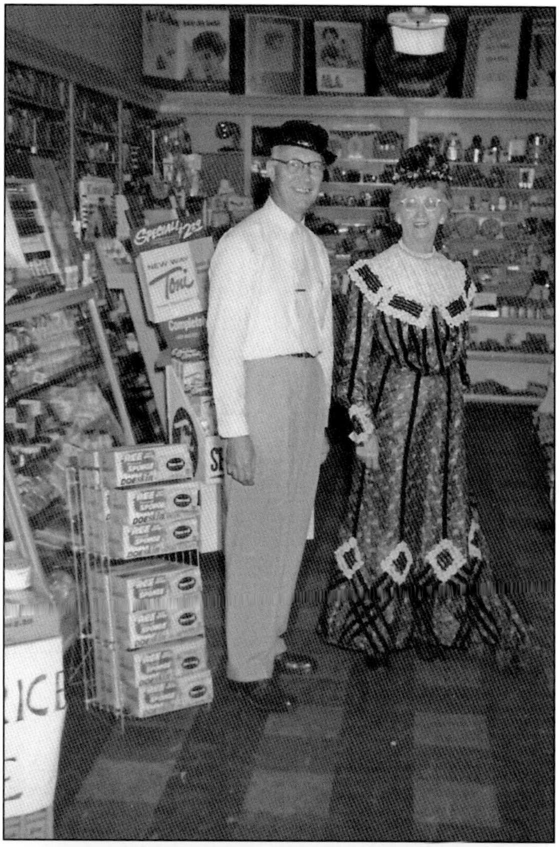

This mid-1940s photograph shows the interior of Lincoln S. "Link" Fogelsanger's Grocery Store and Texaco Station at 245 East King Street. Link is standing on the right. The young man leaning on the counter is Link's son Lincoln B. Fogelsanger, who became a music teacher and band director of the Shippensburg Area School District after World War II. This building currently houses Farner's Billiard Room.

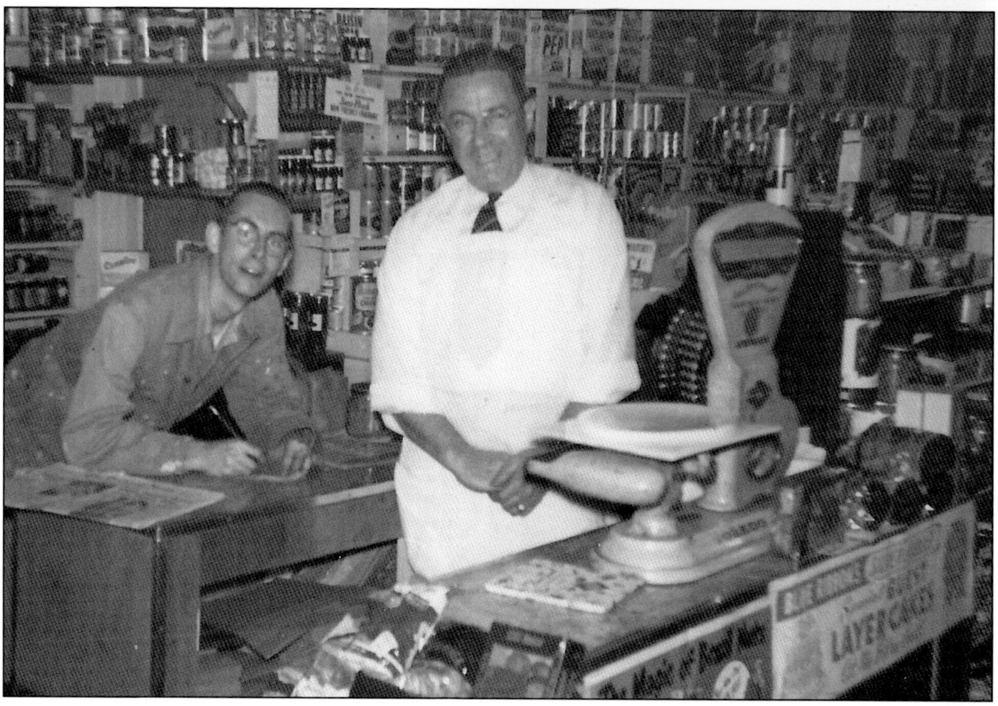

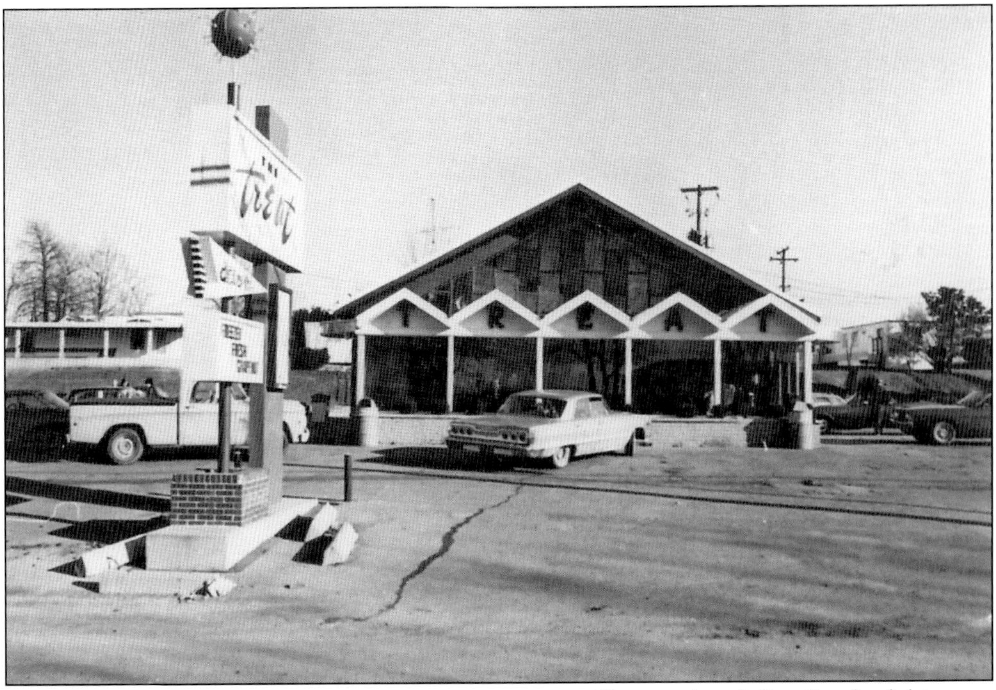

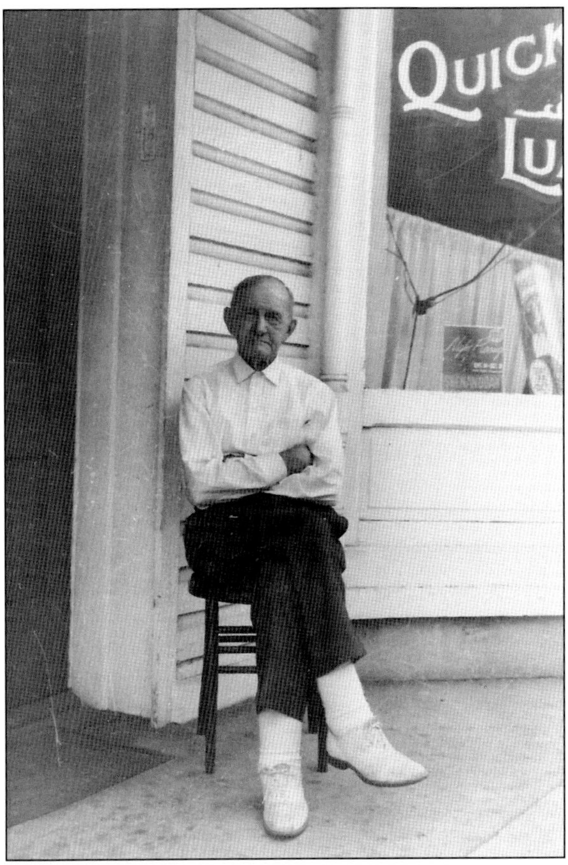

Shippensburg's first fast-food drive-in was built in June 1952 on Route 11 South, about a mile from the borough's business district. At first, it exclusively sold soft drinks and ice cream, closed during the winter, and was called the Tropical Treat. More food items were added during the 1950s and 1960s, when it remained open all year and was renamed the Treat. Most recently, it has become a sit-down restaurant.

Proprietor Hugh Craig Fry sits in front of his Quick Lunch and taproom in about 1950. The Quick Lunch was an orderly establishment where one could enjoy a lunch and a beer without the rowdiness often found in other places that served alcoholic beverages. The Commonwealth National Bank later expanded into this location on the west side of North Earl Street.

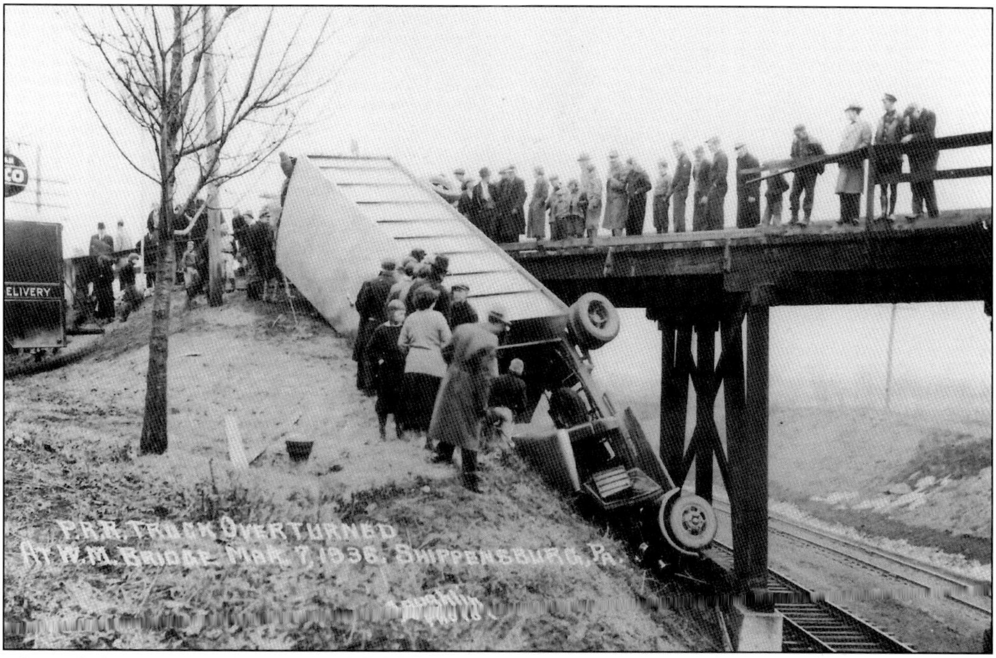

This Clyde Laughlin photograph from March 7, 1936, shows a tractor-trailer that plunged over the east side of the Philadelphia & Reading Railway Bridge (generally called the Baltimore Bridge by locals) as the driver was traveling north towards Shippensburg.

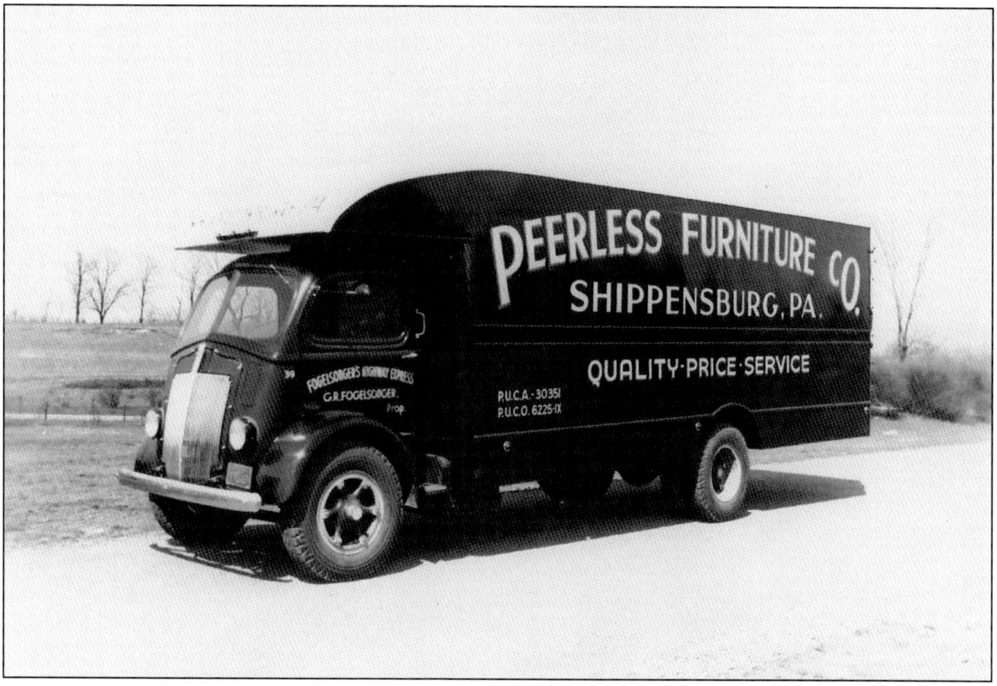

This is one of Shorty Fogelsonger's moving vans from the 1940s. The Peerless Furniture Company was one of Fogelsonger's best customers. Fogelsonger started out with a single wagon and two horses; bought his first truck, a Republic equipped with solid rubber tires, in 1910; and had a fleet of trucks for hire by the middle of the 20th century.

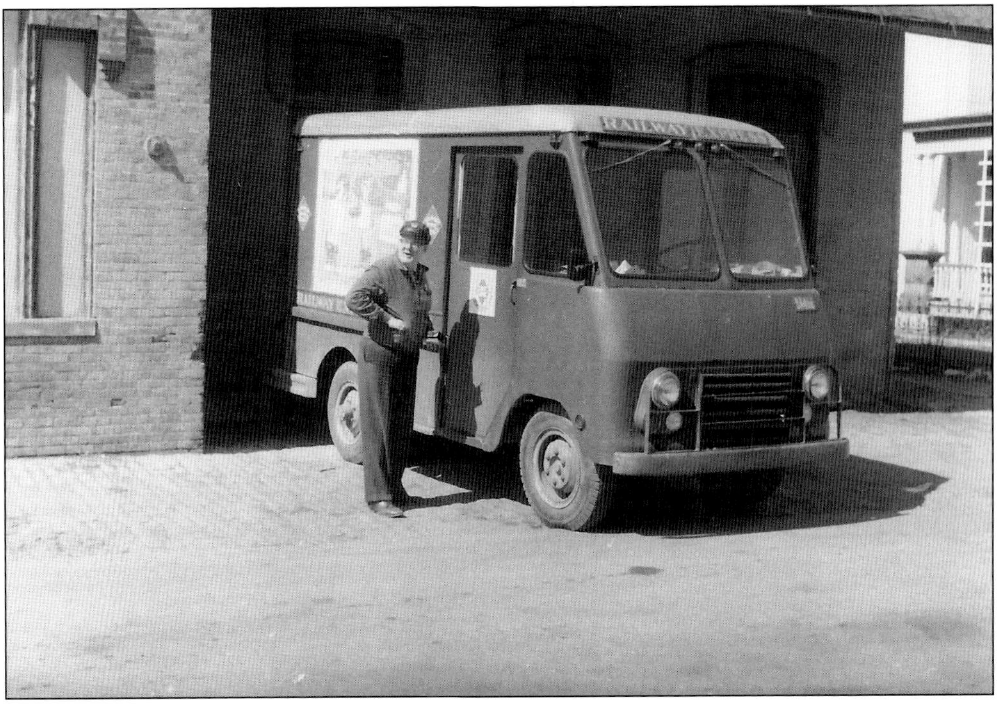

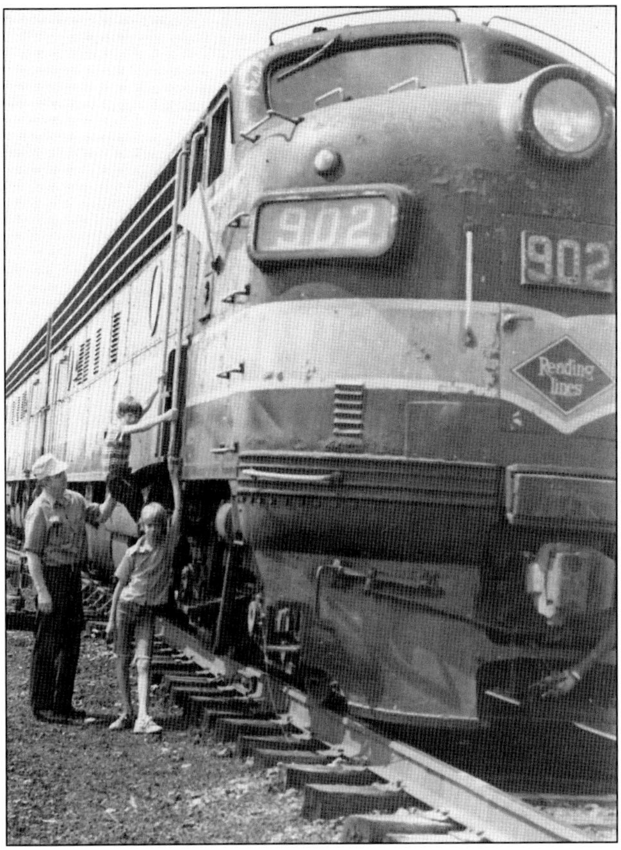

Kenneth G. Wetzel, Shippensburg's last Railway Express agent, stands beside his truck in 1968. Wetzel is in front of the north end of the old railroad passenger station, which was the women's waiting room in the time when travel by rail was popular. The station was torn down in 1969.

On September 18, 1973, this diesel locomotive pulled the last passenger excursion of the Reading Railroad. The young boys are from Shippensburg, where the photograph was taken; the man is a member of the engine crew. In 1985, the railroad tracks were removed from Earl Street after a young man who was holding onto the train as it moved slowly through town was pulled off his bicycle and thrown under the train.

Three

SHIPPENSBURG RESIDENTS RESPOND TO THE CALL TO ARMS

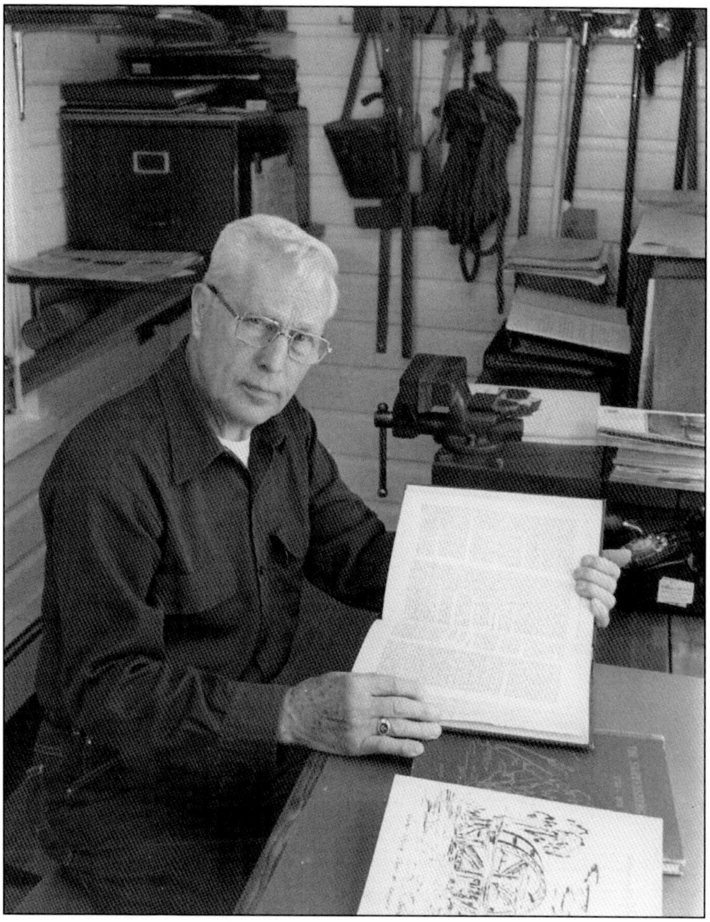

William "Bill" Burkhart is pictured in his study in the late 1970s. Not only was Burkhart a veteran of World War II and a survivor of the Battle of the Bulge, he was Shippensburg's greatest friend of its soldiers, sailors, airmen, and Marines. He wrote histories of Shippensburg's soldiers and collected photographs of them, and he supervised the placing of flags on veterans' graves every Memorial Day.

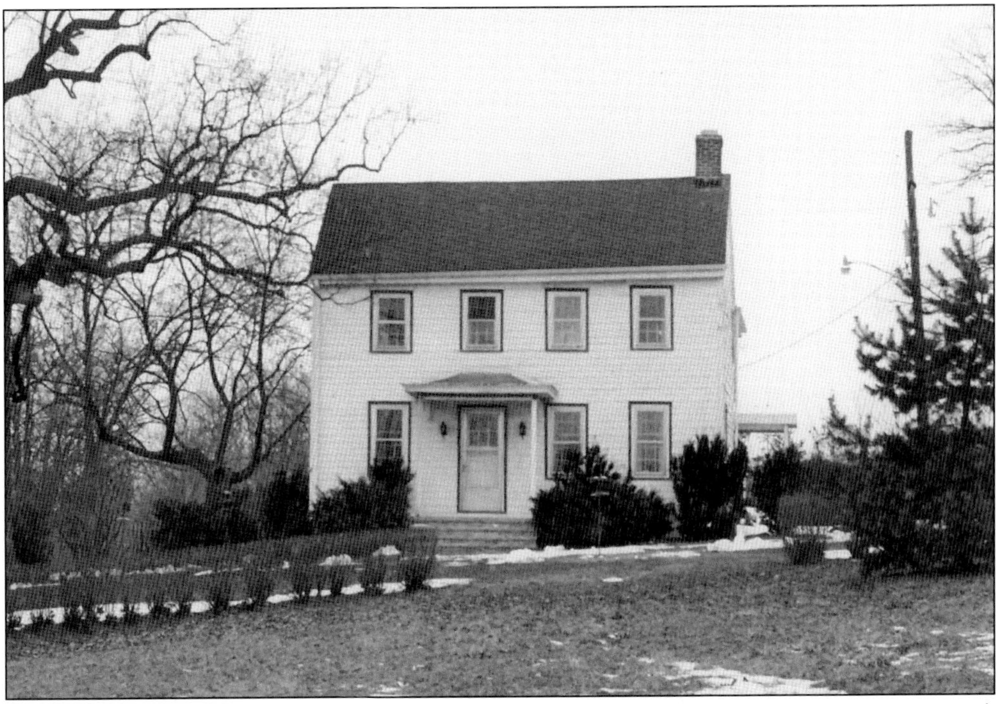

Col. James Burd was married to the daughter of Edward Shippen, for whom Shippensburg is named. Colonel Burd served with Henry Bouquet and George Washington on the Forbes Expedition. He also headed up the project to build Fort Morris in Shippensburg. This 1966 photograph shows the residence that Burd built in 1752 and in which he and his wife, Sally, lived from 1752 to 1756. A street, a stream, and an elementary school in Shippensburg are all named after Colonel Burd.

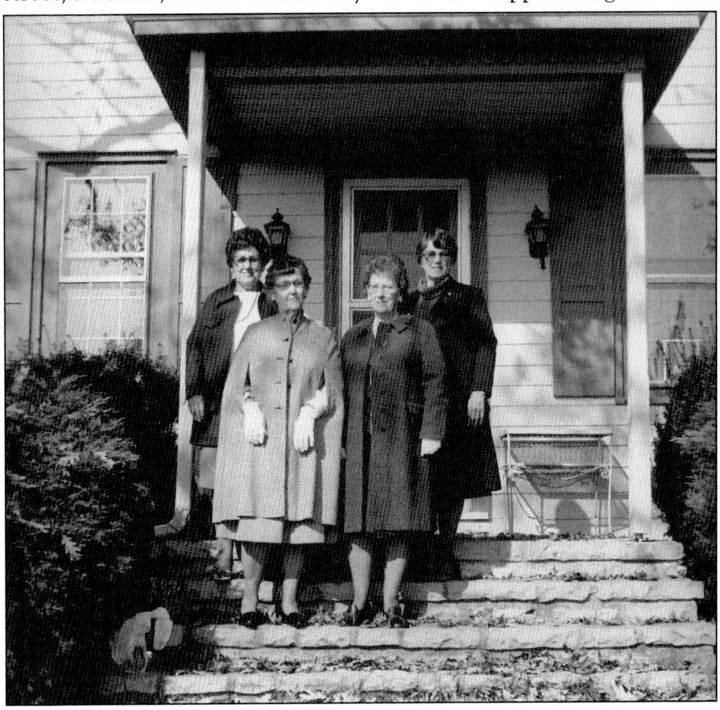

This photograph from October 30, 1979, shows four sisters, all of whom have the maiden name Burd and are fifth-generation descendants of Col. James Burd. Pictured, from left to right, are Leona Burd Butts, Evelyn Burd Parson, Helen Burd Houpt, and Maxine Burd Baker. A fifth sister, Mary Burd Hoover, could not make it to this visit to the Burd homestead.

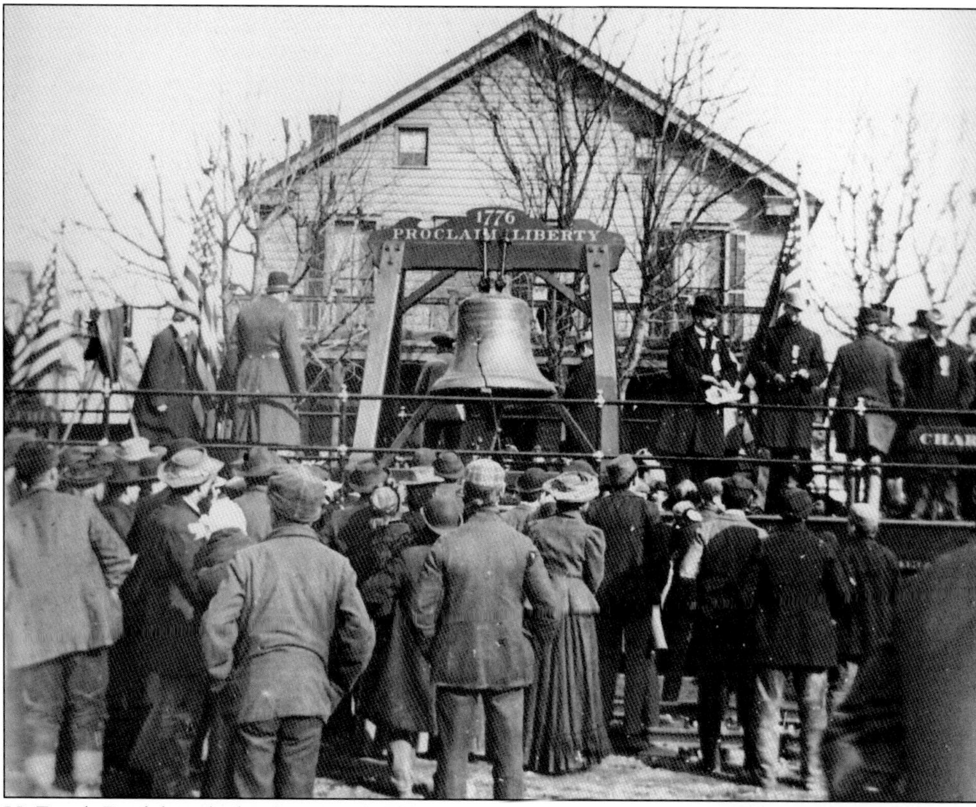

H. Frank Beidel took this January 6, 1902, photograph of the Liberty Bell as it stopped in Shippensburg en route to Charleston, South Carolina. Hauled on a flatcar on the Cumberland Valley Railroad, it passed through Carlisle, stopped at the Cumberland Valley State Normal School for five minutes, and stopped for 15 minutes on South Earl Street before moving on to Chambersburg as it headed south.

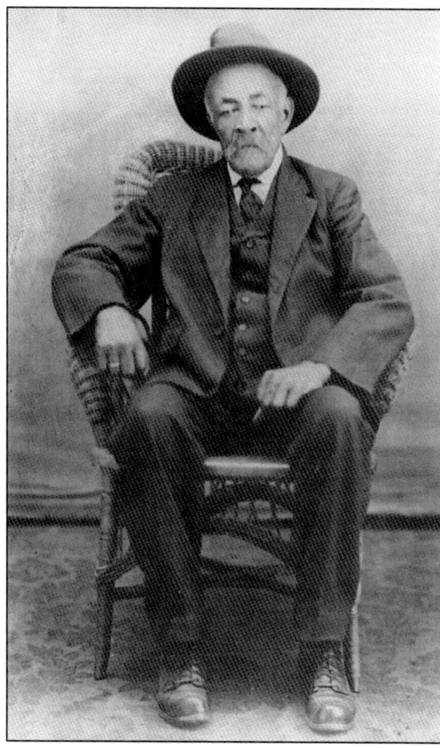

Sgt. Samuel A. Wright enlisted on August 29, 1864, in Company E, 127th Regiment, United States Colored Troops Volunteer Infantry, and served until his discharge on October 20, 1865. He was a stonemason and carpenter's helper in Shippensburg and is buried in Locust Grove Cemetery.

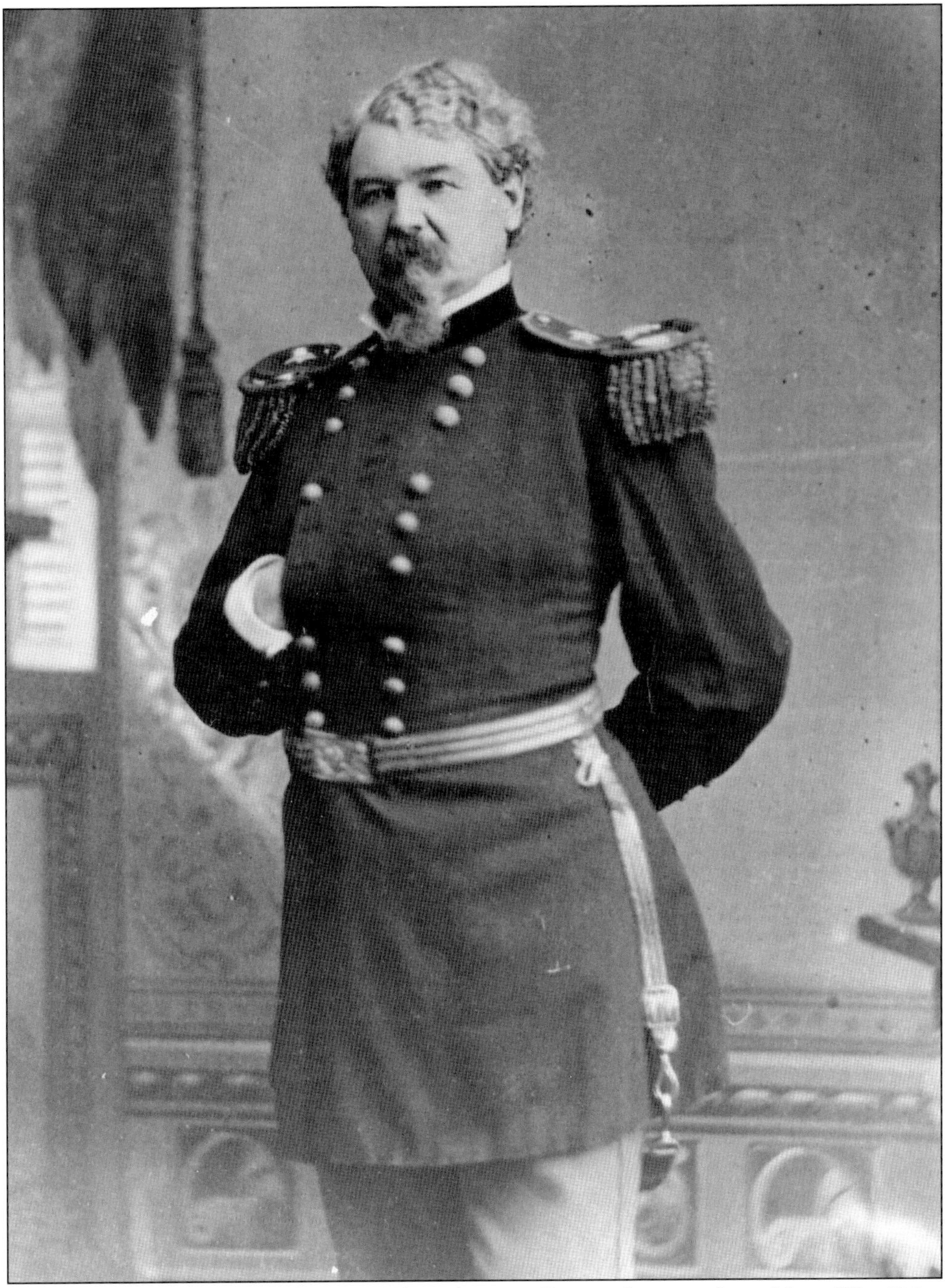

Brig. Gen. Samuel D. Sturgis (1822–1889) was born in Shippensburg, graduated from West Point (USMA), and was the only native of Shippensburg to serve as a general during the Civil War. He commanded troops at Antietam and Gettysburg and fought in other engagements as well. Sturgis remained in the Army after the war and was put in command of the 7th Cavalry, with Lt. Col. George A. Custer as his subordinate. General Sturgis's son, Lt. Richard Sturgis, was killed in the Battle of Little Bighorn. The town of Sturgis, North Dakota, a mecca for motorcyclists, is named for Lieutenant Sturgis. General Sturgis is buried in Arlington National Cemetery.

Pvt. Jacob Agle enrolled at Shippensburg in Company H, 9th Regiment, Pennsylvania Volunteer Cavalry on August 28, 1861. He was killed in action on September 13, 1863, near Lafayette, Georgia.

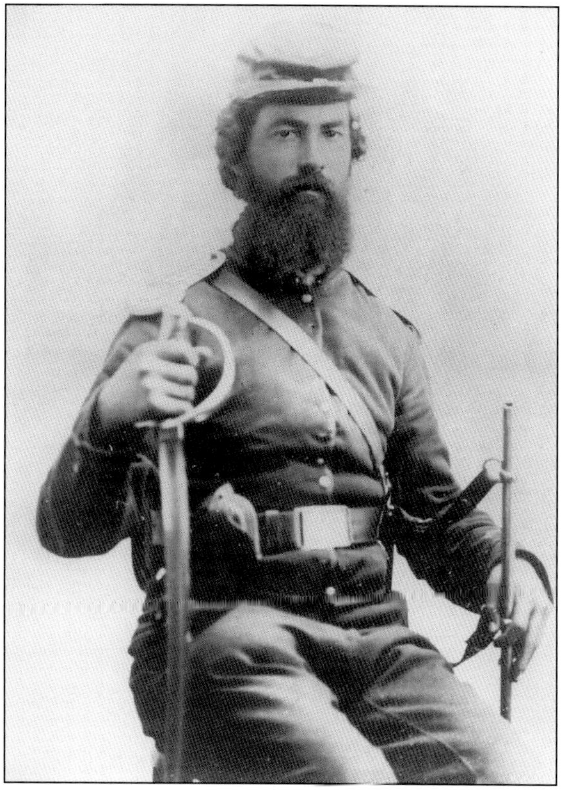

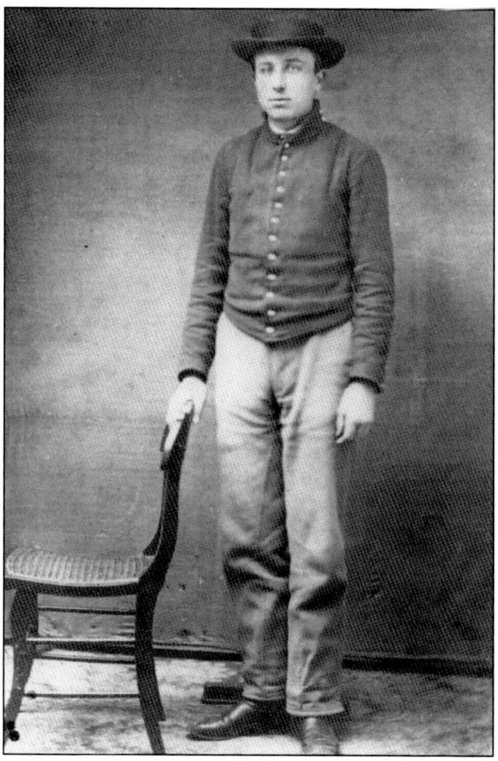

Pvt. James K.L. Mackey enlisted on August 4, 1862, and served in Company D, 130th Pennsylvania Volunteers, Infantry; Company L, 22nd Regiment Pennsylvania Volunteers, Cavalry; and Company L, 3rd Regiment, Provisional Volunteer, and Cavalry. He was discharged on October 31, 1865.

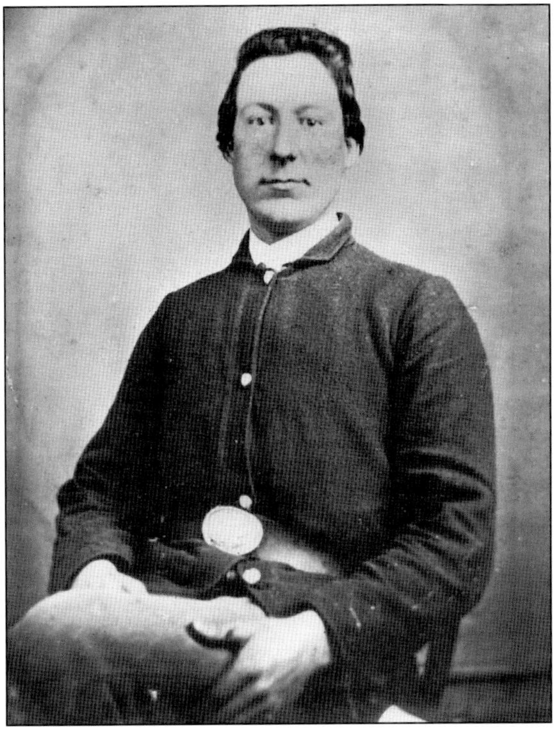

Pvt. William H. Nickles, a Newburg native, enrolled at Shippensburg in Company D, 217th Regiment, Pennsylvania Volunteers and served with that unit until May 16, 1865, when he died of a fever contracted during the siege of Petersburg, Virginia.

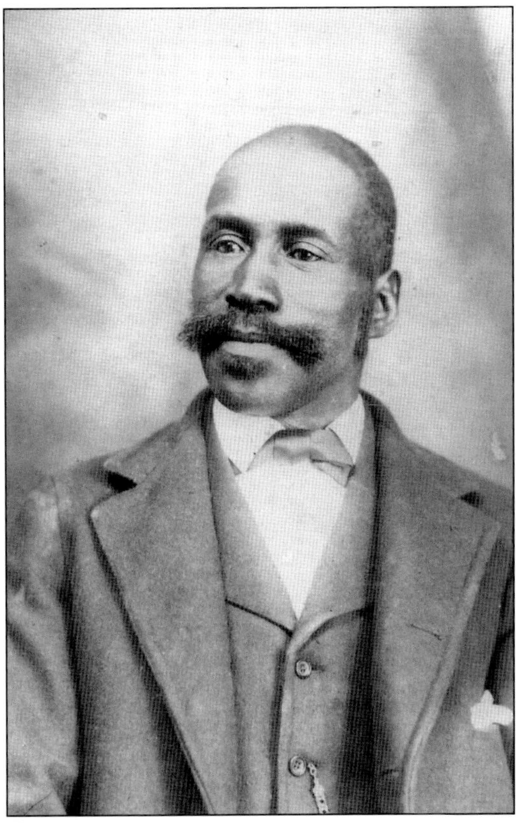

As a boy, Alex Almstead lived in an orphanage in Chambersburg. Johnson Allen, of Shippensburg, took him out of the orphanage to live with the Allen family. During the Civil War, Allen paid $300 so that Almstead could serve in his place in the Union army. Almstead served, and after his discharge he returned to live with the Allen family.

Maj. M.G. Hale was born and raised on a farm in Southampton Township, Cumberland County. He enlisted in Company M, 158th Regiment, and became commander of his regiment.

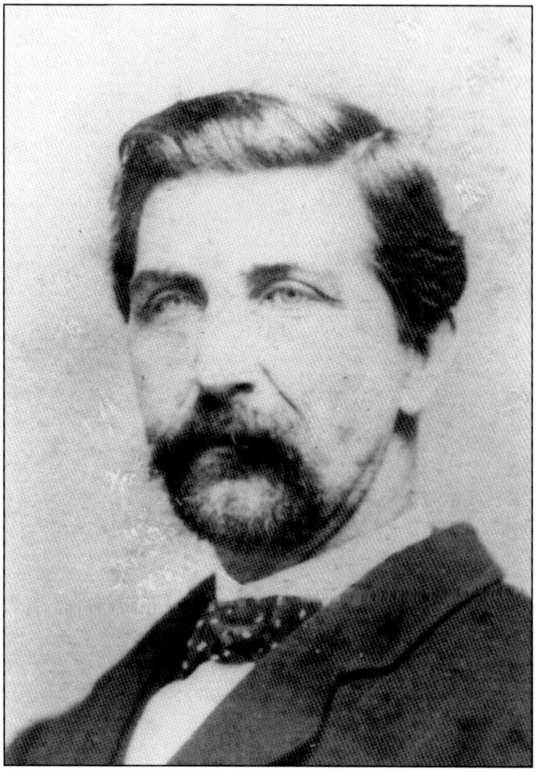

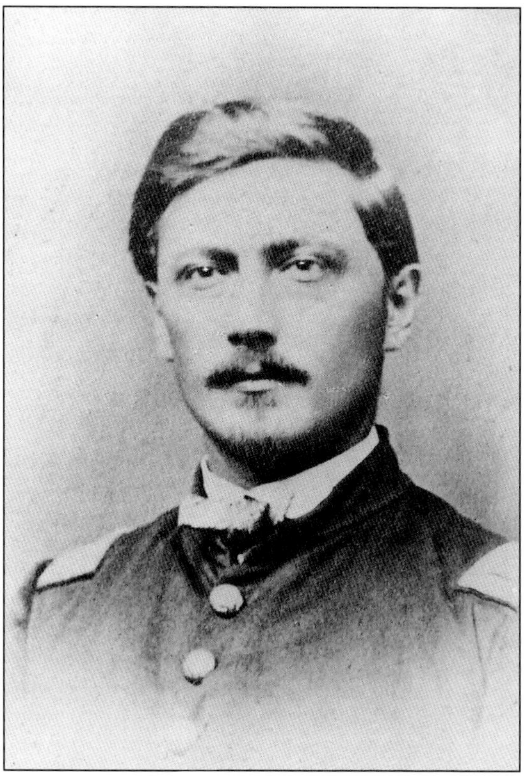

Sgt. John C. Wagner enlisted in the Adamantine Guards, which formed the 3rd Pennsylvania Regiment Cavalry, and was mustered into service on August 17, 1861. Sergeant Wagner was a brother of D.K. Wagner, publisher of the *Shippensburg News*. Together, they published a history of Company H, 3rd Regiment, Pennsylvania Cavalry.

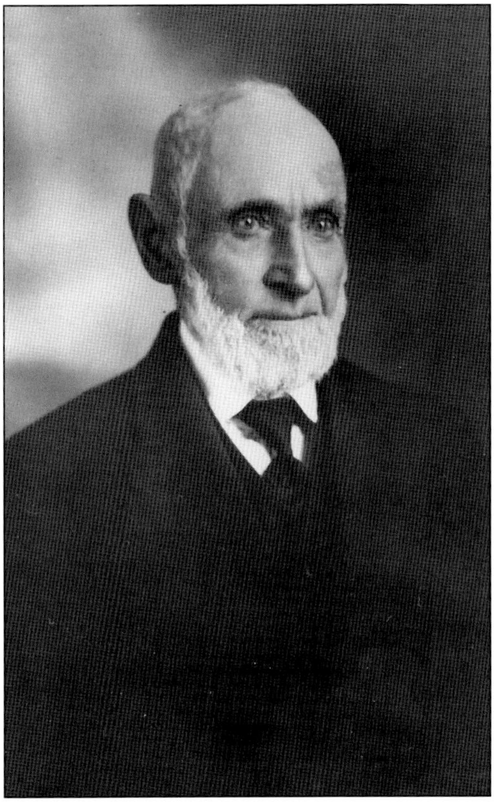

Pvt. Addison Studenroth (1824–1917) enlisted in Company H, 3rd Regiment, Pennsylvania Cavalry. He worked as a machinist after his Civil War service, and in his later years, he was the maintenance manager for the Penn Central Light and Power Company in Shippensburg.

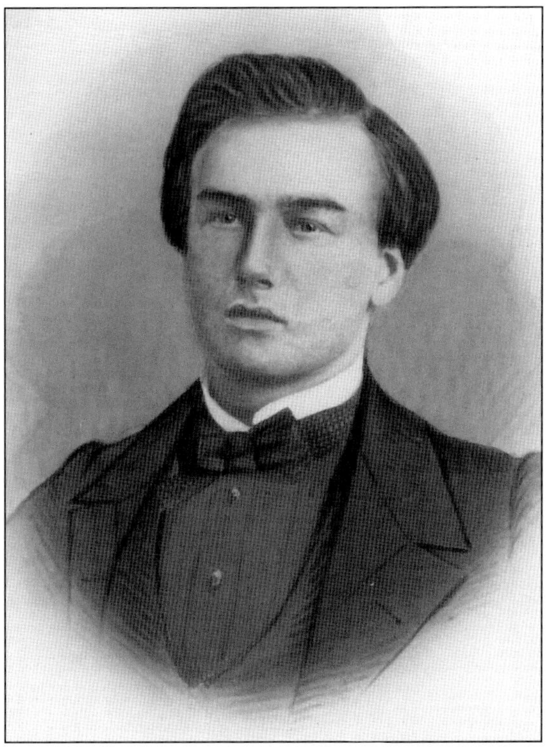

Cpl. George Johnston McLean enlisted from Shippensburg in Company D, 130th Pennsylvania Volunteers Infantry Regiment, on August 4, 1862. He was fatally wounded in the battle at Fredericksburg, Virginia, on December 13, 1862. The Cpl. George Johnston McLean Post 423 of the Grand Army of the Republic (GAR) was named in his honor.

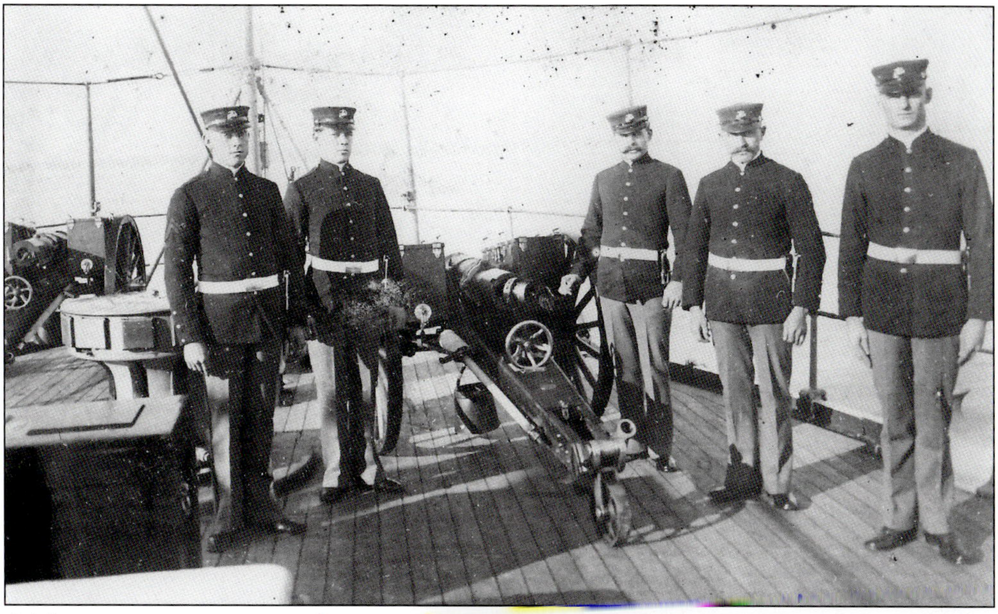

A Marine gun crew is pictured aboard the USFS *Brooklyn*, anchored in Yokohama, Japan. The second man from the right is Pvt. Henry C. Burkholder, who later lived on the road between Mainsville and Shippensburg. Although the picture is dated December 1, 1901, Private Burkholder also served during the Spanish-American War; he is buried in Spring Hill Cemetery.

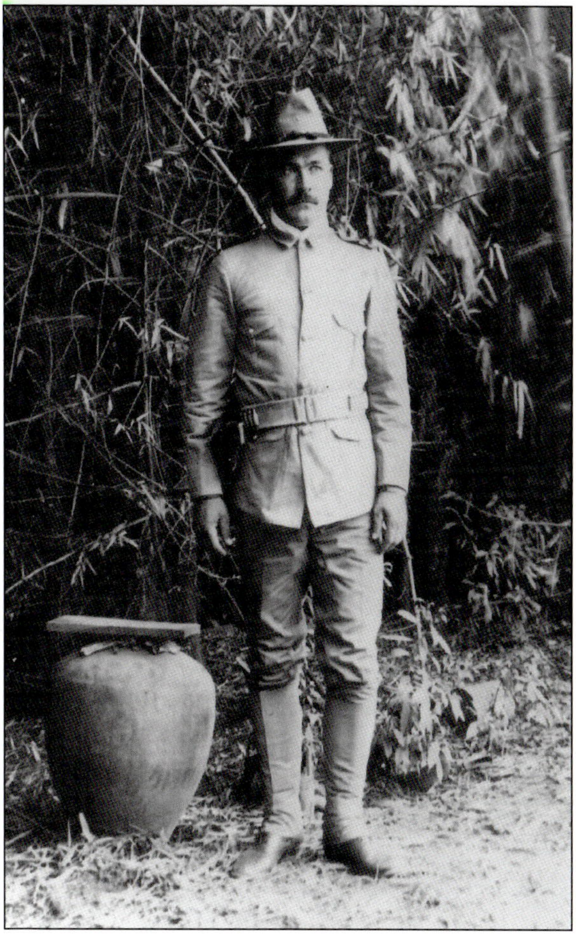

This photograph of Pvt. A. Edward Rosenberry was taken in 1898 in Manila, in the Philippine Islands. Private Rosenberry served with the 14th Battery of Field Artillery during the Spanish-American War.

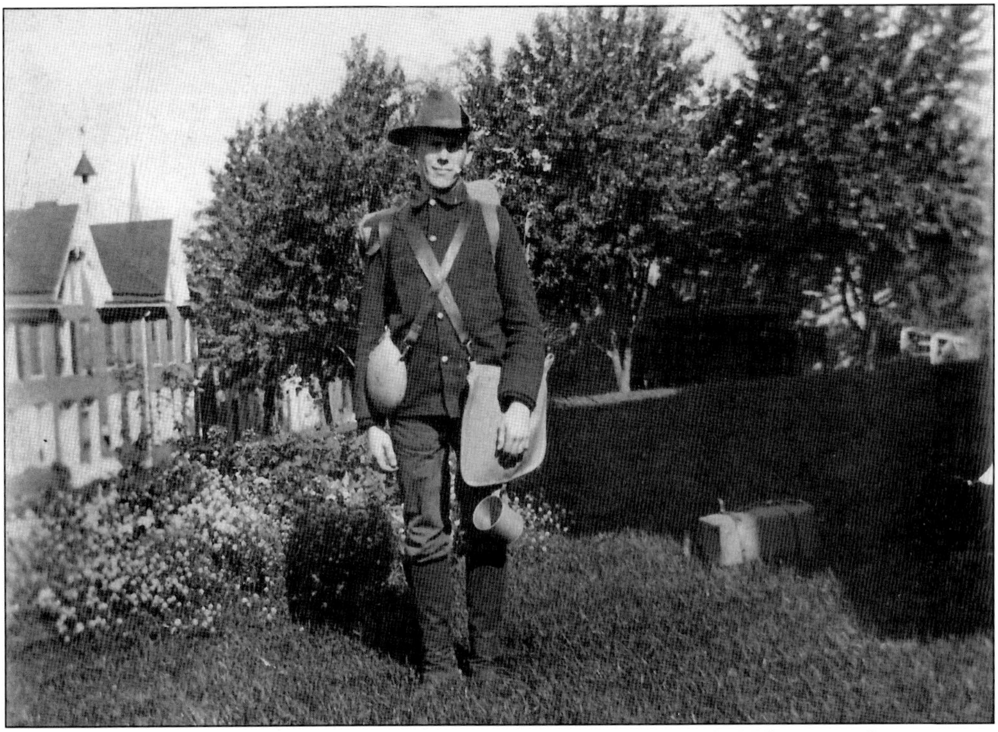

Pvt. George A Walters stands in the backyard of Harry R. Hawk at 100 East Orange Street. Except for the absence of his Krag-Jørgenson .30-caliber rifle, he is equipped with the full uniform and gear of a soldier in the Spanish-American War. Walters served with Company C, 8th Regiment, Pennsylvania Volunteers, Infantry.

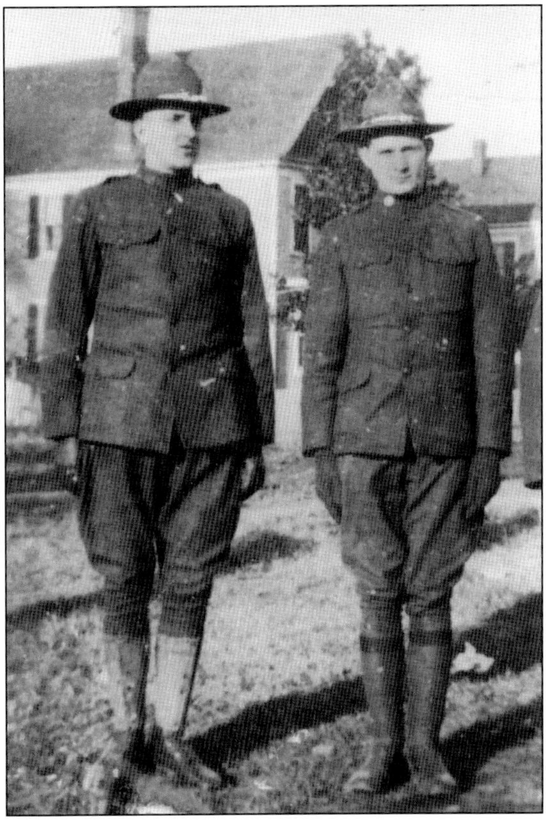

Pvt. Doyle Dunlap Ashburn (left) and Pvt. William H. Durff were both killed in action in 1918 while serving in France with Company I, 4th Infantry Regiment, 3rd Division. Private Ashburn was killed north of Montfaucon on October 20, and Private Durff was killed on the Rhine in Champagne on July 15. The Shippensburg Veterans of Foreign Wars (VFW) Post 6168 is the Durff-Kuhn Chapter, which honors Private Durff's sacrifice as well as that of Frank E. Kuhn, who was killed during World War II.

Brothers Pfc. Ralph (left) and Pfc. William Ashwell both served in France during World War I. William died of spinal meningitis at Aube, France, on January 10, 1918, while serving with Battery G, 7th Regiment, Coastal Artillery Corps; he was the first Shippensburg man to die in a combat zone during World War I.

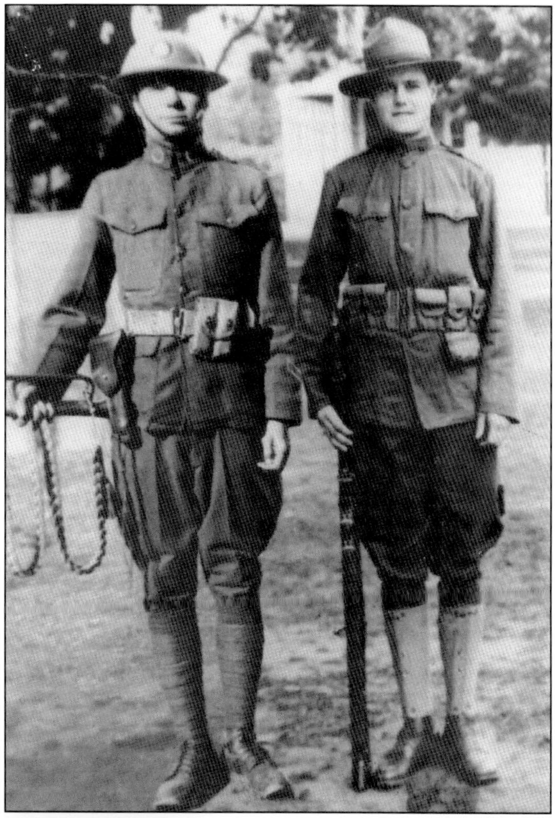

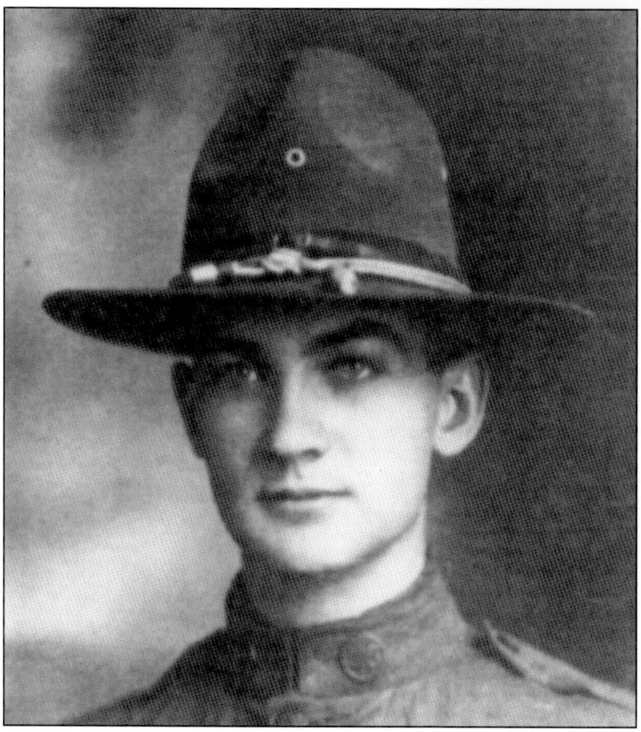

Pvt. Fred Squires, born in Shippensburg, entered the army in May 1918, received his basic training at Columbus Barracks, Ohio, and was discharged in November 1918 after the armistice was signed. He was elected commander of the Shippensburg American Legion in 1938.

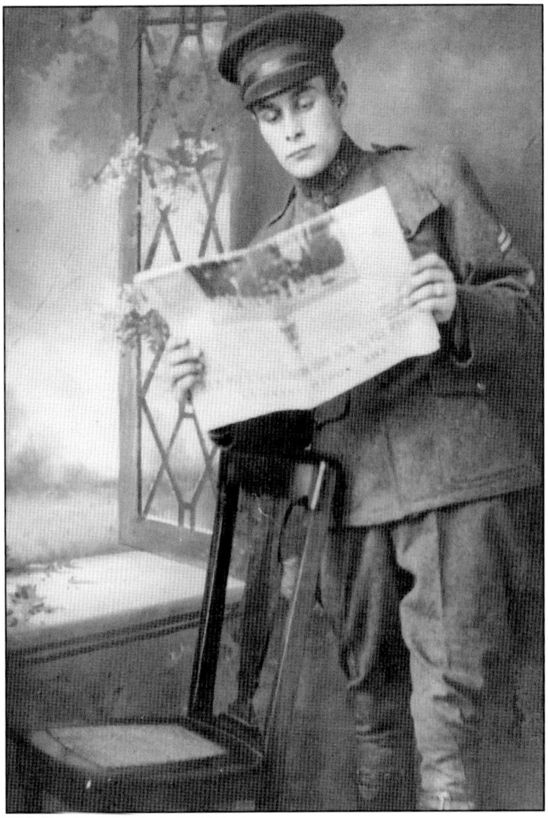

Cpl. Howard P. Booty was killed in action on August 7, 1918, while serving in Company L, 112th Regiment, 28th Division. His body was so badly dismembered that it could not be identified for burial.

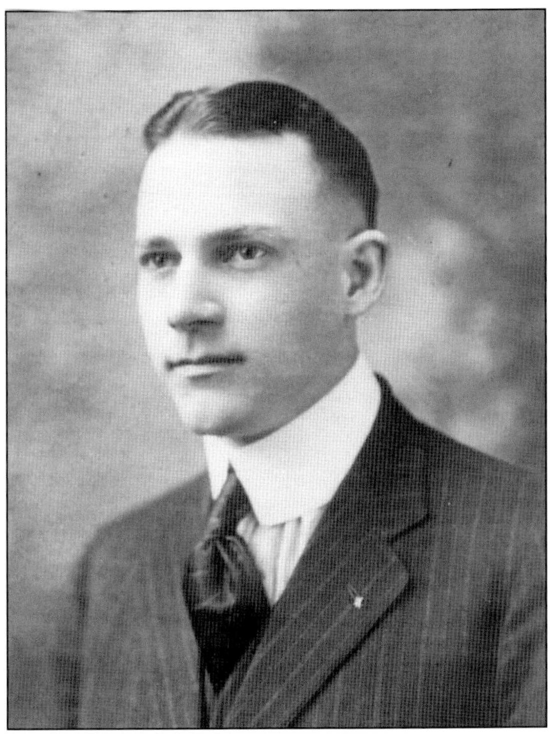

Pvt. Oscar M. Hykes served with Company H, 146th Infantry Regiment, 37th Division, and was fatally wounded on September 27, 1918, during the Meuse-Argonne Offensive. Shippensburg's American Legion Post 223 is named for him.

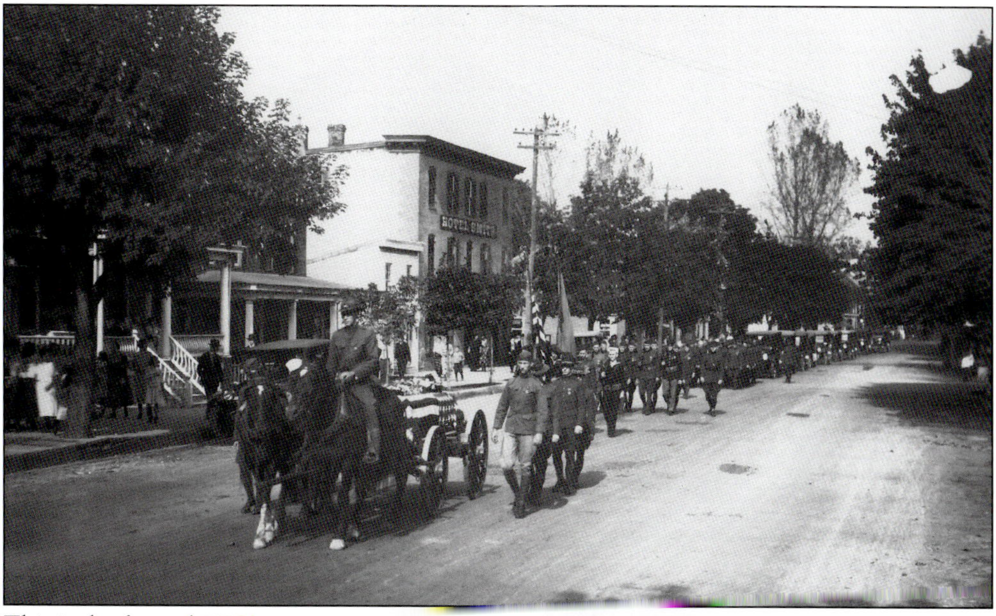

This is the funeral procession for Private Hykes. The hearse has just passed the Hotel Smith. Numerous such processions were held during World War I and afterwards, including two on the same day in 1919.

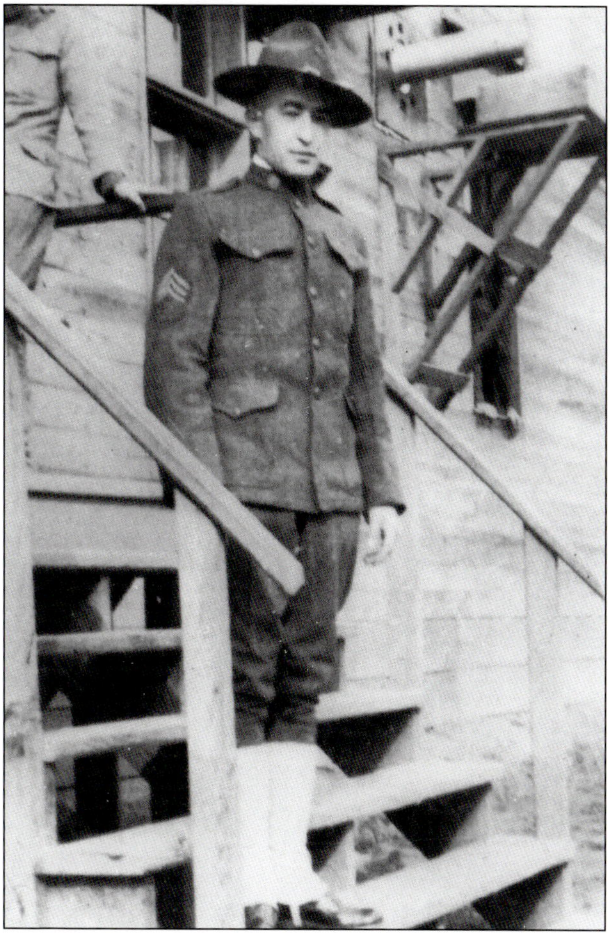

Sgt. Charles E. Newcomer served as a baker in Company 314 while attached to the base hospital 108 at the Meuse Hospital Corps in France during World War I. Several days before his discharge, he died while swimming at Fort Ontario, New York.

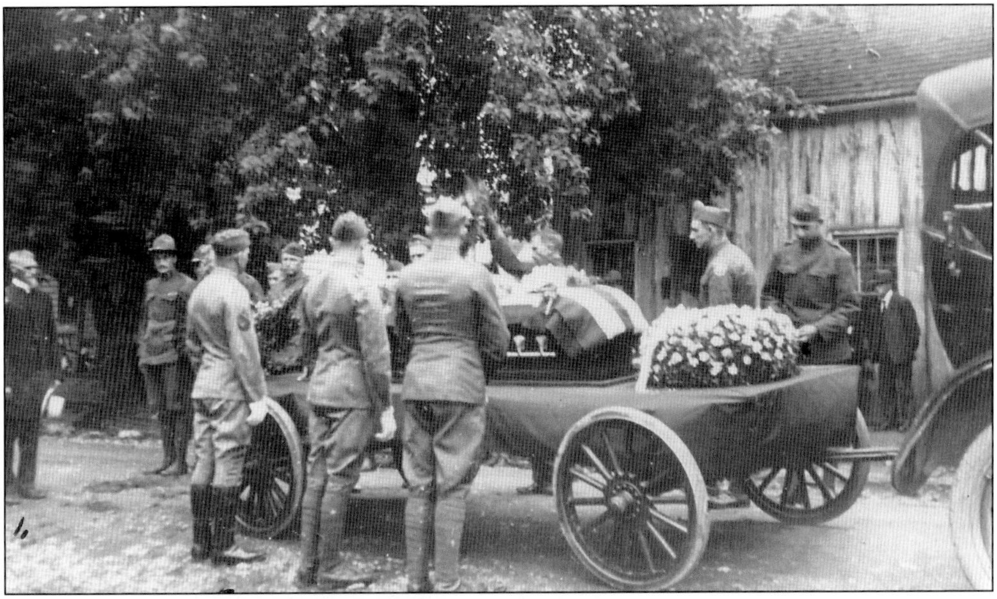

This photograph shows the funeral procession for Sgt. Charles E. Newcomer in front of his mother's house at 127 North Penn Street. His mother lived there with her sons, three of whom served in World War I. This was the first military funeral in Shippensburg after World War I.

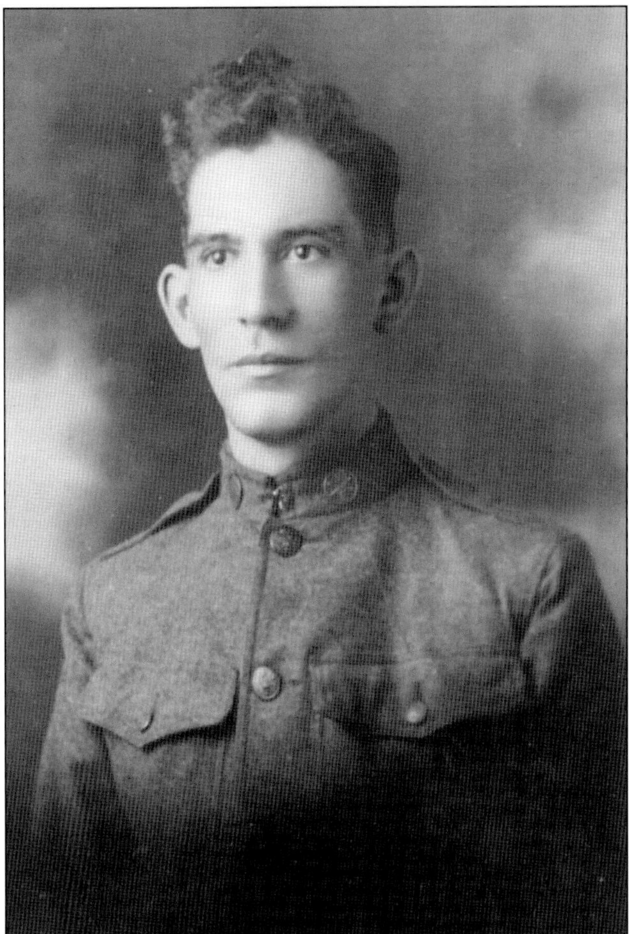

Pvt. Robert J. Price served with Company G, 148th Infantry Regiment, 37th Division. Fatally wounded on October 15, 1918, at Pagny-sur-Meuse, northwest of Verdun, France, he died the same day.

Pvt. Calvin Lee Sharp was killed in action on September 27, 1918, while serving with Company H, 118th Infantry Regiment, 28th Division. His unit was participating in the push into Chateau-Thierry in the beginning of the Meuse-Argonne Offensive.

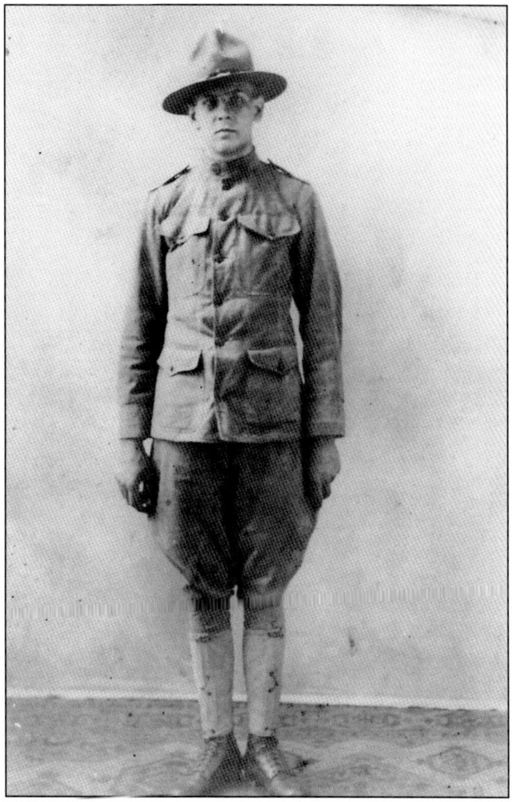

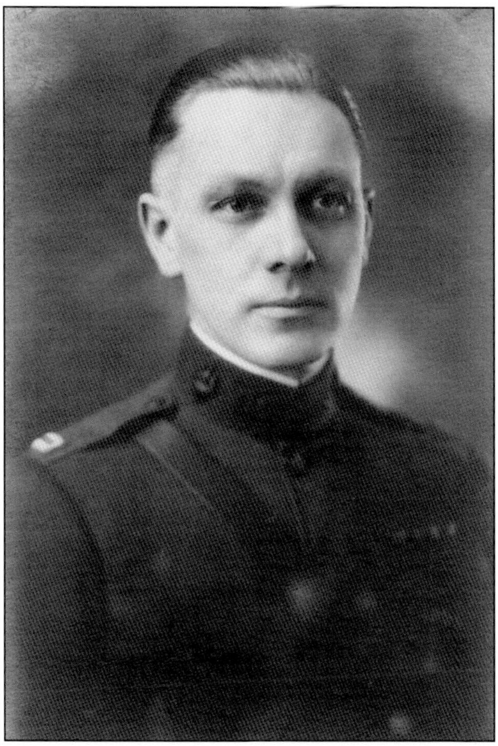

Capt. George H. Stewart Jr. served in the Transportation Corps of the Army during World War I. Following Captain Stewart's military service, Pennsylvania governor William C. Sproul appointed him a member of the five-man Battle Monuments Commission in France to select sites and erect monuments to honor the soldiers, sailors, and Marines who served there. In 1919, Stewart was chosen the first commander of the newly formed Shippensburg American Legion Post 223.

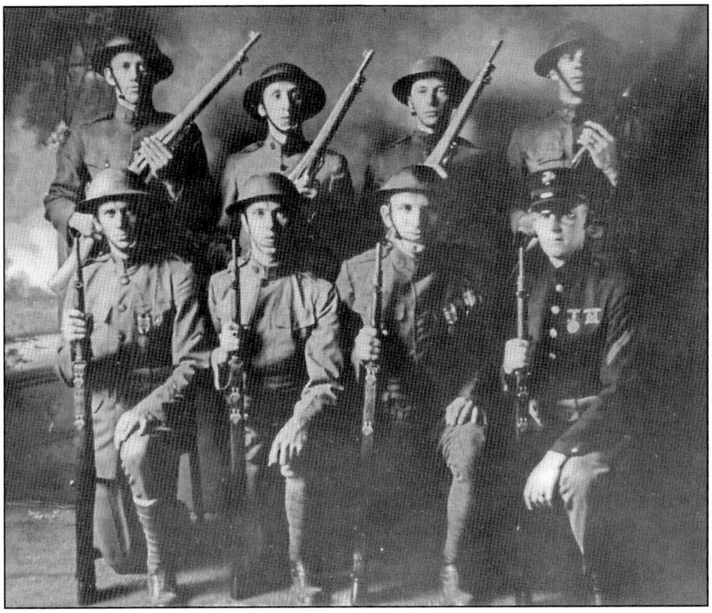

This was the first Shippensburg American Legion Firing Squad that participated in a public ceremony. Made up of World War I veterans, all except one are wearing the World War I US Army uniforms in which they were discharged. Lee M. Hale (first row, far right) was a Marine.

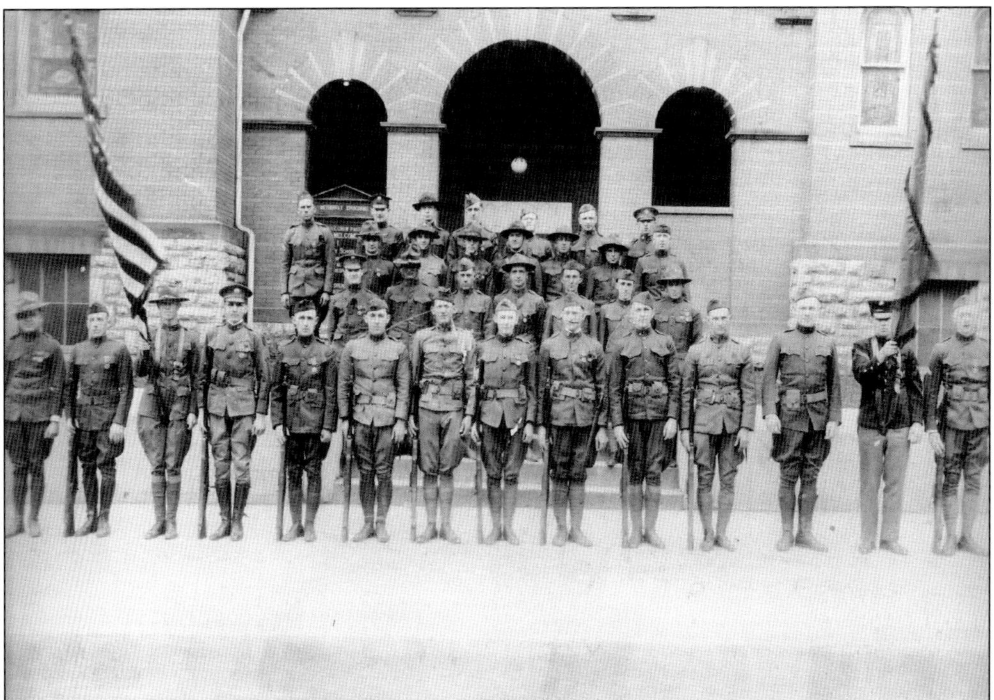

The American Legion Marching Unit was assembled to march in the 1920 Memorial Day parade. The unit stands in front of what is now Christ United Methodist Church at 47 East King Street. Traditionally, the marching units of both the American Legion and Veterans of Foreign Wars participate in Memorial Day parades and other functions.

Wilber E. and Mildred I. Goodhart both served in World War I. She was in the British military service, while he was in the American Air Service. Wilbur served as commander of the Shippensburg American Legion.

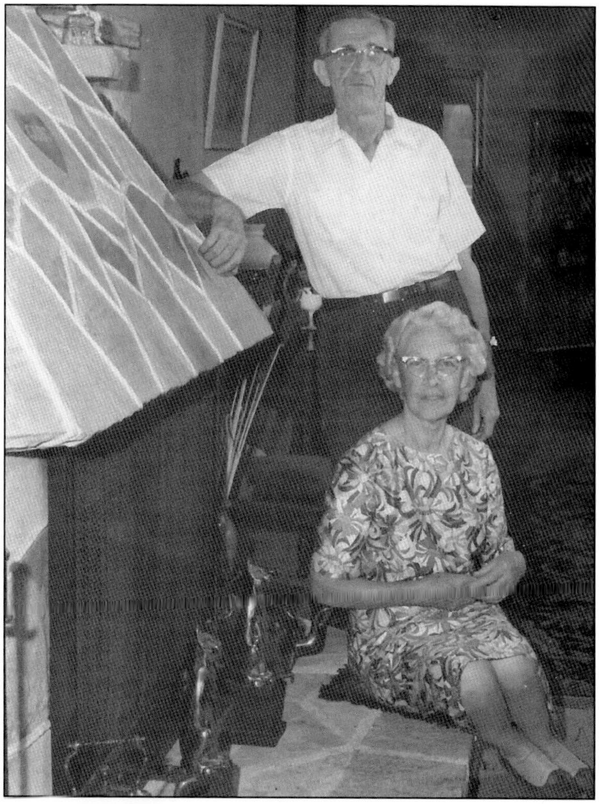

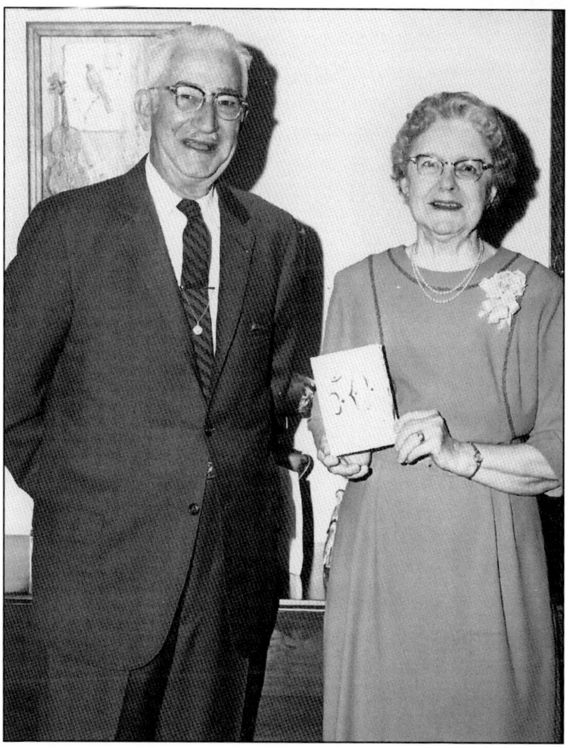

Kenneth J. and Helen M. Jacobs are pictured in 1968. After his military service in World War I, Kenneth was elected post commander of the Shippensburg Veterans of Foreign Wars Post 6168. Kenneth died on August 10, 1973.

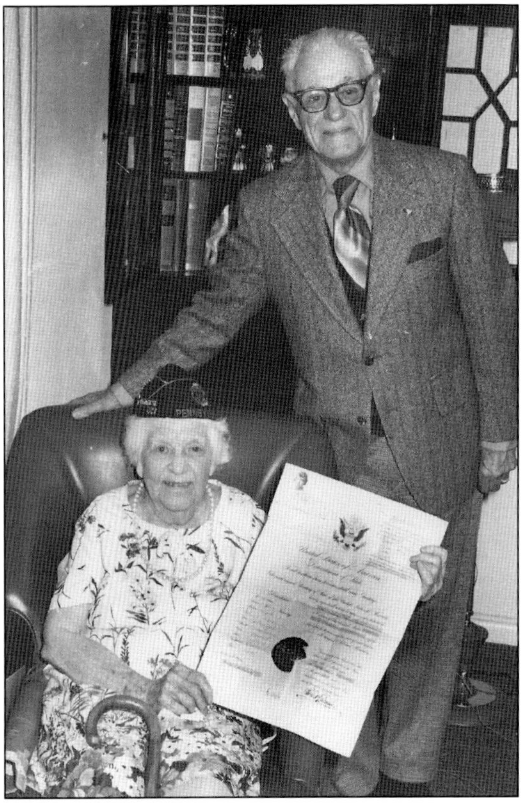

The woman in this photograph is Anna Fellows, an Army Reserve nurse who performed her duty in France during World War I. The gentleman is Russell L. Kent, who served with the Army in France in World War I. The photograph was taken on January 28, 1980, in the Episcopal Home on East Burd Street, where Fellows was a resident. Both are now deceased.

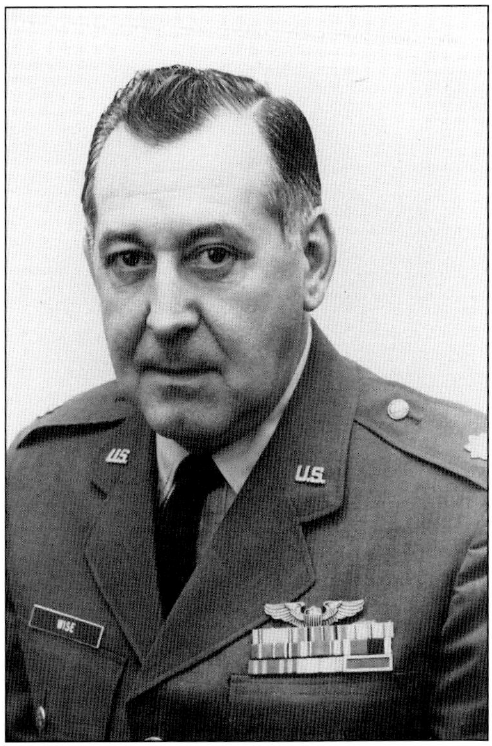

Lt. Col. Raymond T. Wise, of the US Army Air Forces, served from December 1940 to March 20, 1946, during World War II. He was elected commander of the Shippensburg American Legion for 1947.

Michael "Mike" Shaner participated in several operations with the Marine Corps in the Pacific during World War II. He commanded the Shippensburg American Legion in 1963 and 1964. He was extremely popular with the veterans and was one of the few elected to a second term.

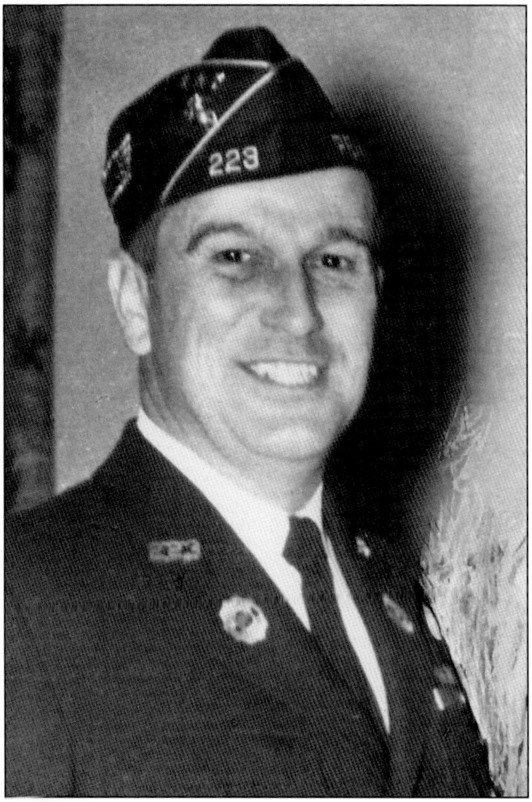

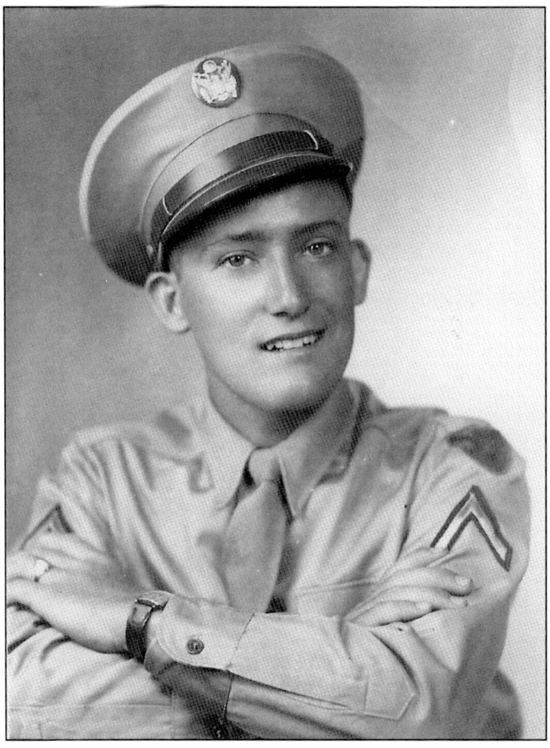

Pfc. Wilbur C. Burkholder was an infantryman in the Fifth Army and participated in landings in North Africa and Italy. He was killed in action in Italy on October 15, 1944.

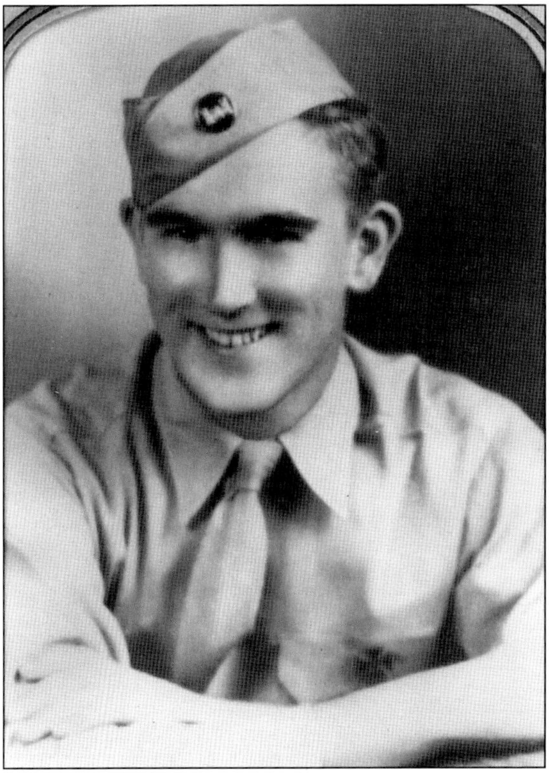

John A. Fogelsanger was the son of Ross and Martha Fogelsanger, who had a farm on Rowe Road. Ross served in France in World War I and was gassed. His son John was killed in action in France during World War II.

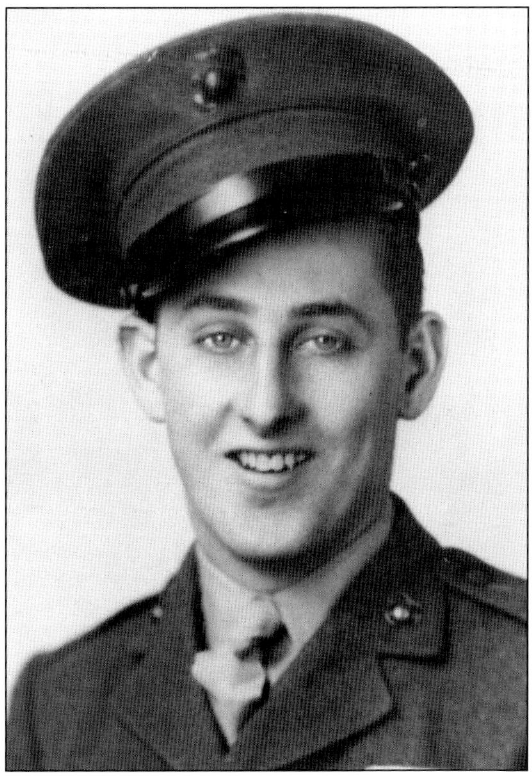

Pfc. Clyde Marshall Klenzing, US Marine Corps, was killed in action while fighting on the island of Peleliu on October 6, 1944. Peleliu was one of the bloodiest battles in the Pacific theater. Many survivors of this campaign later landed at Okinawa on April 1, 1945.

Pfc. Robert C. Mitten, US Army, took part in the D-Day landing at Normandy and continued fighting until he was killed in action on August 11, 1944, at St. Lô, France.

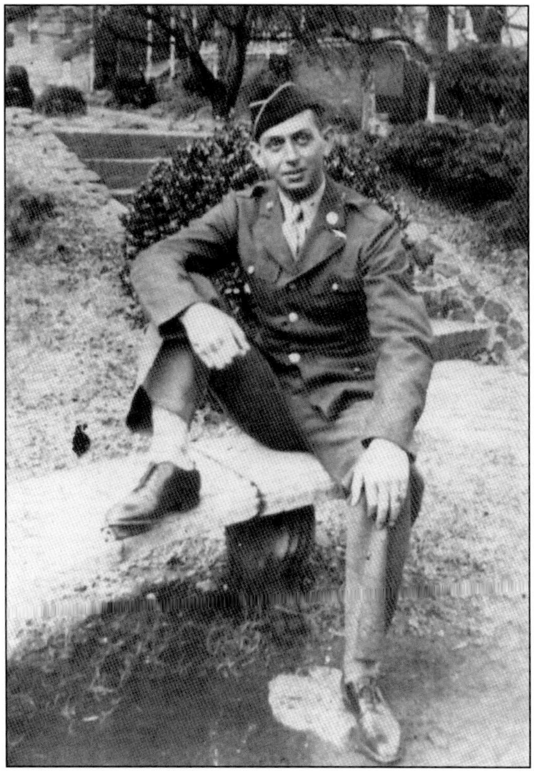

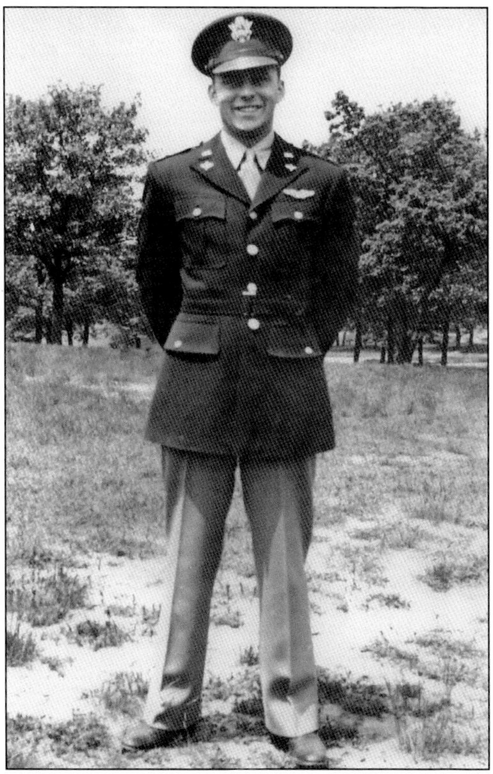

Capt. Richard Bruce Ott, a member of the Army Air Force troop carrier *Cornwall*, was killed in action when the plane he was piloting crashed as he was returning to base in Sicily on November 22, 1943.

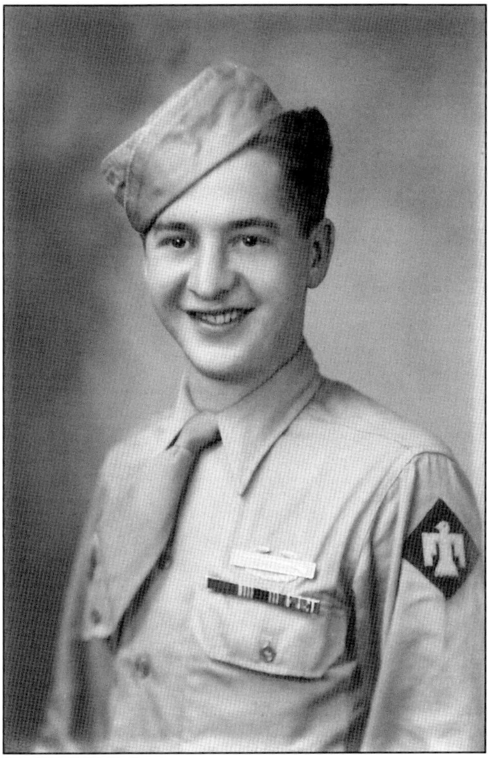

Pfc. Robert E. "Bob" Palmer, US Army, was with the 45th Infantry Division when it landed at Oran, Algeria; Salerno, Italy; and finally, at Anzio, Italy, where he was captured on February 15 or 18. He and other American soldiers who participated in the landing spent the next 14 months as prisoners of war. Palmer was wounded in battle and was awarded the Purple Heart. (Courtesy of Ethel Palmer.)

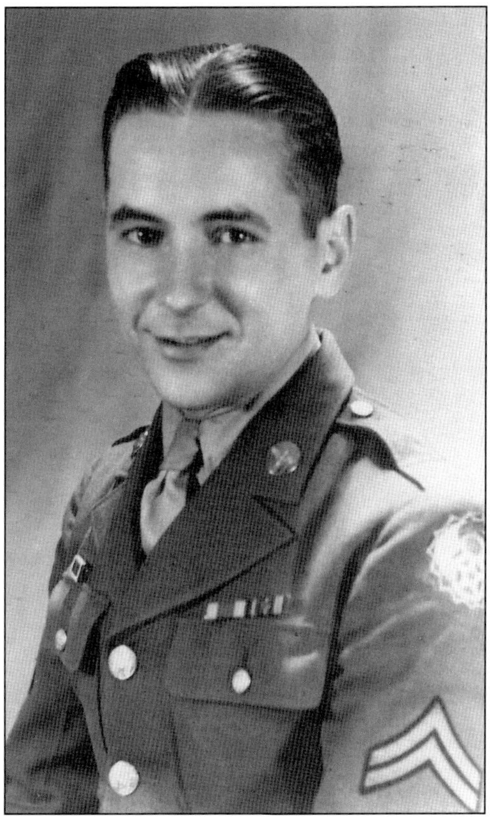

Cpl. Roy Dubbs served in the Army Air Forces in England and France, where he worked as an aircraft mechanic during World War II. He returned to the United States after the war and, in 1948, brought his future wife, Christina—whom he had met in Scotland during the war—to the United States, where they were married. He retired from Letterkenny Army Depot. His widow, "Chris," survives. (Courtesy of Christina Dubbs.)

Army staff sergeant John W. Fague participated in the Battle of the Bulge with the 11th Armored Division and, after the Ardennes Campaign, served with the Third Army in the Rhineland, Central Europe, and Austria. His memoirs of the Battle of the Bulge have been published in both French and English. The photograph was taken in July 1945 at the Berghof, Hitler's mountain retreat near the town of Berchtesgaden. (Courtesy of John Fague.)

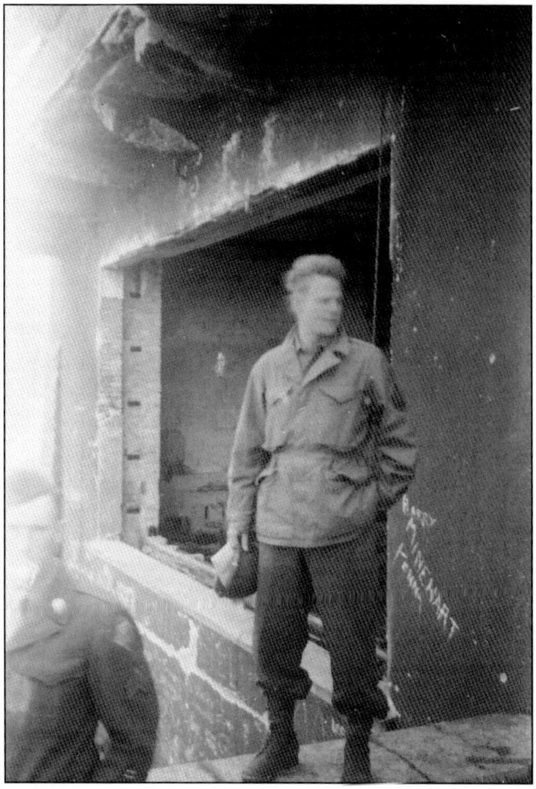

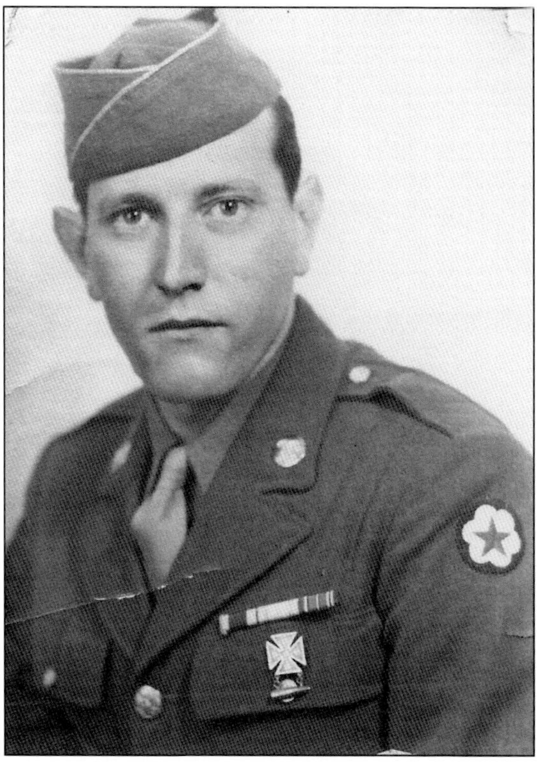

Cpl. Samuel Reed was assigned to the 3882 Quartermaster Truck Company, where he took part in the Normandy Invasion on June 6, 1944, and the Battle of the Bulge. He helped keep 40 Army trucks in working order as they drove thousands of miles to deliver munitions and supplies to the front lines. He entered Berlin as the war was coming to an end. (Courtesy of Samuel Reed.)

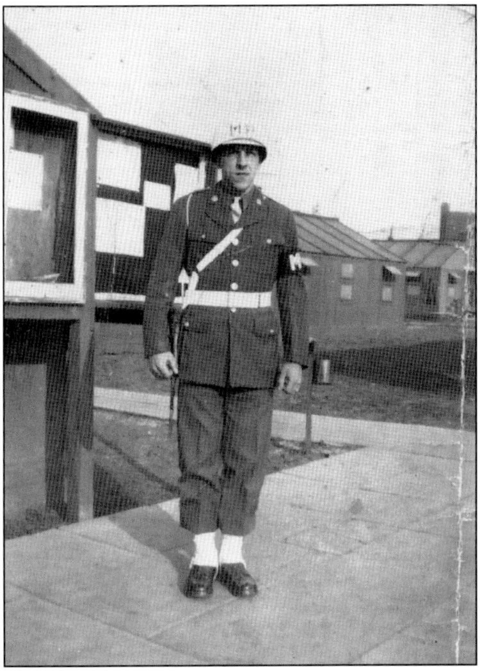

Pfc. Rodney W. Kauffman, of Cleversburg, entered the US Army on July 3, 1942. After basic training, he was selected to go to Columbus, Ohio, to train in the Army Air Forces as a military policeman. Initially stationed in England, Kauffman's unit was renamed the 1145th Police Aviation unit just before D-Day (June 6, 1944). By September, he was in Belgium, followed by movement into Germany in 1945 at the conclusion of the war in Europe. (Courtesy of Joan Coy.)

The Mitten-Stouffer Chapter 265 of the Military Order of the Purple Heart is seen here parading on West King Street on May 30, 1948. The *Purple Heart*, the official publication of the Military Order of the Purple Heart Inc., features this photograph on the cover of its August 1948 issue.

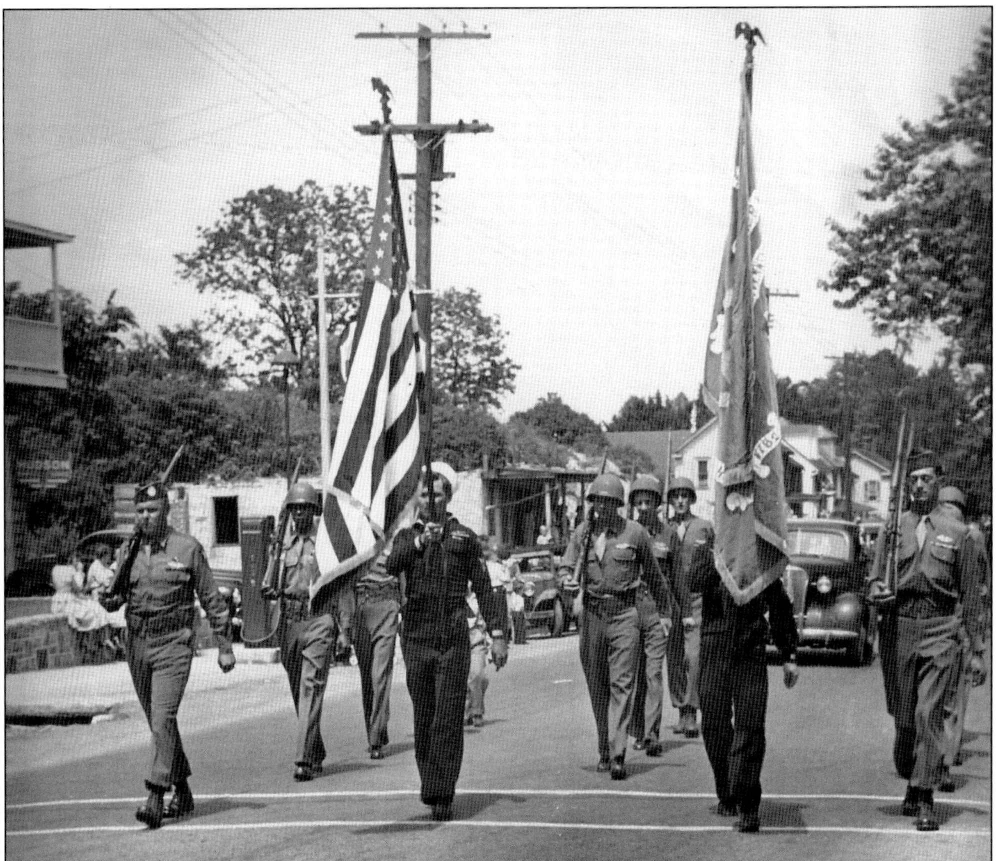

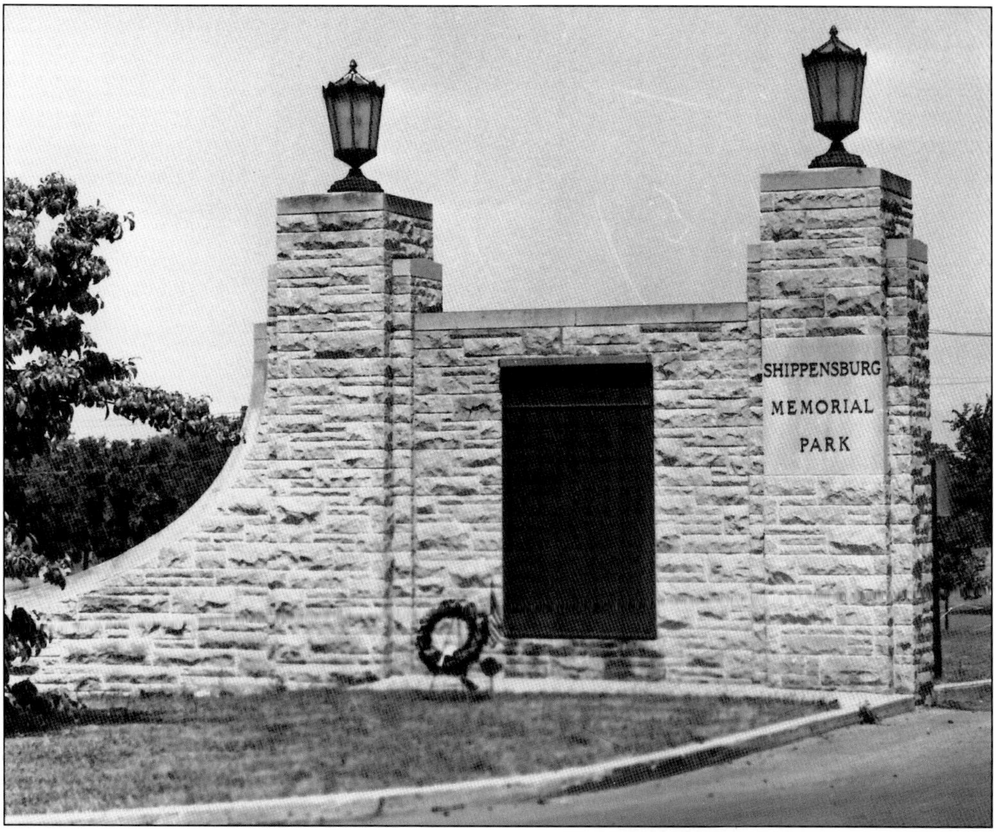

This photograph shows the west tablet of the World War II Honor Roll (the other half is on the right side) at the entrance to Shippensburg Memorial Park. The tablets list 1,491 World War II veterans from Shippensburg. Among these veterans, 49 died during the war. This memorial was dedicated on Labor Day in 1950.

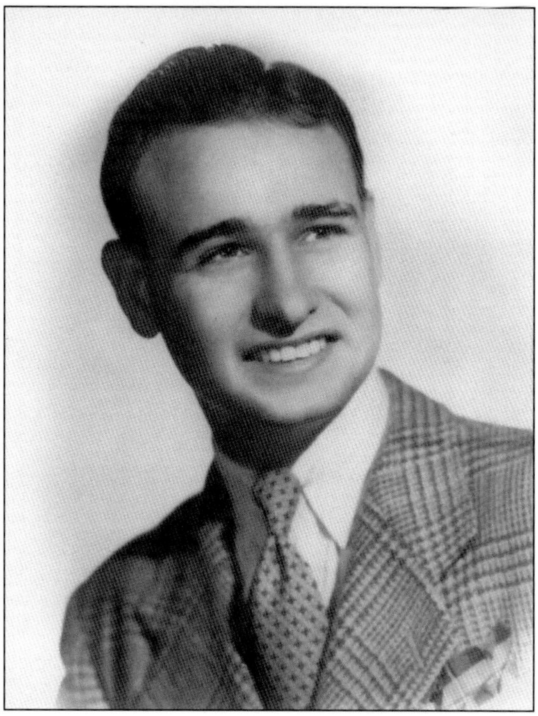

Gordon L. Eyer, a member of the 29th Infantry Regiment of the US Army, was the first Shippensburg soldier killed in the Korean War. He was killed at Hadong Pass, South Korea, on July 27, 1950, shortly after hostilities broke out following the North Korean invasion of South Korea.

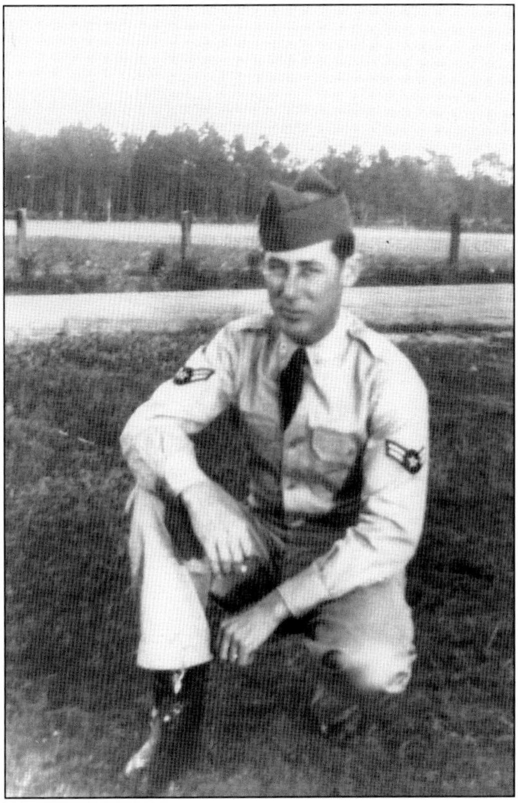

A1c. (later S.Sgt.) Thomas "Tom" A. Payne served in the Army Air Forces and the renamed US Air Force from September 1946 through the Korean War until June 1956. He commanded the Shippensburg American Legion in 1971 and served as legion delegate to the 19th District from 1973 to 1975.

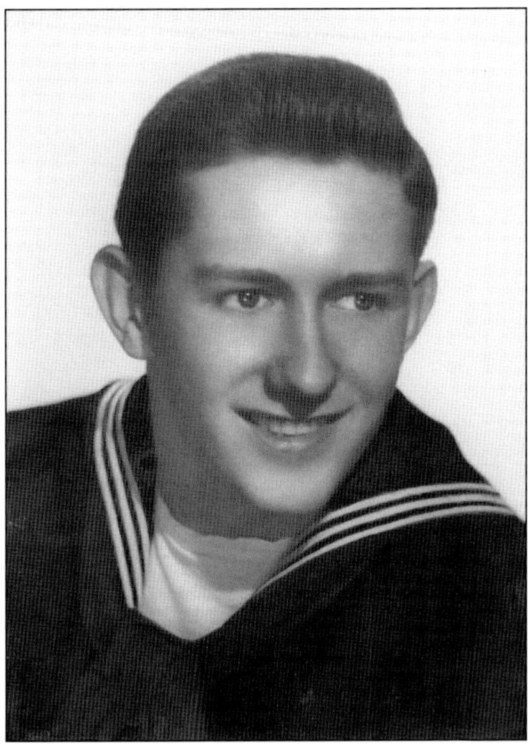

Carl L. Cramer served with the US Navy for 28 years, with four years of active duty from 1952 to 1956. He received a promotion to chief sonarman in 1965. A life member of the Shippensburg American Legion Post 223 and the Shippensburg Veterans of Foreign Wars Post 6168, Cramer has been a member of the American Legion's "Minutemen" for 35 years. In civilian life, he operated an insurance agency and served as mayor of Newburg, Pennsylvania, for 32 consecutive years. (Courtesy of Carl Cramer.)

Cpl. Gerald Eldon Crider served with the 24th Signal Company, 24th Infantry Division, Korea, for 17 months during the Korean War. He was discharged on November 10, 1954. (Courtesy of Gerald Crider.)

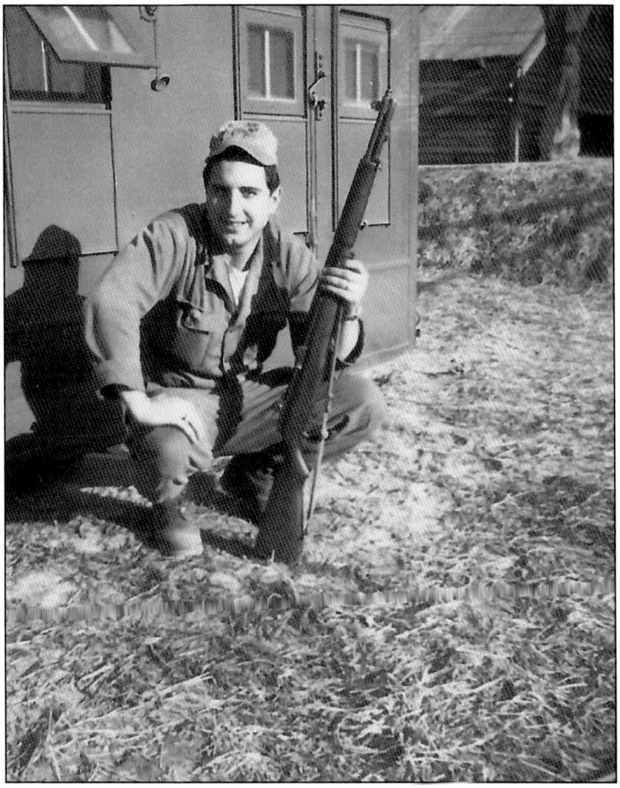

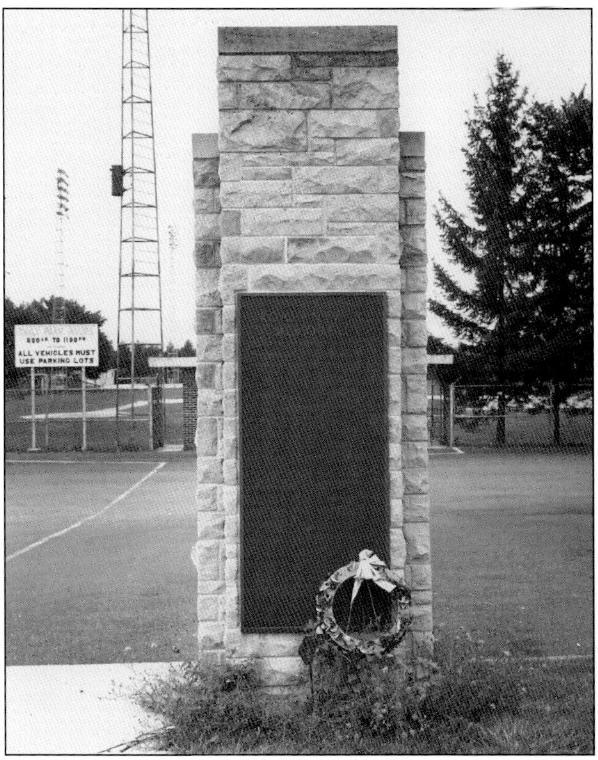

This Korean War Honor Roll, listing 472 names of Shippensburg residents who served during the Korean War, was installed in 1958 in Memorial Park by the Shippensburg Veterans Council, representing the American Legion and the Veterans of Foreign Wars.

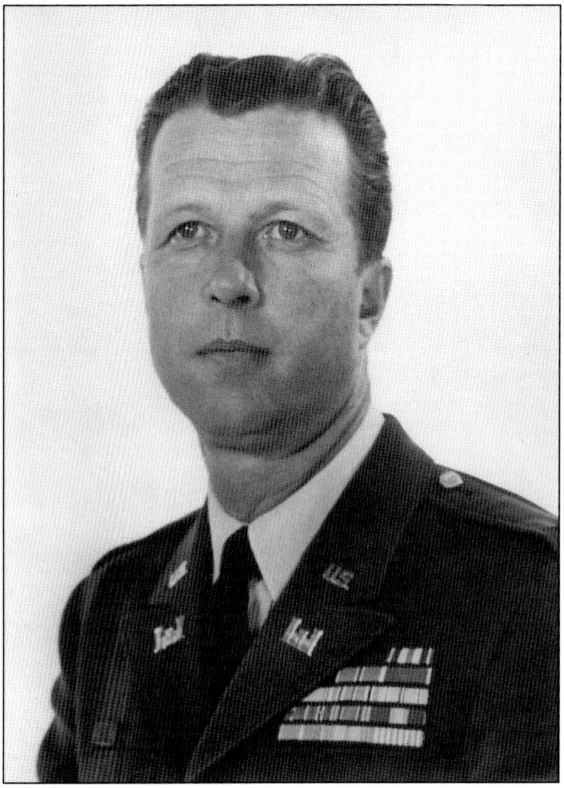

Maj. Courtney P. Hollar was drafted into the US Army in 1941. He served in the Army Corps of Engineers in World War II, the Korean War, and Vietnam. He lost his life in a plane that was shot down by guerilla fire on May 5, 1964, becoming Shippensburg's first fatality in the Vietnam War.

Loetta G. Hollar, widow of Maj. Courtney Hollar, is being presented her late husband's Legion of Merit Award. Major Hollar died when the twin-engine plane in which he and nine other Americans and five Vietnamese soldiers were riding was shot down by enemy forces south of Saigon.

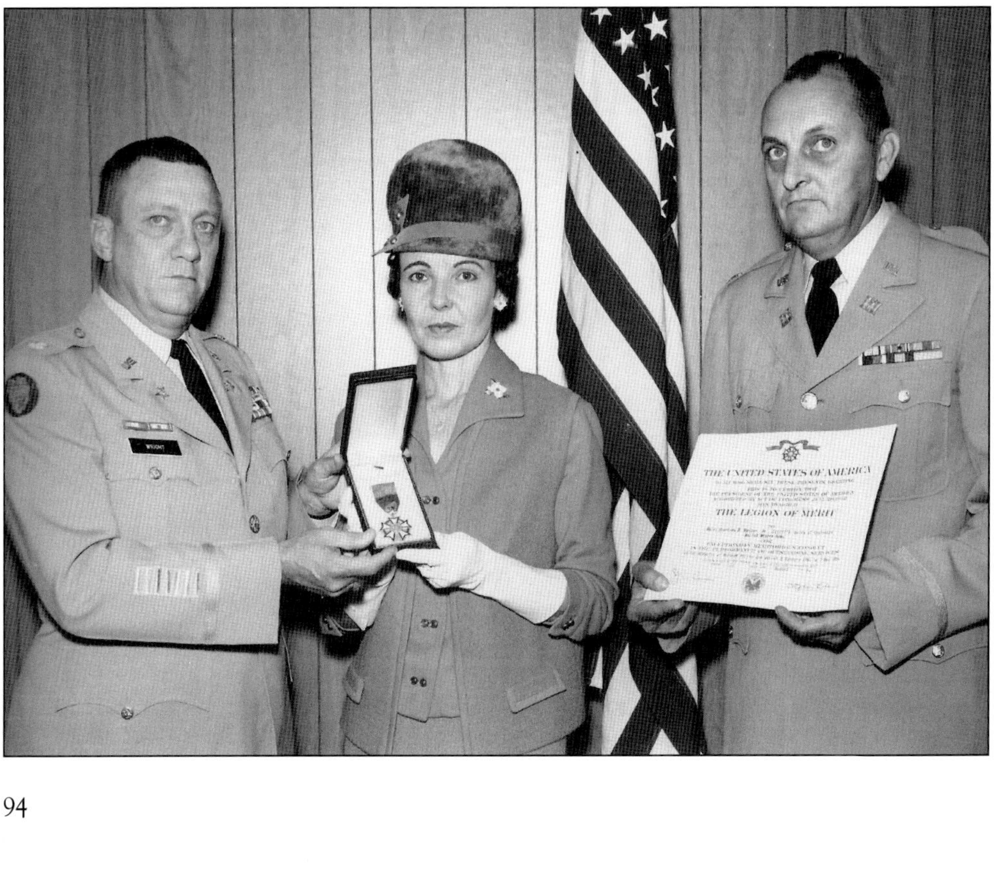

Freddie Maley served in the US Navy as an aviation boatswain's mate (AB) during the early days of the Vietnam War. He commanded the Shippensburg American Legion in 1988.

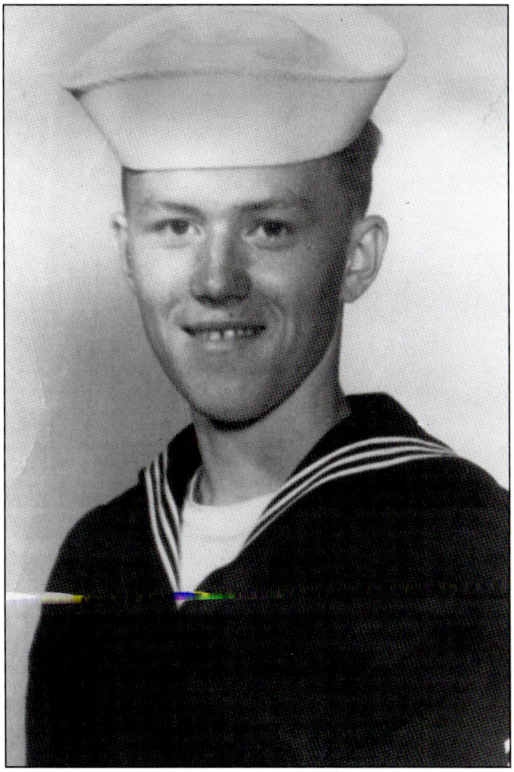

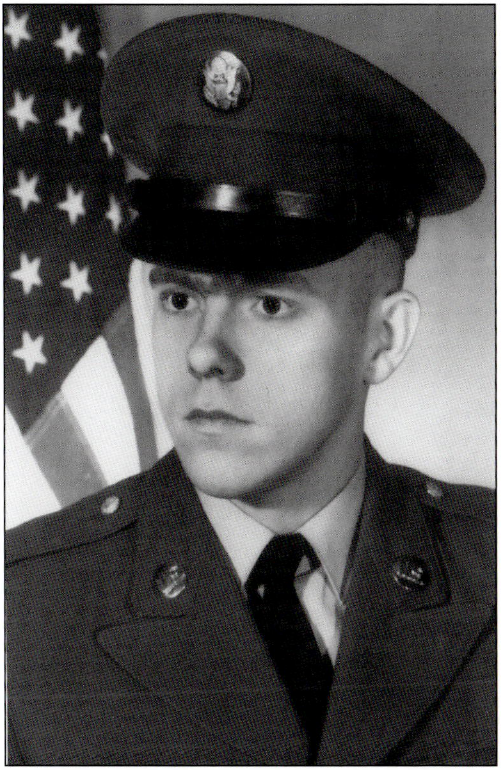

SP4 (specialist fourth class) Jules F. Clugh, US Army, served during the Vietnam War from 1969 to 1976. He was commander of the American Legion in 1978.

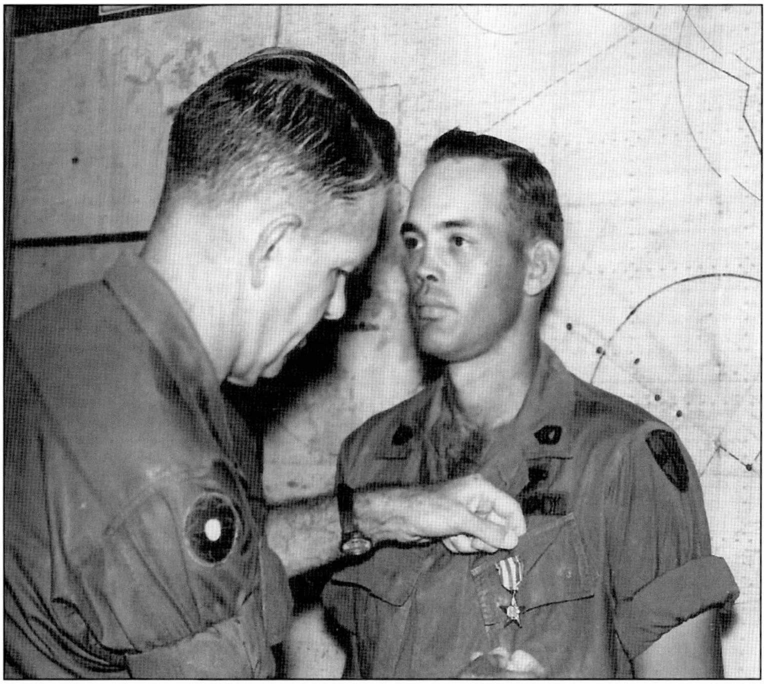

Army sergeant first class Jimmie E. Watt, of 24 South Washington Street in Shippensburg, was awarded the Silver Star for heroism against the enemy on August 30, 1967. The award was made in September 1968. The Silver Star is the third-highest award for bravery in the US Army.

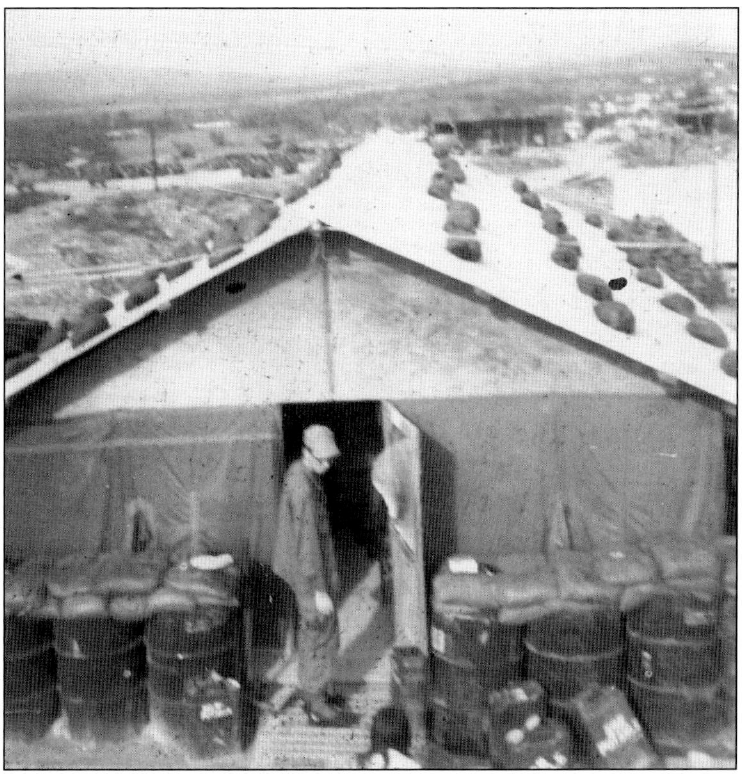

This 1970 photograph shows Sgt. Donald F. Dagenhart at Chu Lai in South Vietnam. He was attached to Headquarters Battery of the 3rd Division, 16th Artillery. He served as an artillery surveyor, or fire direction control computer, in which capacity he computed fire missions for the 155-mm battery. (Courtesy of Donald Dagenhart.)

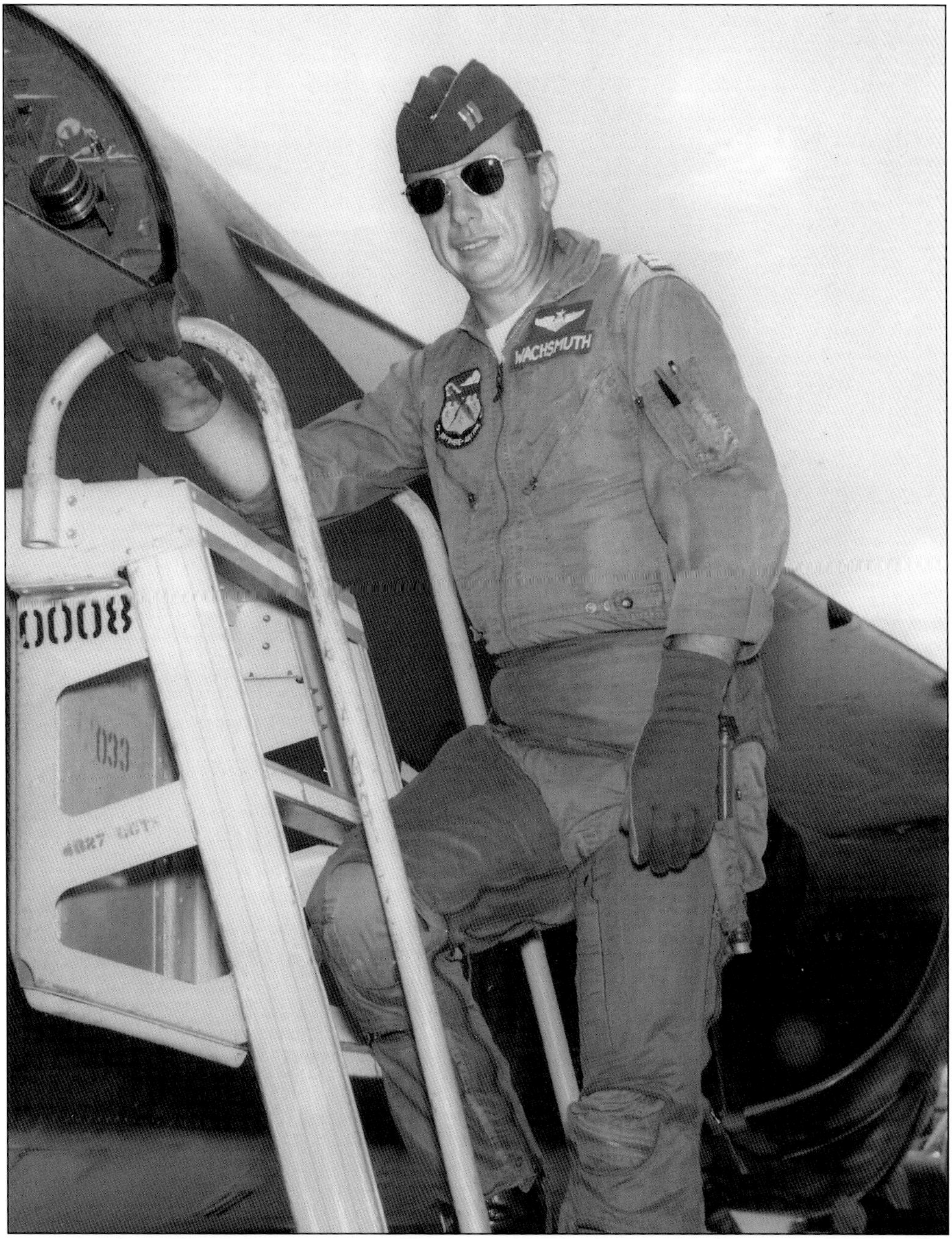

Lt. Col. Wayne Wachsmuth (pictured here as a captain) served in the US Air Force from 1957 to 1987. Among his many other flying missions, he flew 133 as a B-52 pilot in the Vietnam War; altogether, he has over 6,000 flight hours. Upon retirement, Colonel Wachsmuth became a licensed battlefield guide at Gettysburg National Park. He has served in numerous capacities as a Civil War consultant. (Courtesy of Wayne Wachsmuth.)

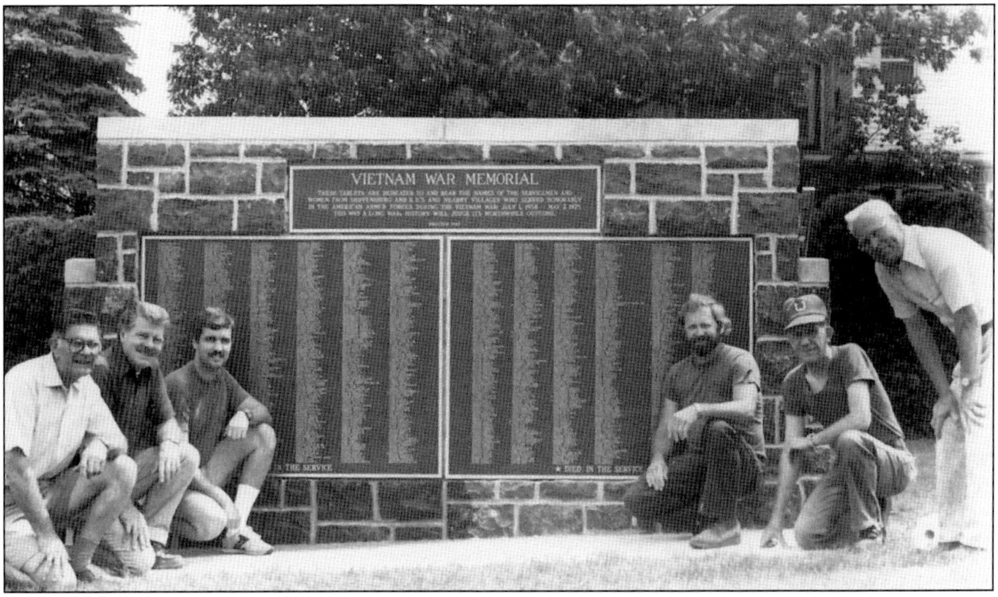

This Vietnam War Memorial is located on the east side of the entrance to Shippensburg Memorial Park. The three bronze plaques list all of the residents of Shippensburg who served in the war from 1958 to 1975. Pictured here are the men who fastened the plaques to the marble marker on June 13, 1987. They are, from left to right, B.W. Brechbill, Thomas G. Everett, Richard Bonitz, William "Jim" Yohe, Barry Hippensteel, and William "Bill" Burkhart. All are veterans.

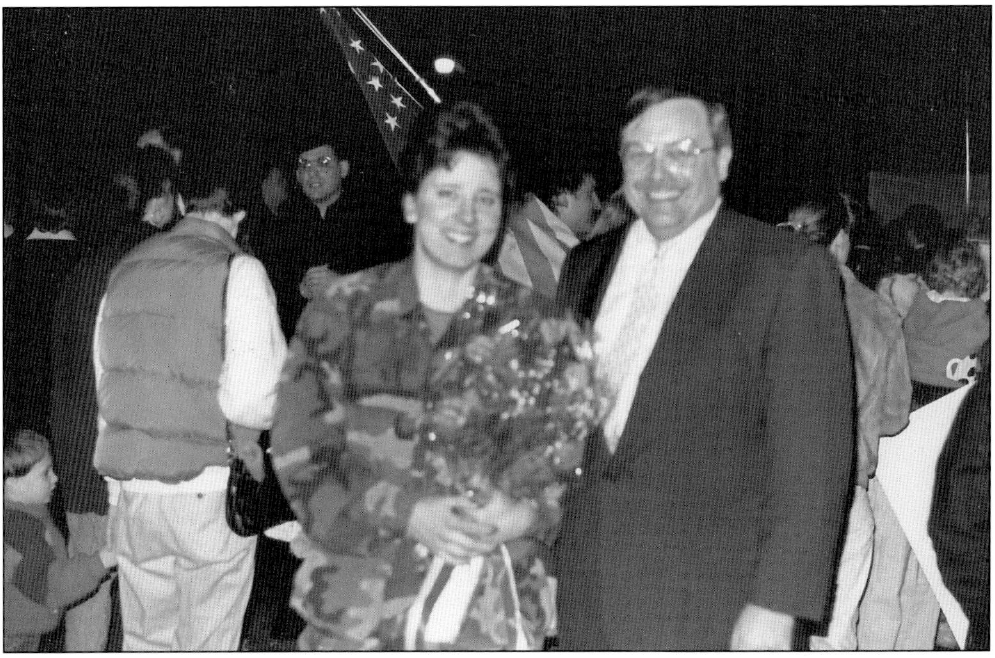

Sgt. Jacqueline Gill, member of the 316th Station Hospital in Riyadh, Saudi Arabia, is welcomed home by Harrisburg mayor Stephen Reed on the return of the Harrisburg unit from Operation Desert Storm in 1991. The joyous receptions for returning Desert Storm veterans stood in sharp contrast to the unusually cool or indifferent receptions given to many returning Vietnam veterans in the 1960s and 1970s. (Courtesy of Jacqueline Gill.)

This April 6, 1968, image shows the ground-breaking ceremony for the new post home of the Shippensburg Veterans of Foreign Wars. Manning the shovel is post commander Arthur Tagenborg.

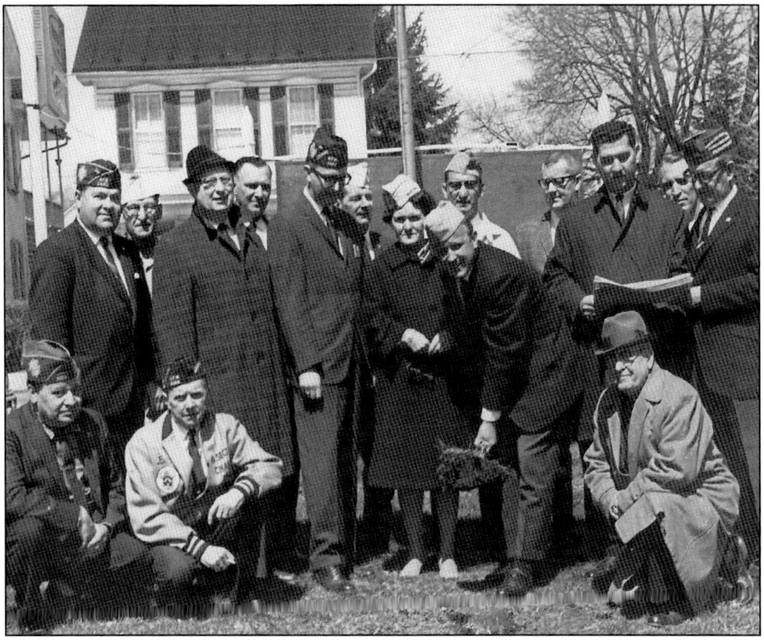

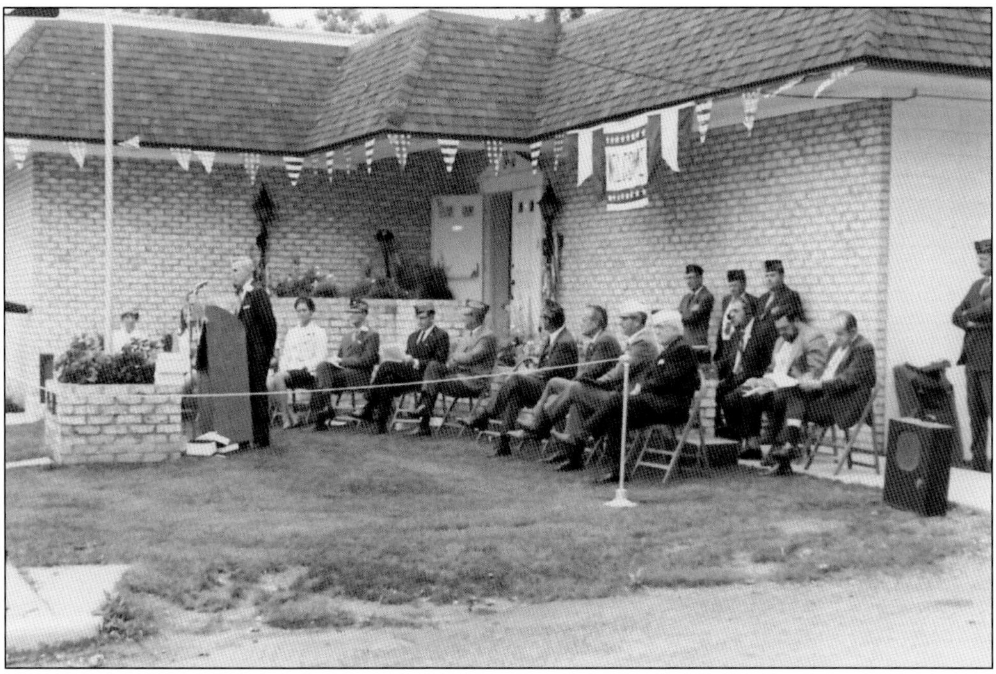

This July 14, 1977, photograph shows the dedication ceremony for the Shippensburg Veterans of Foreign Wars at 130 West King Street. The ceremony was accompanied by the marching units of both the Shippensburg VFW and the American Legion. Here, life member and World War II veteran William Burkhart addresses the audience.

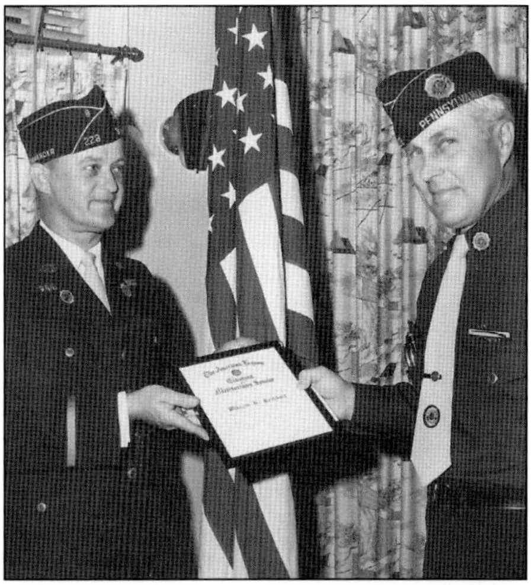

William H. Burkhart (right), historian for Shippensburg's 240th anniversary celebration, made brief remarks and presented a commendation to the Shippensburg Veterans of Foreign Wars at the dedication of their new post home. This July 14, 1977, photograph shows Comdr. Erwin Mears receiving a commendation.

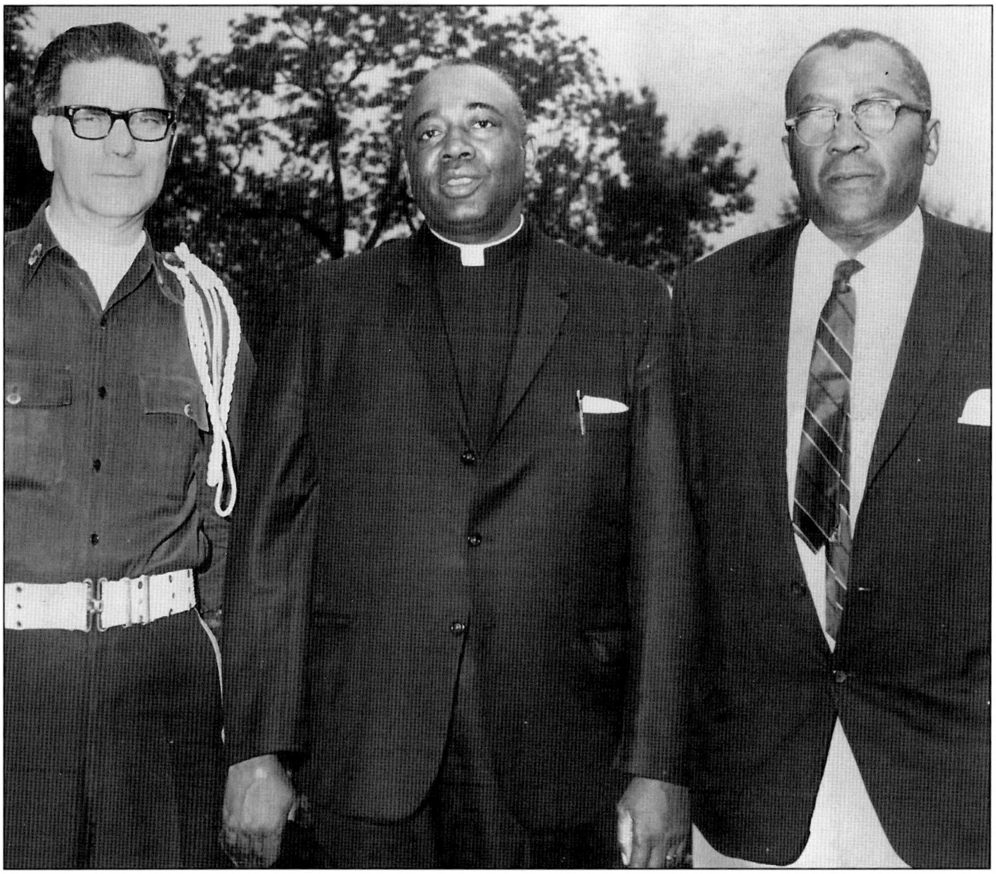

This 1970s photograph includes the leading participants in the annual Memorial Day service held at the Locust Grove Colored Cemetery. Locust Grove is the final resting place of 23 veterans of the US Colored Troops who served in the Civil War. In the 21st century, these heroes of the Civil War have been honored by a Pennsylvania historical marker, a restoration of the cemetery, and a wrought-iron fence surrounding the hallowed ground. Pictured are Benjamin Brechbiel (left), Rev. George Spells (center), and David Coleman.

Four

CHURCHES OF SHIPPENSBURG

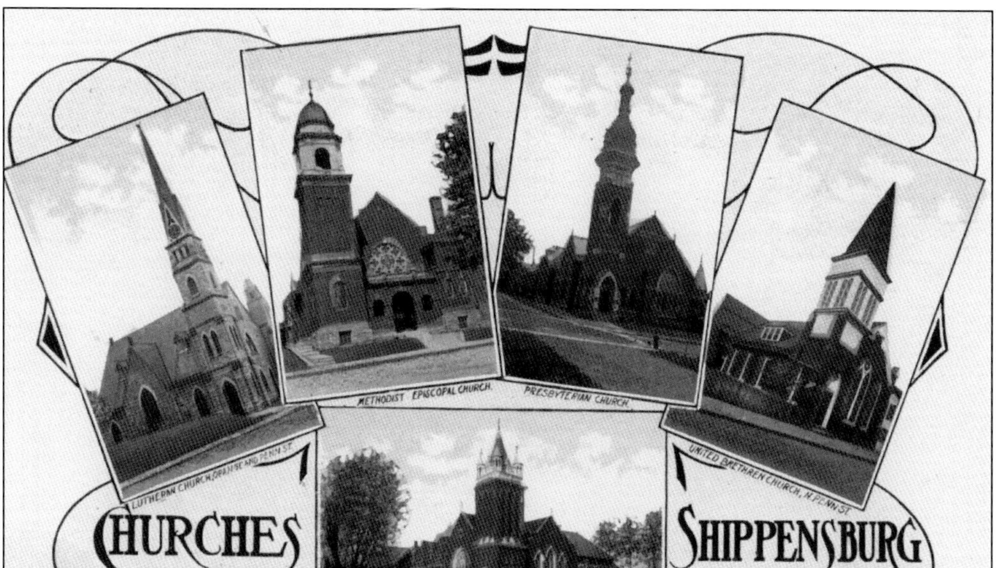

This early-1900s Clyde Laughlin postcard depicts the five largest churches in Shippensburg: the Lutheran, the Methodist Episcopal, the Presbyterian, the United Brethren, and the Church of God.

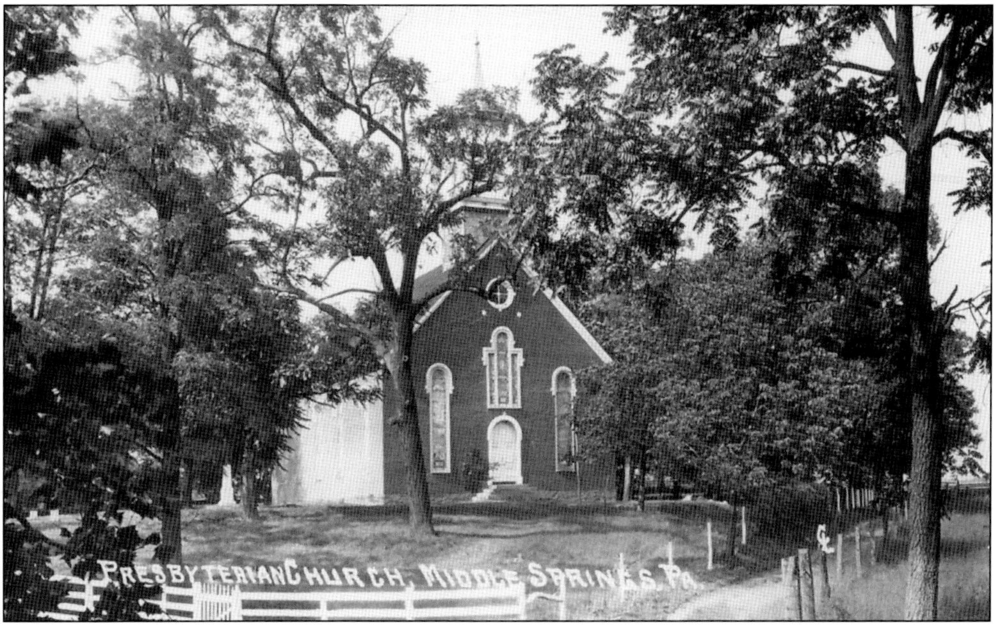

This is the Middle Spring Presbyterian Church as it appeared on an early-1900s Clyde Laughlin postcard. Middle Spring was the first church for Scots-Irish Presbyterians in Shippensburg. It was not until 1799 that Shippensburg Presbyterians would see the beginnings of a separate congregation. The foundation date for Middle Spring Presbyterian Church is 1738. The church building pictured was built in 1847 and is still standing and in use.

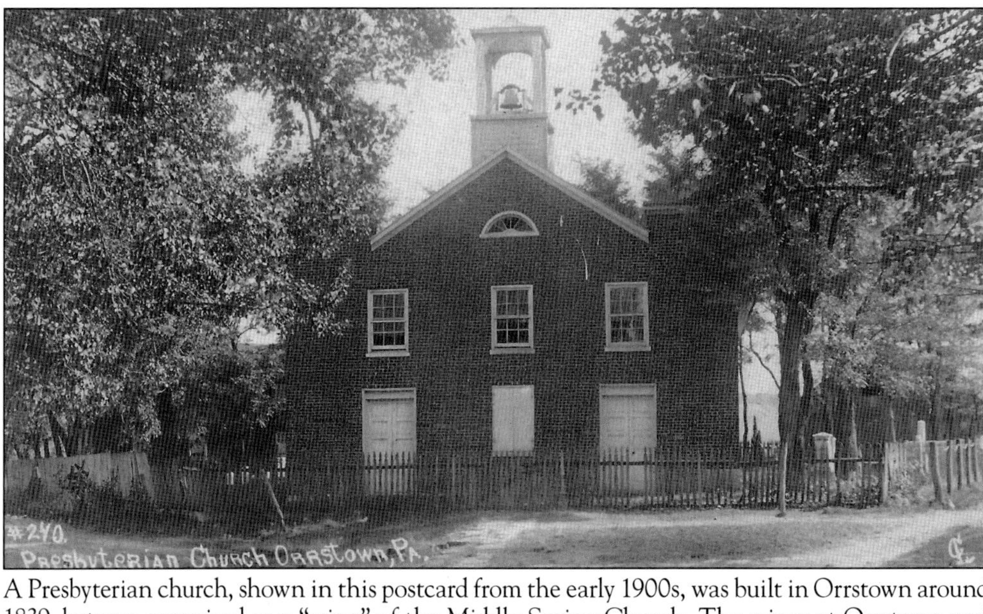

A Presbyterian church, shown in this postcard from the early 1900s, was built in Orrstown around 1839, but was organized as a "wing" of the Middle Spring Church. The wings at Orrstown and Newburg were served by the same pastor as the Middle Spring Presbyterian Church; he visited the wings on alternate Sunday afternoons for services. The Orrstown wing was torn down in 1968.

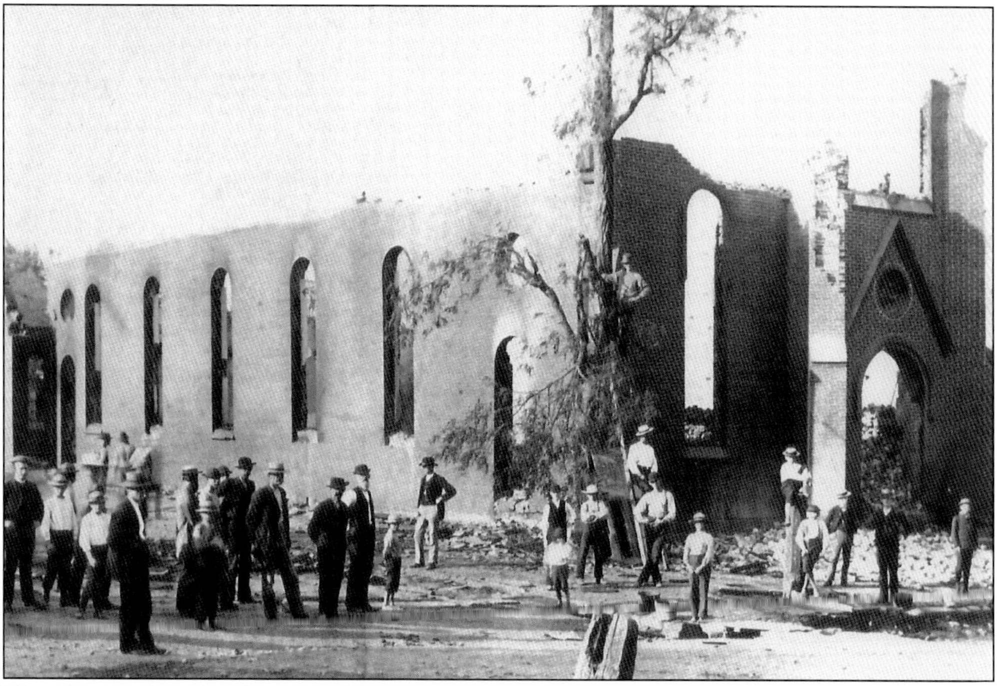

The Shippensburg Presbyterian Church, which was built in 1843 on the corner of East King and South Prince Streets, was destroyed during a thunderstorm on the afternoon of June 14, 1885—the aftermath is pictured here. Shippensburg did not have a public water system or powered pumpers, only wells and cisterns, so there was little onlookers could do as the fire burned down the steeple to the shingle roof.

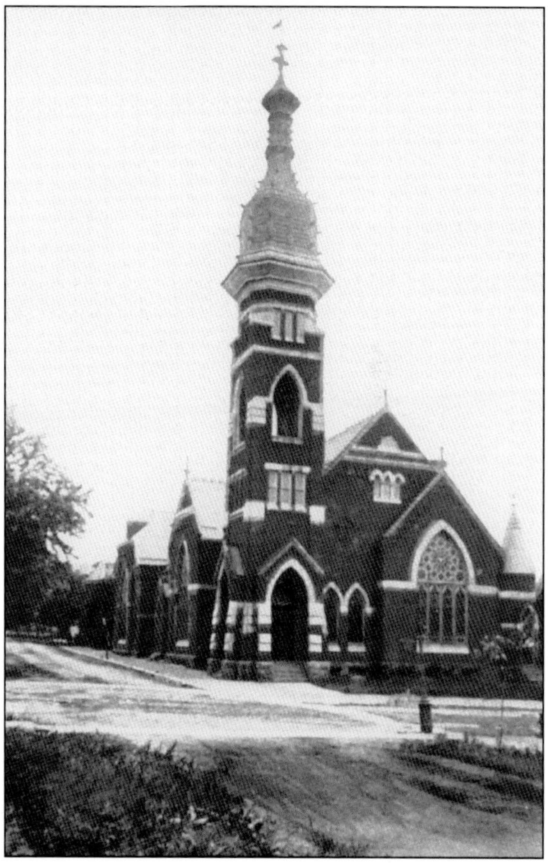

This 1907 Clyde Laughlin postcard shows the Shippensburg Presbyterian Church building that replaced the one that burned down in 1885. The galvanized iron steeple was removed in 1936, and numerous other modifications have been made since that time.

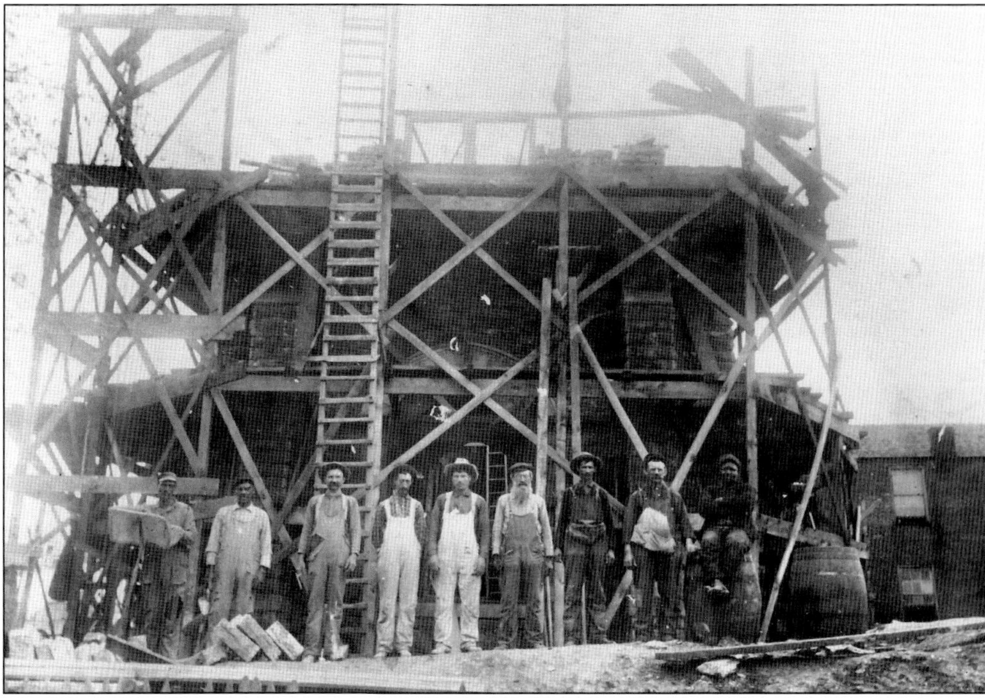

In 1906, J.W. Trough took this photograph of John Richard Gruver's crew of stonemasons who were building St. Andrew's Episcopal Church on the southeast corner of East Burd and North Prince Streets.

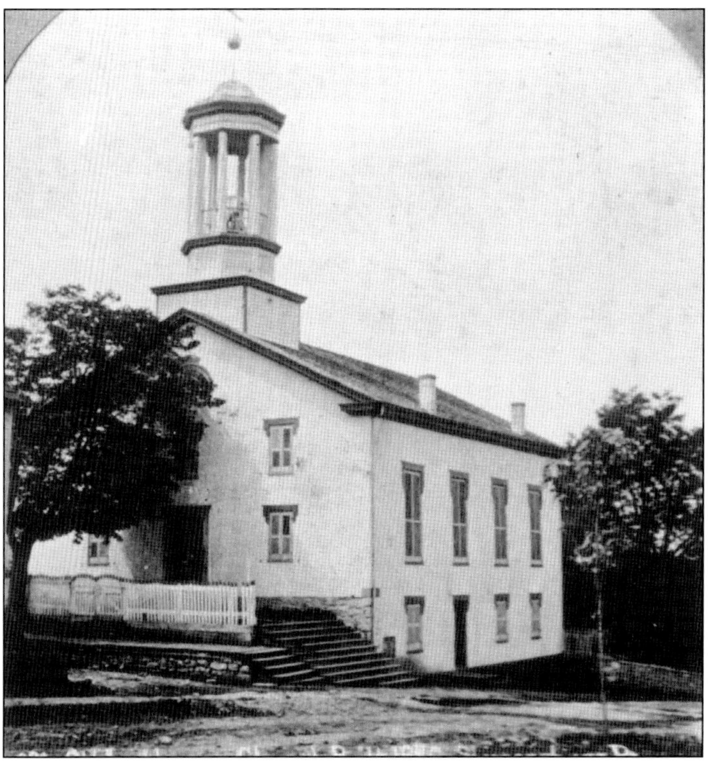

The Old Lutheran Church, built in 1846, was the first building the Shippensburg Lutherans constructed for their own use. It was located on the southwest corner of South Penn and East Orange Streets, where the current church was built in 1882 or 1883.

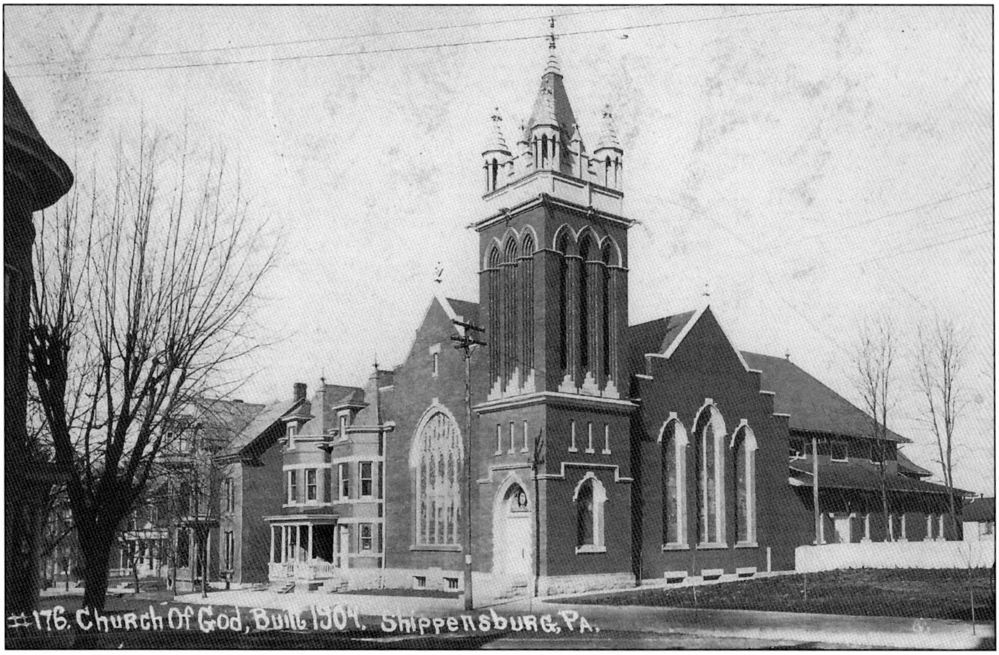

Located at 123 East King Street, this building was erected in 1904 by the congregation of the First Church of God. Additions in the 20th century extended the church buildings to the north and west.

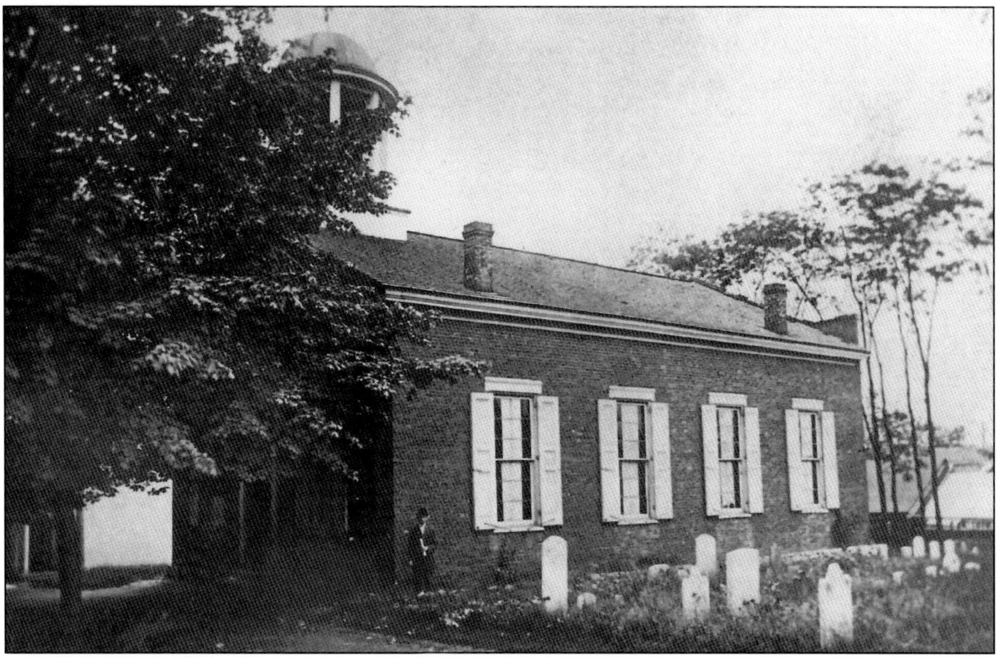

The German Reformed Congregation built this church in 1849. After the Reformed congregation built a new brick church on the corner of South Prince and East Orange Streets in 1890, the United Brethren in Christ first rented this church and then bought it in 1893. The Christian Missionary Alliance bought it from the United Brethren in Christ in 1950. The cemetery in the picture belonged to the Reformed congregation.

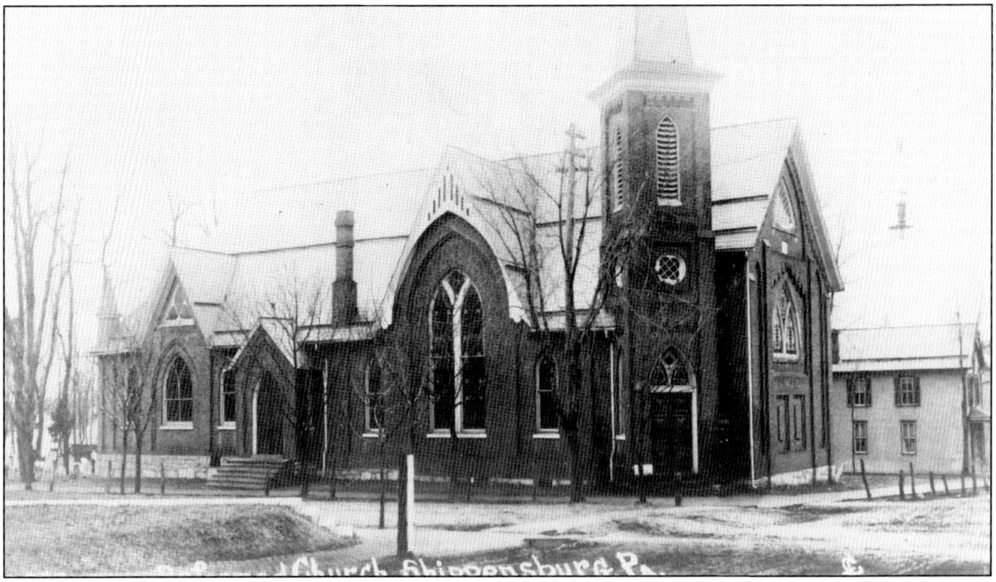

The building in this 1912 photograph was constructed in 1890 for the Reformed Congregation (changed to Grace Reformed in 1898) and was located on East Orange and South Prince Streets. This church building was torn down in 1924, owing to structural defects, and a fourth church was constructed on the site. After 1957, this congregation was known as Grace United Church of Christ.

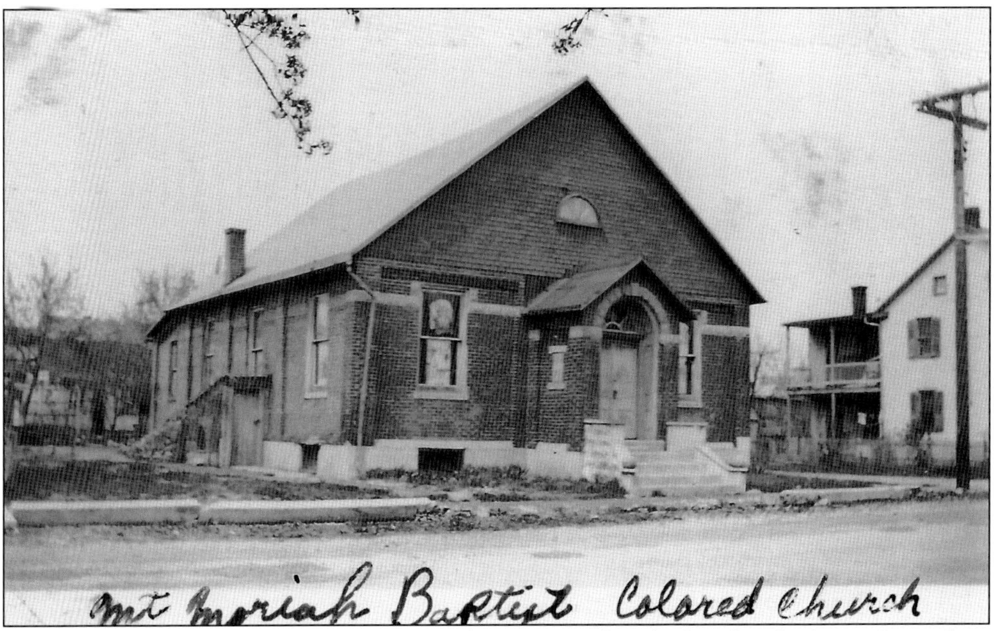

This 1936 photograph shows the Mt. Moriah Baptist Colored Church, which was located on the north side of West Orange Street and the west side of the Locust Street intersection. It was dedicated on May 22, 1921, by the church's pastor, Rev. Joseph Robinson. In 1951, it was sold to the Church of God Pentecostal, who worshipped there until it blew down in 1964.

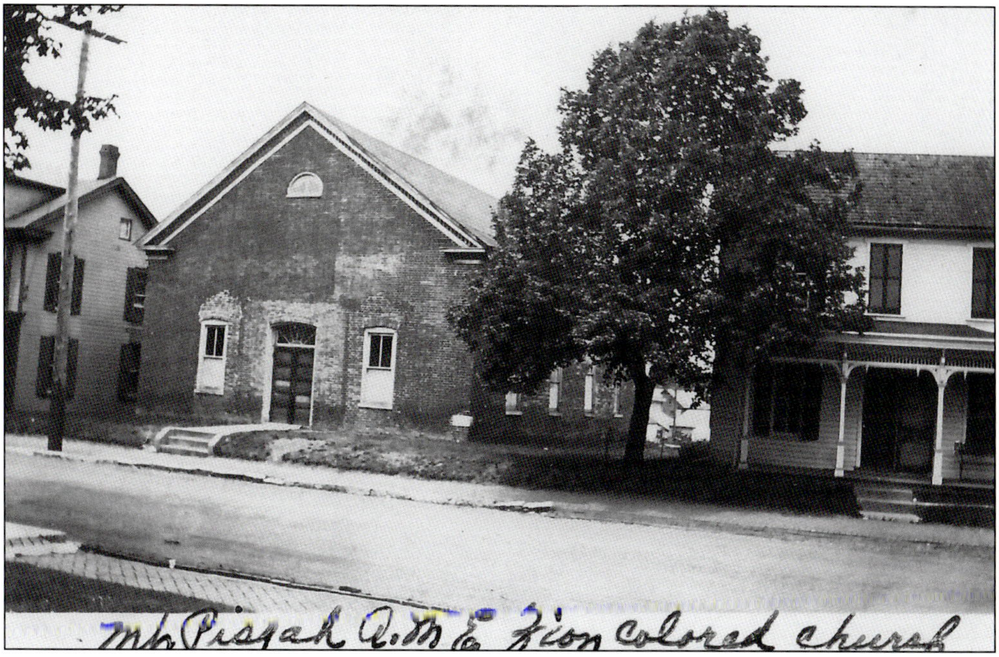

This 1936 photograph shows the Mount Pisgah African Methodist Episcopal Zion Church, located at 205 East Orange Street. This church, built in 1825, is believed to be the oldest church building in Shippensburg. The African American congregation bought it from the Methodists in 1872. It still stands and serves a congregation, although a quite small one.

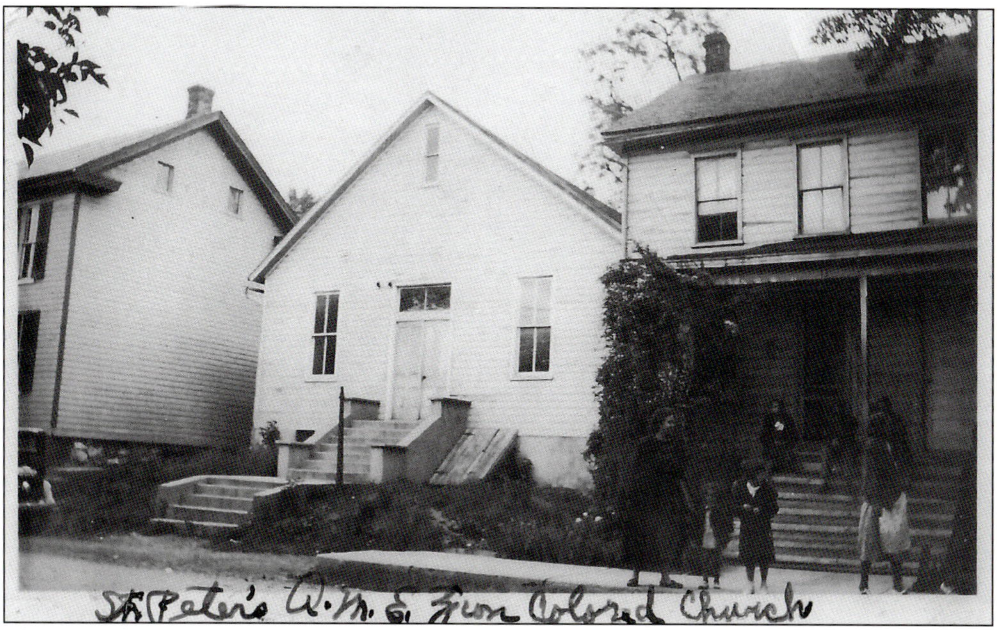

This 1936 photograph shows St. Peter's African Methodist Episcopal Zion Church, located at 119 South Penn Street, which was dedicated (and the cornerstone laid) on April 10, 1892. It served most of the African Americans of Shippensburg until the 1970s, when the congregation moved to a new location at Stewart Place.

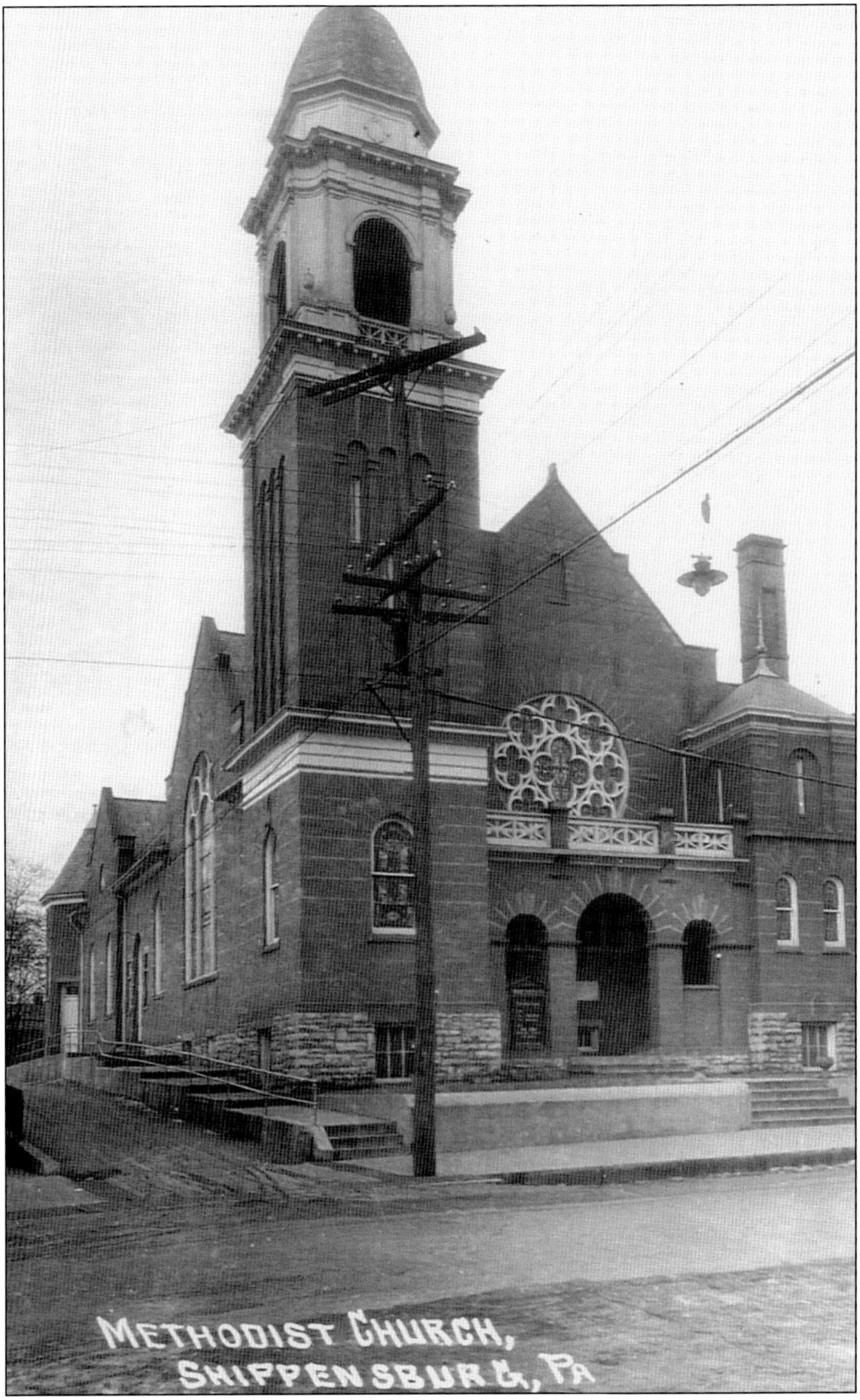

On July 28, 1901, the Methodist Episcopal church at 47 East King Street was destroyed by a fire that began in the furniture factory on the church's right and spread to the building to the east and to the church on the west side. This 1902 photograph was made when the church was newly reconstructed after the devastating fire. Today, after additional modifications, this is the Christ United Methodist Church.

Five

SCHOOLS OF SHIPPENSBURG

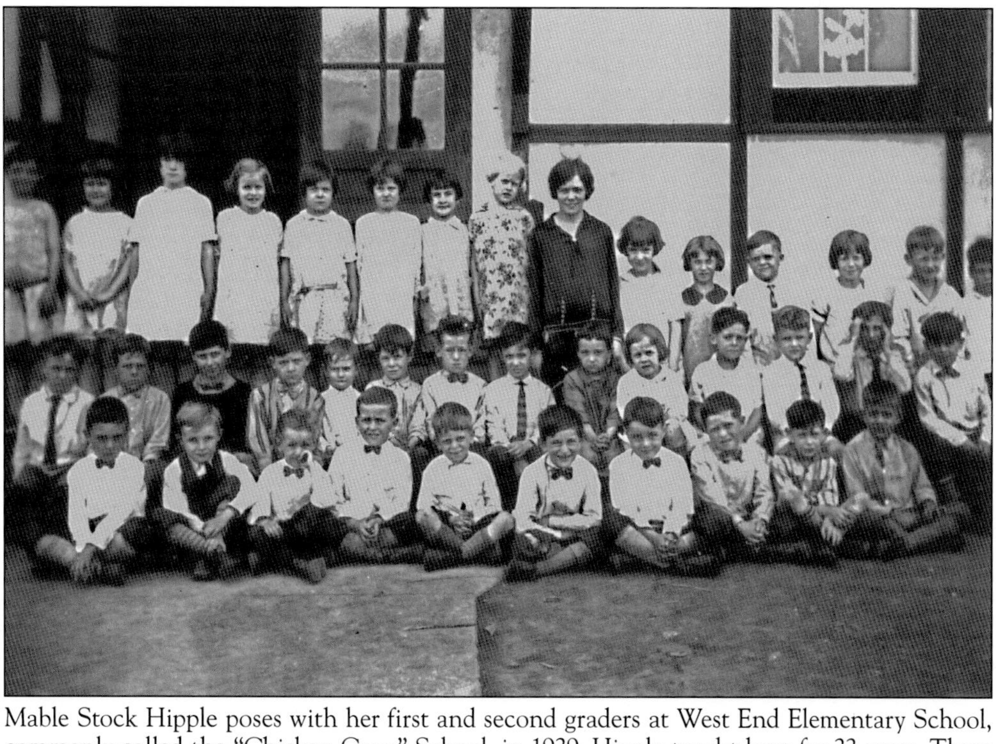

Mable Stock Hipple poses with her first and second graders at West End Elementary School, commonly called the "Chicken Coop" School, in 1929. Hipple taught here for 22 years. There were just two teachers in the building—one for first and second grades, and one for third and fourth grades. After 1960, it was no longer used as a schoolhouse.

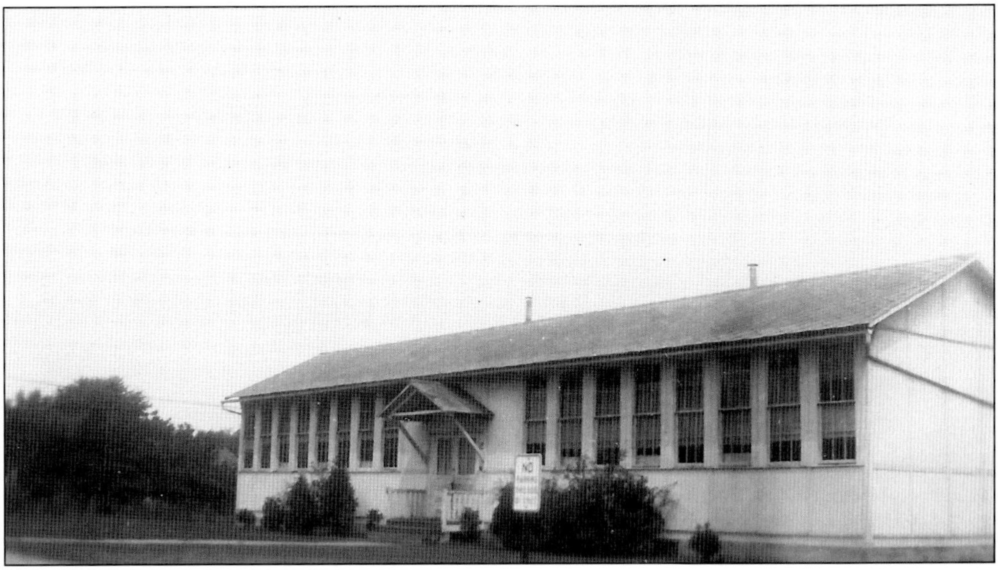

After fire destroyed the Central Public School in 1925, the school board decided to build an elementary school at the northeastern corner of West Orange and South Morris Streets to accommodate students from the west end of Shippensburg. In 1926, the school board purchased a portable school building that became known as the Chicken Coop School. This photograph is from September 7, 1948. The building was torn down in 1979.

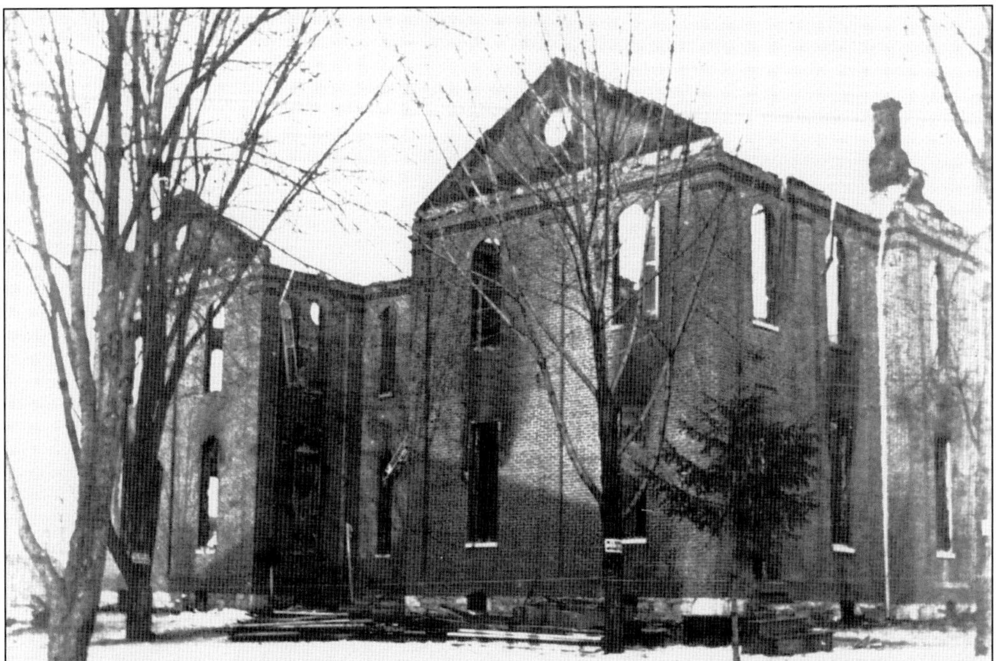

The first Shippensburg High School class graduated from this building in 1881. Known as the Public School Building, it sat on the north side of Burd Street between Prince and Washington Streets. The elementary grades were housed on the first floor, and the higher grades were on the second floor. This building burned in February 1902 and was replaced by a new Shippensburg High School in 1905. This photograph shows the aftermath of the blaze.

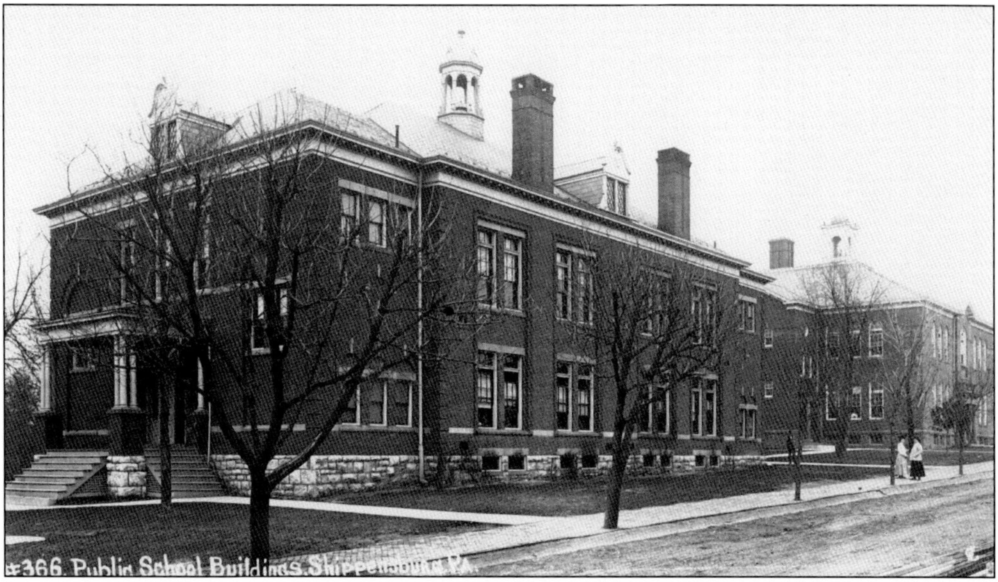

Education Hall was built on the north side of Burd Street between Prince and Washington Streets. It was used as an elementary school and high school until a new high school was built in 1905. This building burned down on New Year's Eve in 1925. This photograph shows Education Hall with the high school in the background.

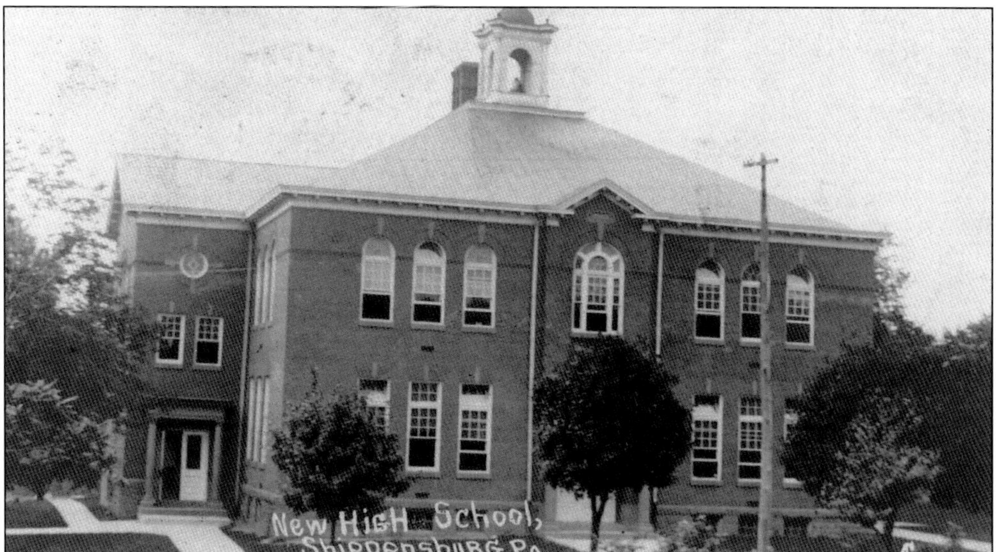

The new high school was opened in 1905, just east of Education Hall. A narrow strip of grass separated the two buildings. When Education Hall burned in 1925, the high school building was unscathed. It served as the high school until a new, larger high school opened around the corner on Prince Street—this then became the junior high building.

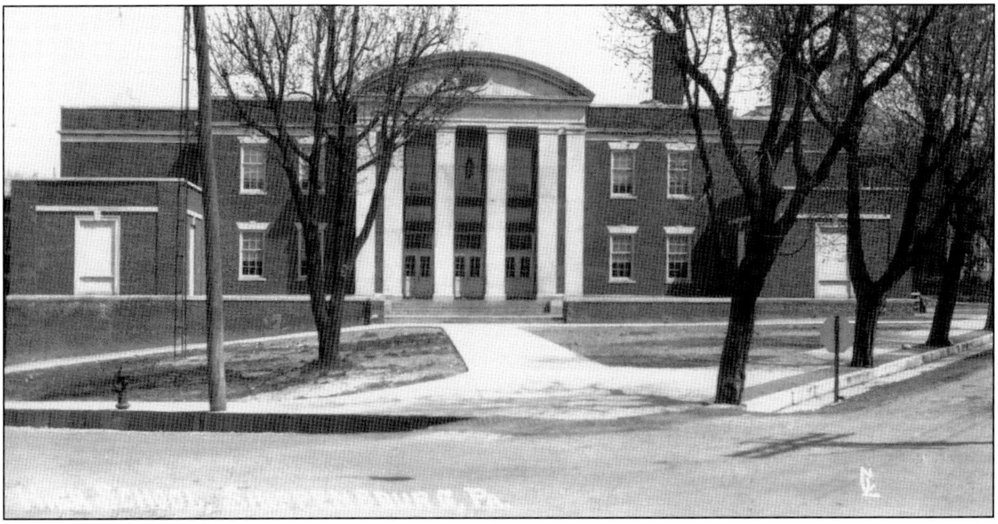

Central Public School opened in 1925 and served as the high school until 1955, when Shippensburg Area Senior High School was built along Route 11, west of the borough. This structure became the junior high until 1970, when yet another high school was constructed behind the building on Route 11, and the school in front became the junior high. The building pictured was torn down in 1979. The Episcopal Square Apartments now occupy this site.

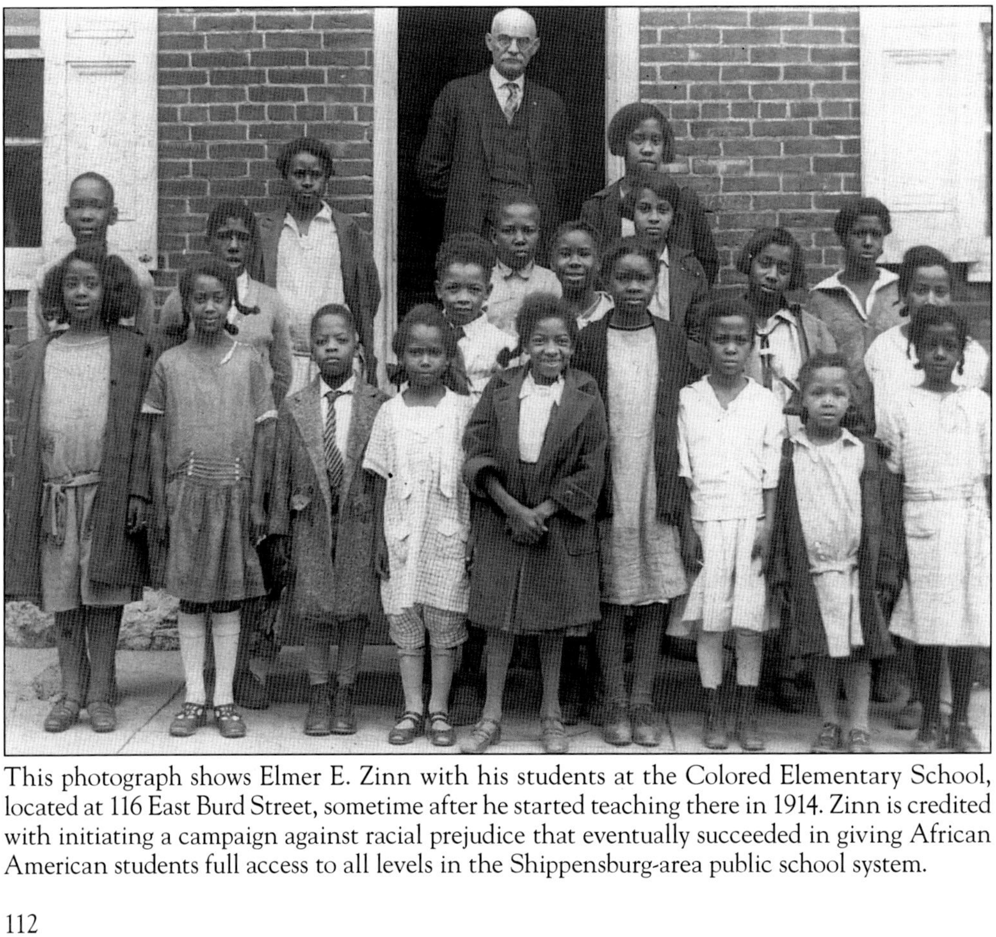

This photograph shows Elmer E. Zinn with his students at the Colored Elementary School, located at 116 East Burd Street, sometime after he started teaching there in 1914. Zinn is credited with initiating a campaign against racial prejudice that eventually succeeded in giving African American students full access to all levels in the Shippensburg-area public school system.

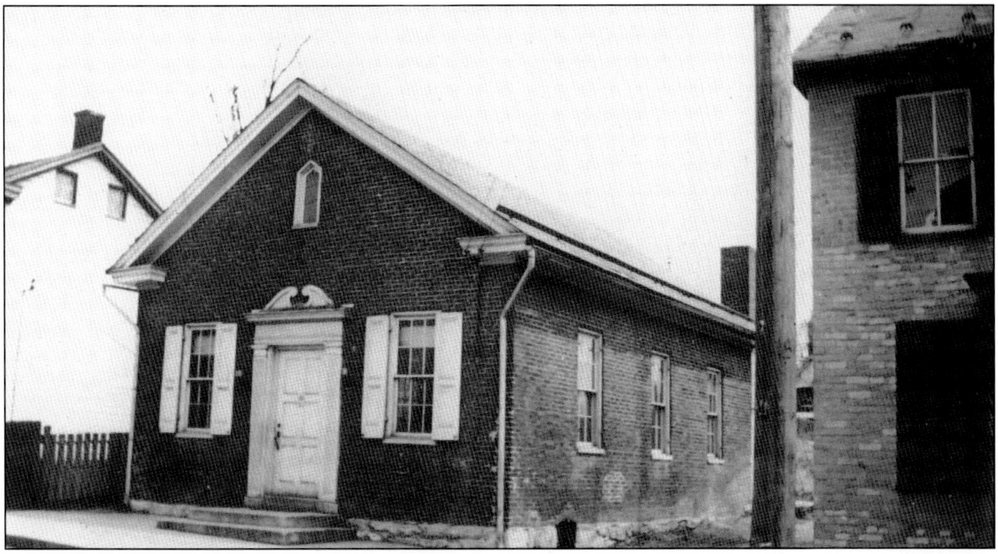

This 1936 photograph shows the Colored Elementary School; the school operated from 1900 until 1934, when it was closed and schools were integrated. From 1937 to 1948, this building served as Our Lady of the Visitation Catholic Church. In 1961, it was bought by the Prince Street United Brethren in Christ Church and made into a church office. It still stands today.

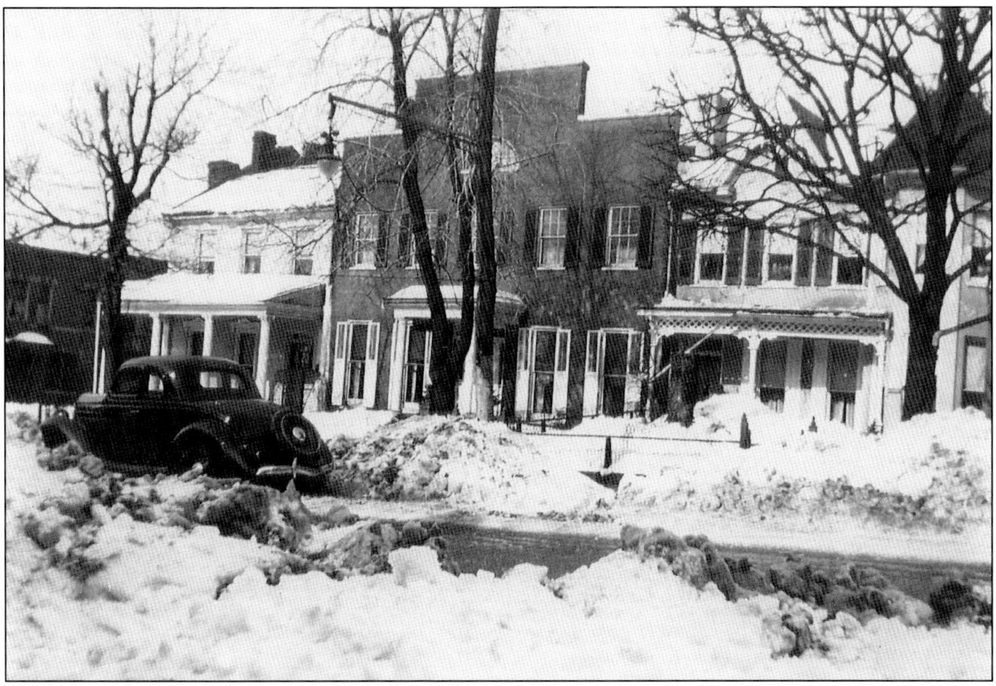

This photograph from the 1930s shows a part of the former Shippensburg Academy, a two-story brick building located at 103 East King Street, which opened in 1845. According to an 1849 advertisement, the school was a first-class boarding and day school that offered a course of study embracing all branches of a complete English and classical education. After several name changes, it ceased to function during the Civil War and became a private residence owned by the Shapley family. It was torn down in 1956 to make way for a gas station.

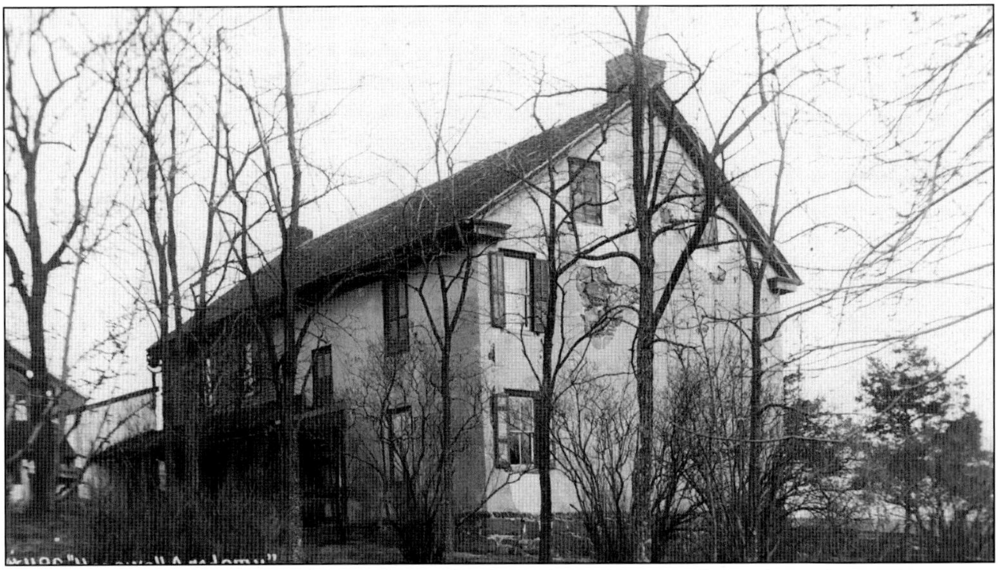

This Clyde Laughlin postcard from the early 1900s shows Hopewell Academy, located between Shippensburg and Newburg on Newburg Road. It was founded around 1810 by John Cooper, who served as its first and only teacher. Liberally educated and qualified for the ministry, Cooper seemed to find his true calling in preparing young boys for the challenges life might bring their way. He was the son of Middle Spring minister Dr. Robert Cooper

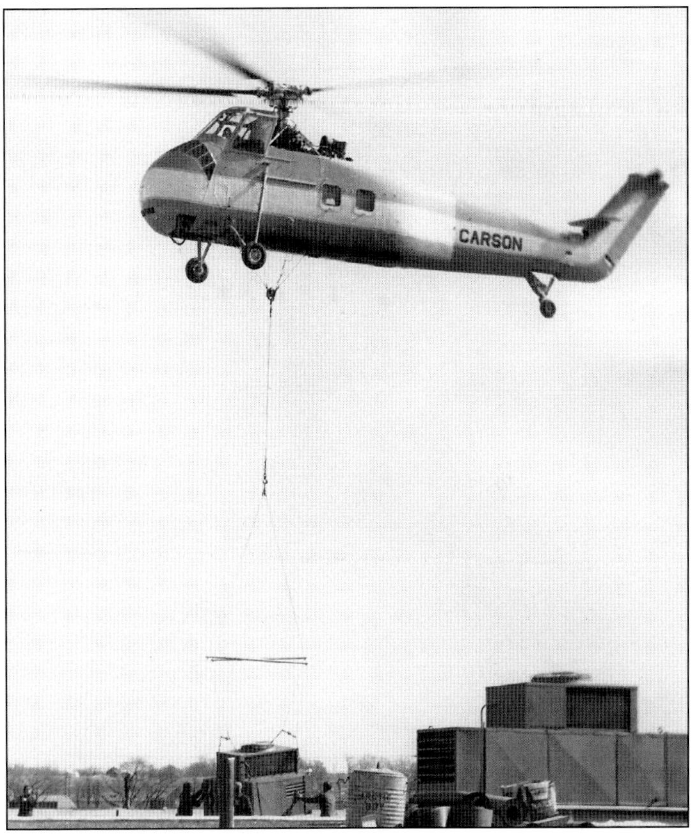

This May 1, 1970, photograph shows a Carson Helicopter Service craft lowering a part of the cooling system onto the roof of the newly built Shippensburg Area Senior High School on Rowe Road, west of the borough. One unit was 600 pounds over the helicopter's lift capacity and had to be disassembled into two parts for lifting it to the roof.

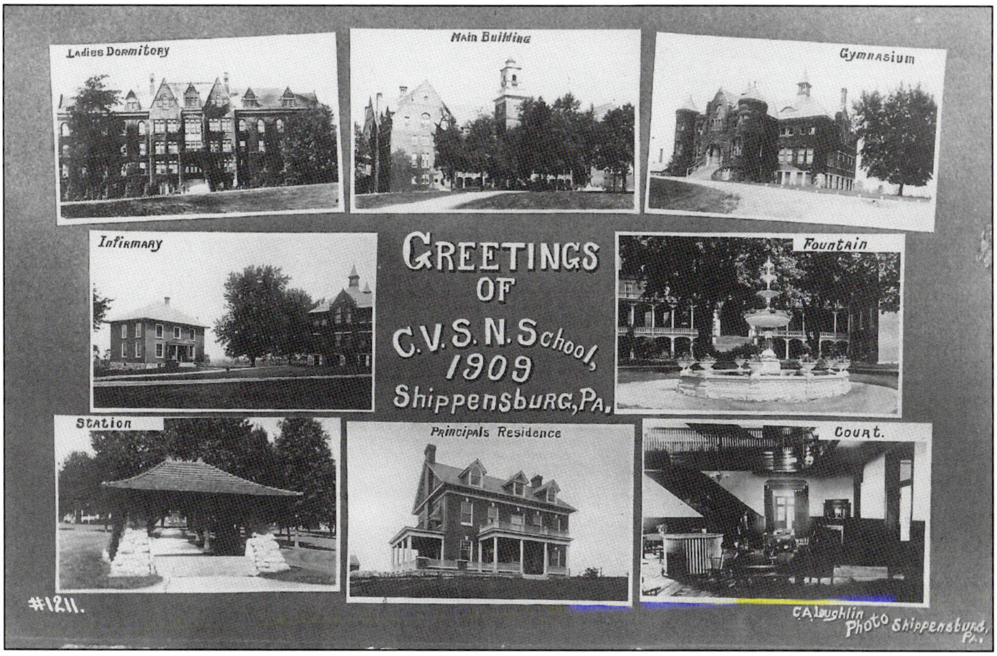

A 1909 Clyde Laughlin postcard shows some of the main buildings on the campus of the Cumberland Valley State Normal School. The first classes were held in the spring term of 1873. Free tuition was offered to all students over 17 who intended to teach. There are now 14 such state schools included in the Pennsylvania State System of Higher Education.

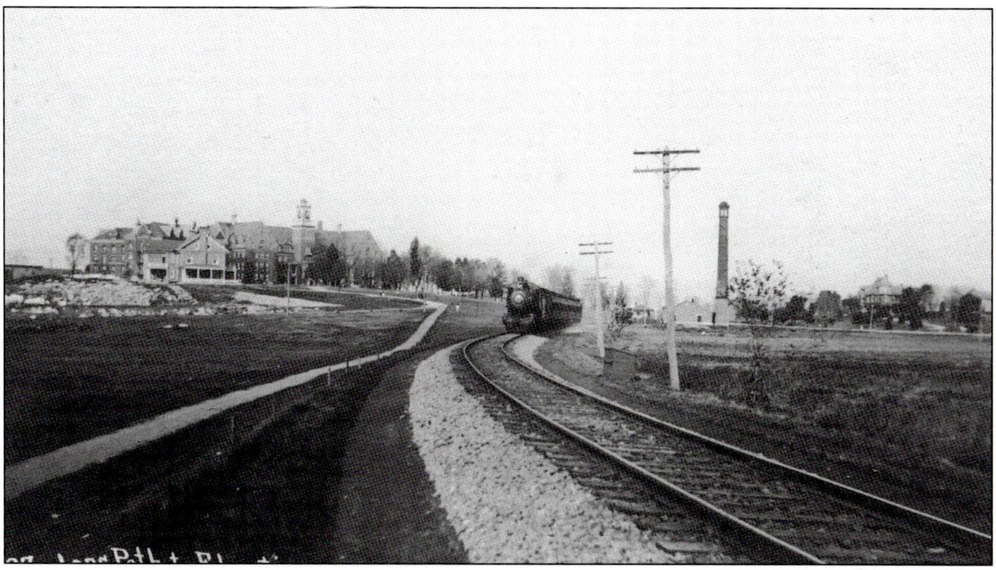

This early 1900s photograph, entitled "Long Path to Education, C.V.S.N.S., Shippensburg, Pa" shows the footpath used by students walking between the normal school and the town. The railroad tracks are now gone, but the path—which has been slightly moved—is now paved and still used by many pedestrians.

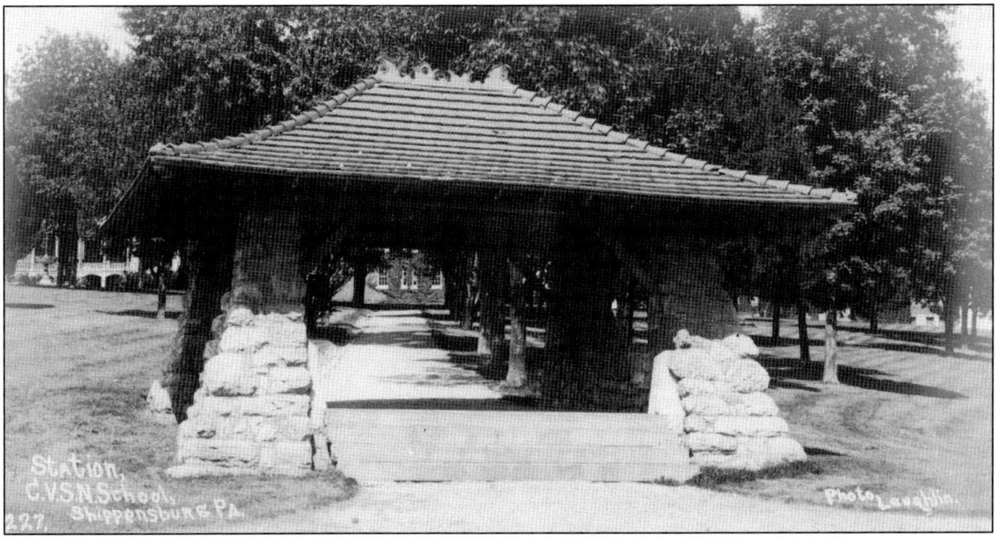

Many students from beyond Shippensburg arrived at and departed from the campus by train. This "station" offered shade or shelter to traveling students. The Pennsylvania Railroad discontinued passenger service through Shippensburg in 1962.

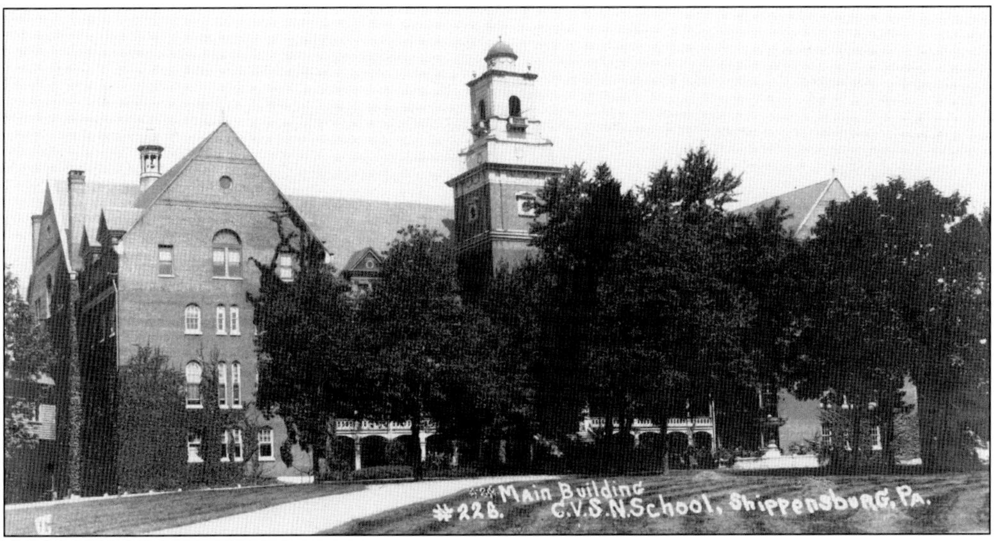

This is the administration building or Old Main, as it has been called by many since it was erected in 1871. Through the 1970s, it housed classrooms, faculty offices, conference rooms, a chapel, student quarters, and administrative offices. Today, it primarily houses administrative offices, a cafeteria, and Old Main Chapel, which is used for public lectures and performances.

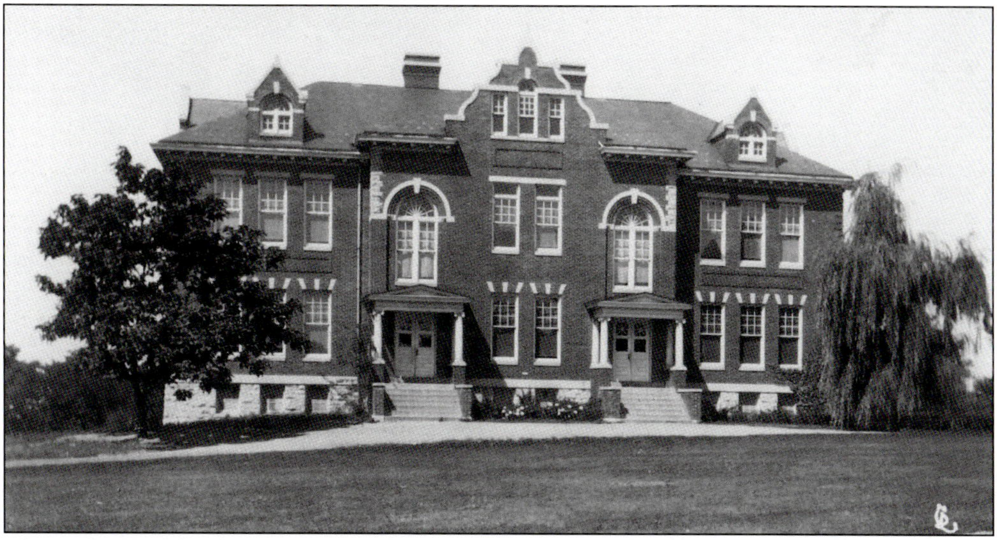

This is the Model School on the CVSNS campus. The school contained primary, grammar, and high school departments. It was here that many prospective public school teachers completed part of their training by observing skilled teachers with students. Now called Gilbert Hall, this structure contains university classrooms and faculty offices.

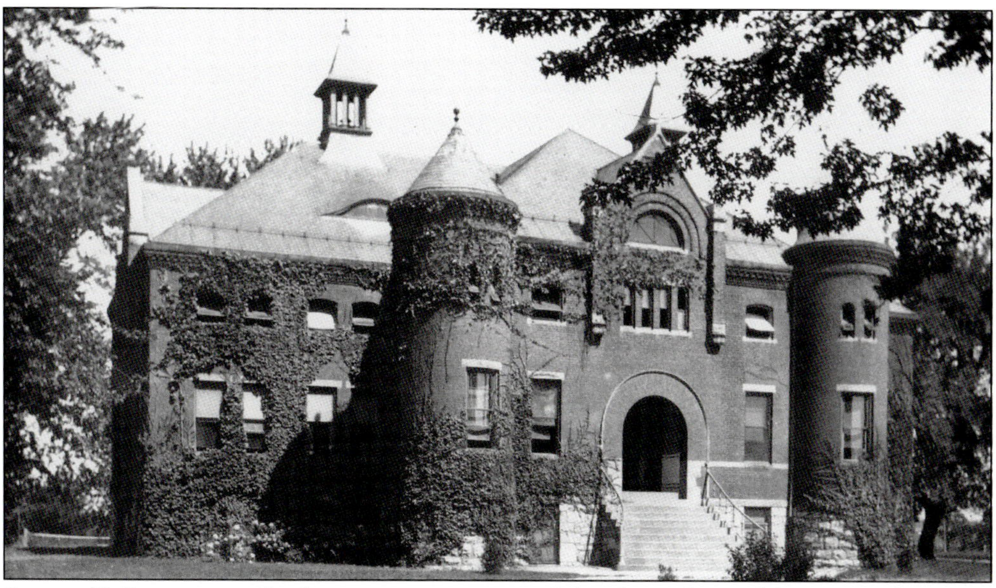

Stewart Hall was originally the campus gymnasium. It has been thoroughly renovated over the years and now houses art studios and a theater. University students put on several plays here each year for the entertainment of young children.

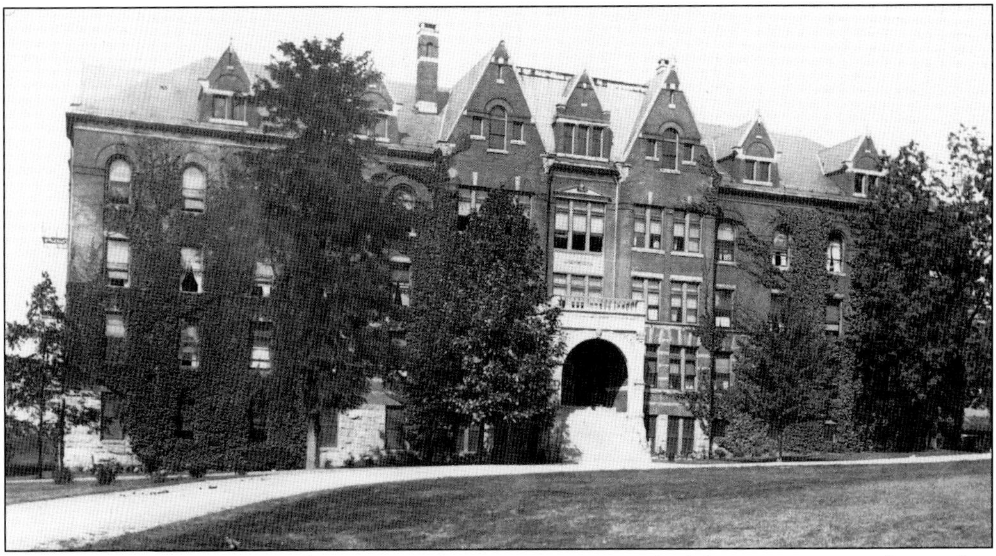

To the left of Old Main sits the women's dormitory. It was readied for occupancy in September 1894. A bridge was later built to connect the two buildings over the roadway that passes between them. Beginning in 1938, it was called Horton Hall to honor Ada V. Horton, one of the early deans of women. It now houses faculty and administration offices.

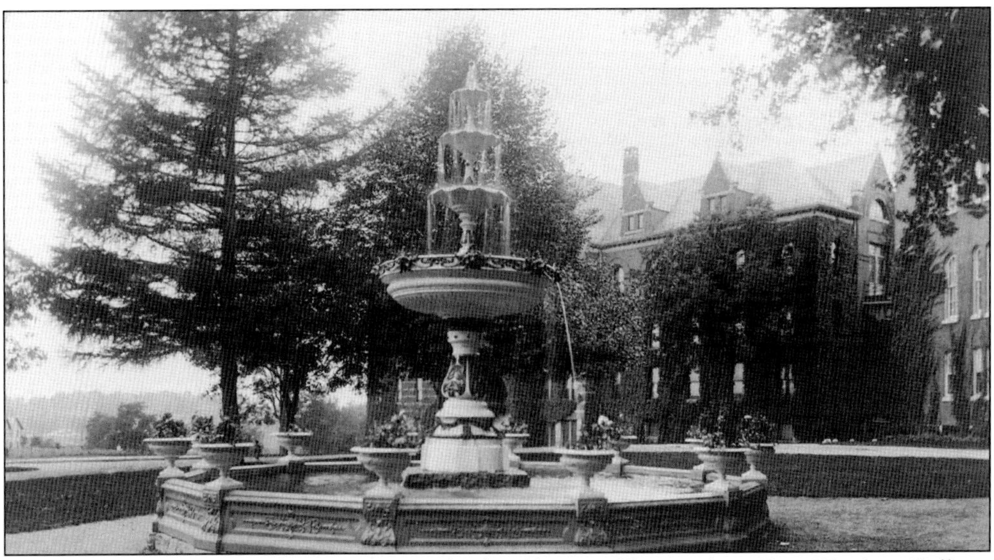

In 1927, the Cumberland Valley State Normal School became Shippensburg State Teachers College; in 1960, the name was changed to Shippensburg State College, and it became Shippensburg University in 1983. Through all the name changes, the appearance of the fountain in front of Old Main has barely changed. In early 2012, it is being renovated.

Six

Historic and Unusual Buildings of Shippensburg

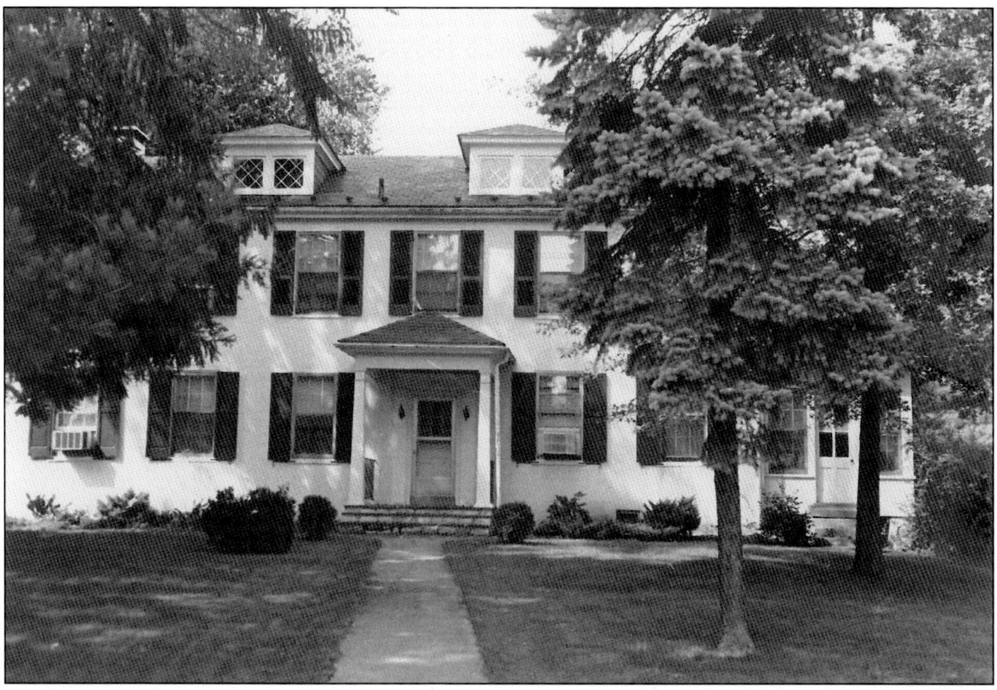

Old Pines, a stone house located at 317 West King Street, is the birthplace of George Balch Nevin (1859–1933), a nationally known composer of choir music in the early decades of the 20th century. The house originally belonged to a farm that bordered the west end of Shippensburg in Franklin County.

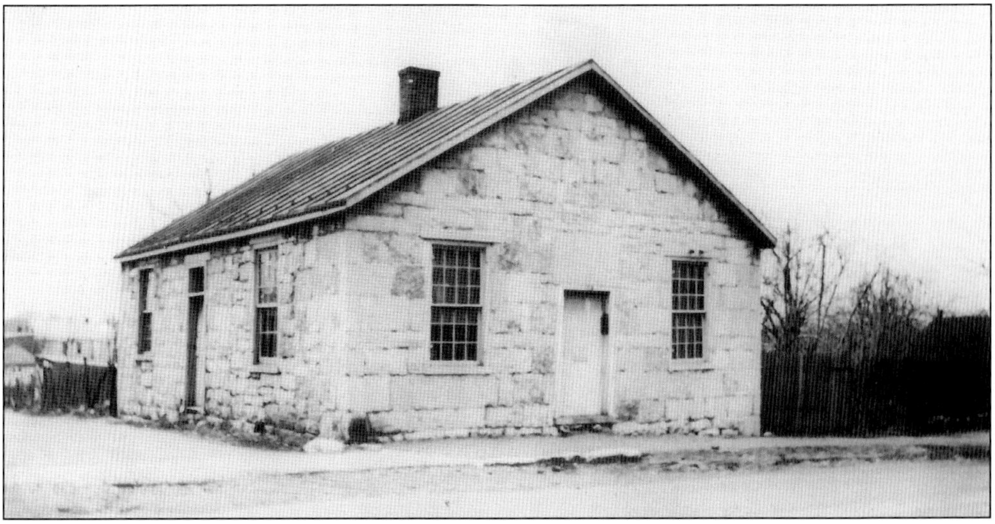

A small stone house that once stood at 18 North Prince Street was built by Col. Paul Martin before the Civil War, probably as the shop for his butchering business. During the Prohibition era, it became an all-male social club known as the Nest of Owls—it was well known that bootleg liquor could be obtained there. The building was torn down in 1950 to make way for the United Brethren Church.

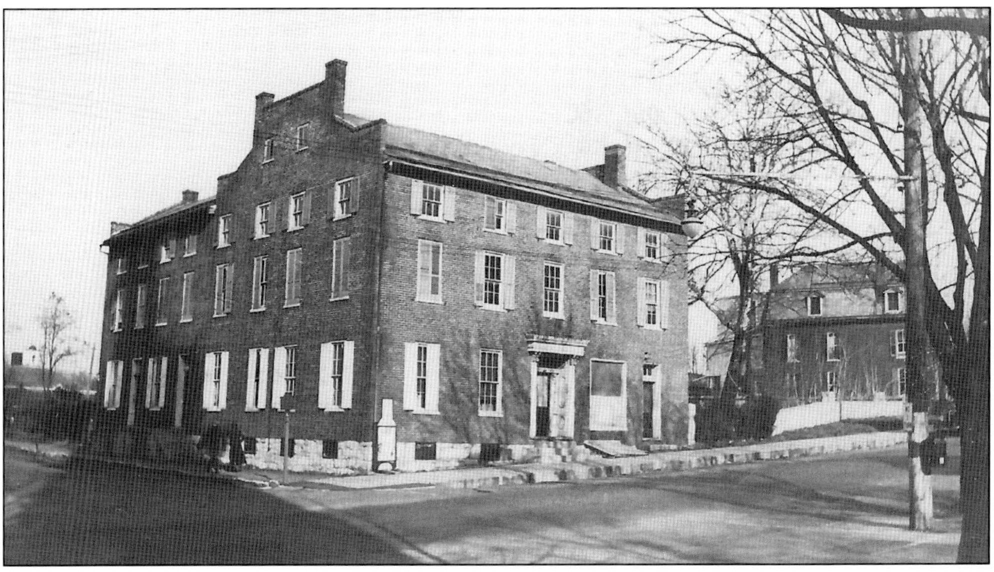

This three-and-a-half-story building, generally referred to as the Martin House, was located at 200 East King Street on the northwest corner of King and Prince Streets. It was built by Col. Paul Martin in the 1830s. Colonel Martin was a veteran of the War of 1812 and served as the sheriff of Cumberland County during the 1840s. This stately building was torn down in 1968.

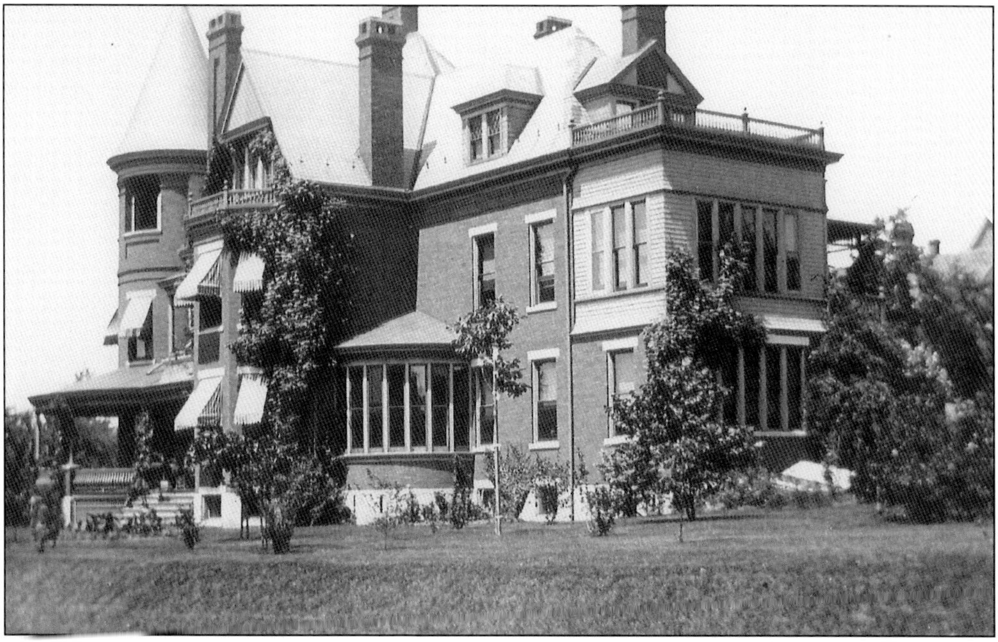

In 1893, Harry Hawk, who owned a lumberyard in Shippensburg, bought properties on the southeast corner of Orange and Penn Streets and tore down the old buildings. In their place, Hawk constructed this commodious house in 1896. Stories were told of how he made frequent and unexpected trips to the house as it was under construction and, if he noticed any errors, would make the builders tear out inaccuracies and correct them.

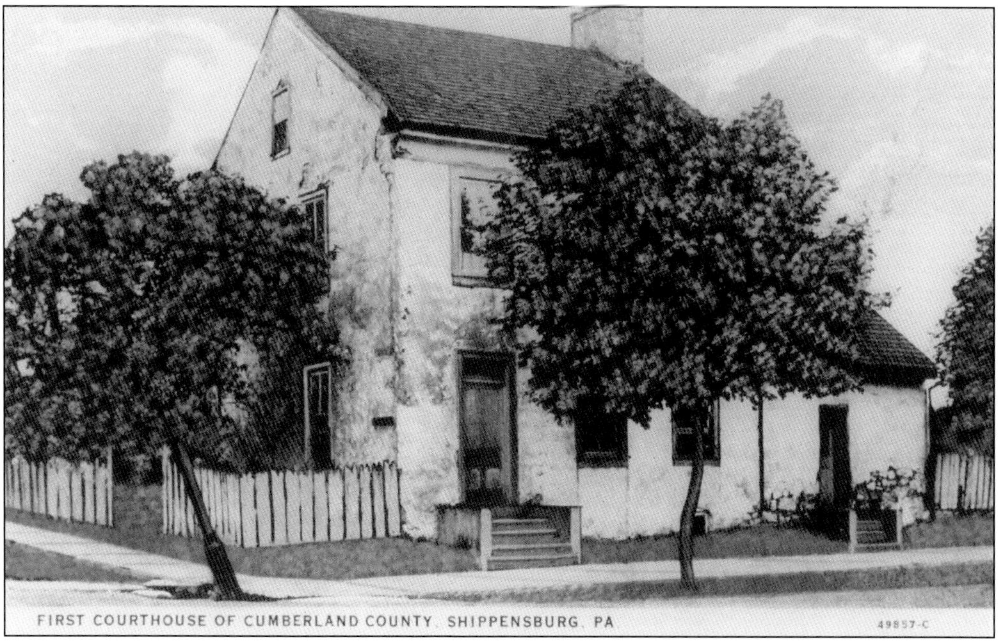

The Old Courthouse, located at present-day 352 East King Street, was allegedly built in Shippensburg by Samuel Perry. It is now known as the Widow Piper's Tavern and is the home of the Shippensburg Civic Club. In 1750 and 1751, four sessions of the Cumberland County Court were held here. In 1751, the county courthouse was transferred to Carlisle.

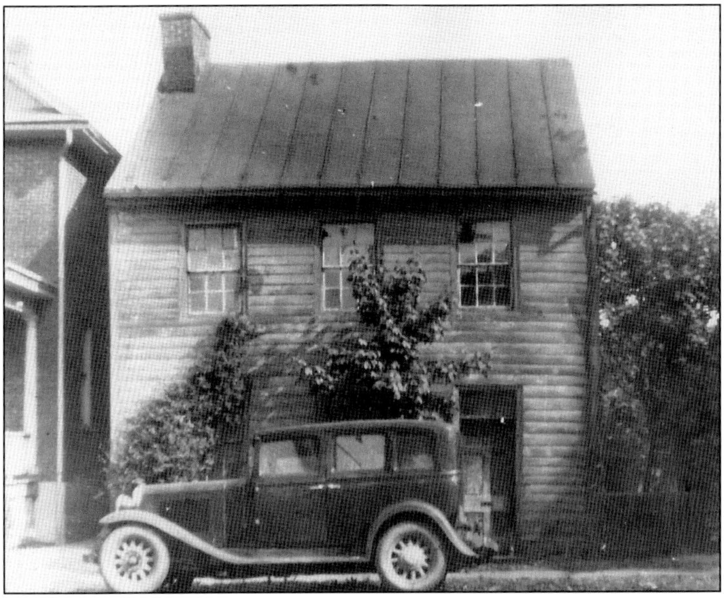

The William H. Boher home, formerly located at 118 West King Street, was a two-and-a-half-story, weatherboarded log house. The original deed dated to 1836 and was later transferred to Samuel Boher, a Civil War veteran and cooper by occupation. James Hockersmith purchased the property in 1942 and razed it to enlarge the lawn of his home. This photograph is from 1924.

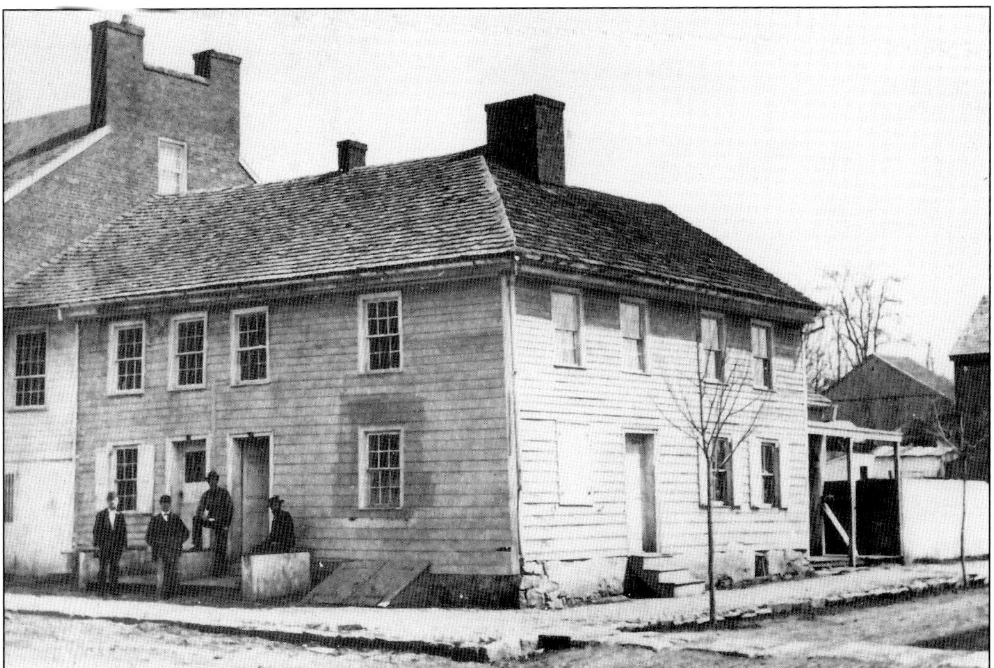

The clapboard-covered building on the southeast corner of King and Penn Streets is pictured here in 1874, when it was a residence (the next two photographs shows the changes to the site).

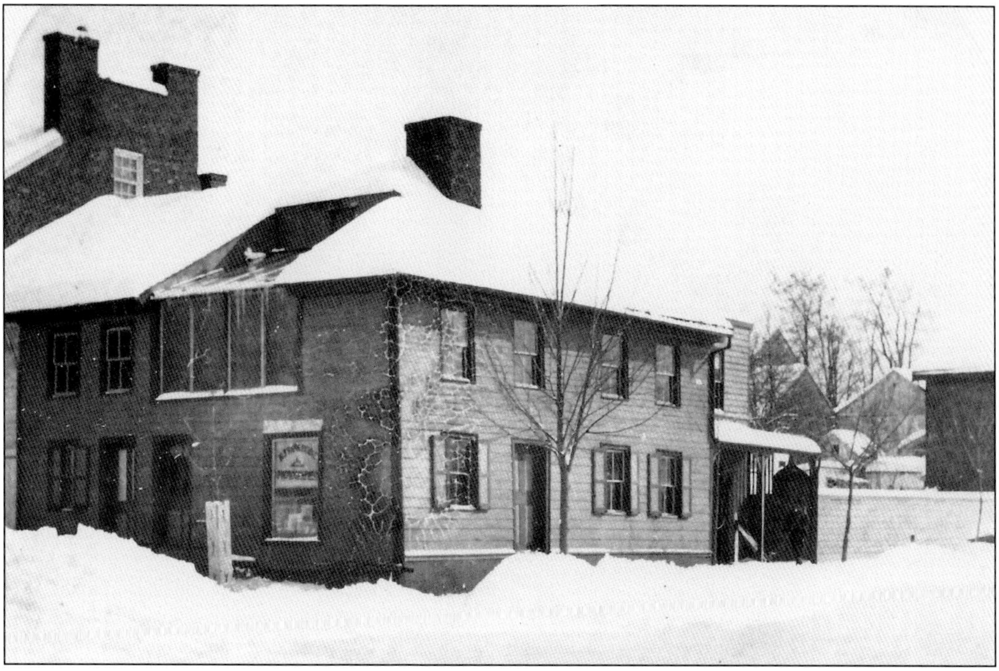

In 1878, the house on the previous page was converted into a photographic studio by cutting a skylight into the front of the roof. Today, the Shippensburg Historical and Architectural Review Board (HARB) would not allow such a drastic modification to the original appearance of the building.

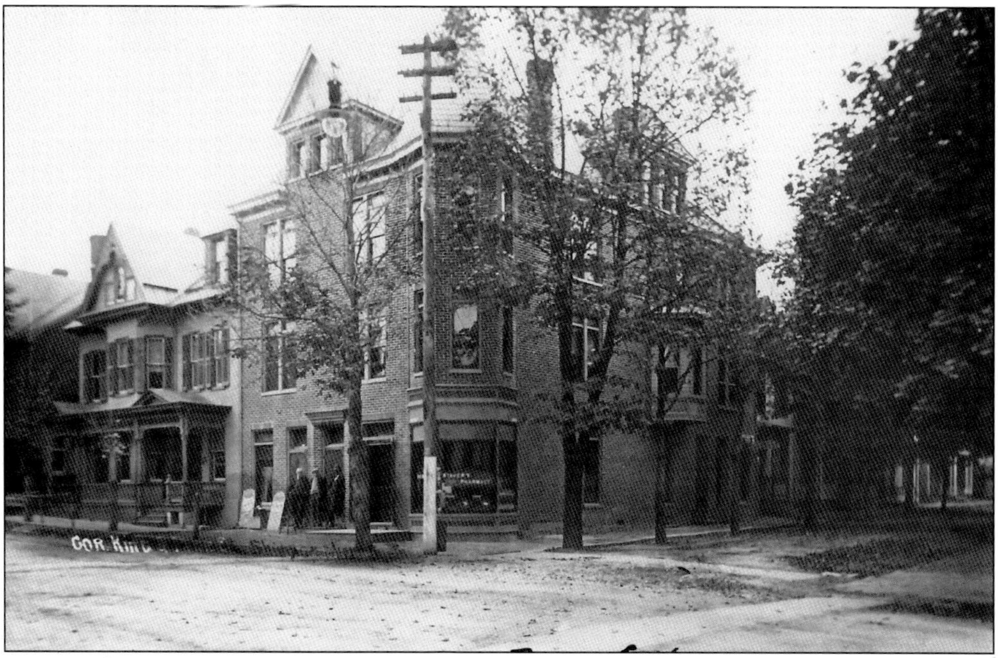

In 1901, the wooden structure had been razed, and this stately brick building was erected. The last occupants operated a pizza restaurant. It is currently unoccupied, and a For Sale sign in the window advertises it as a historic house.

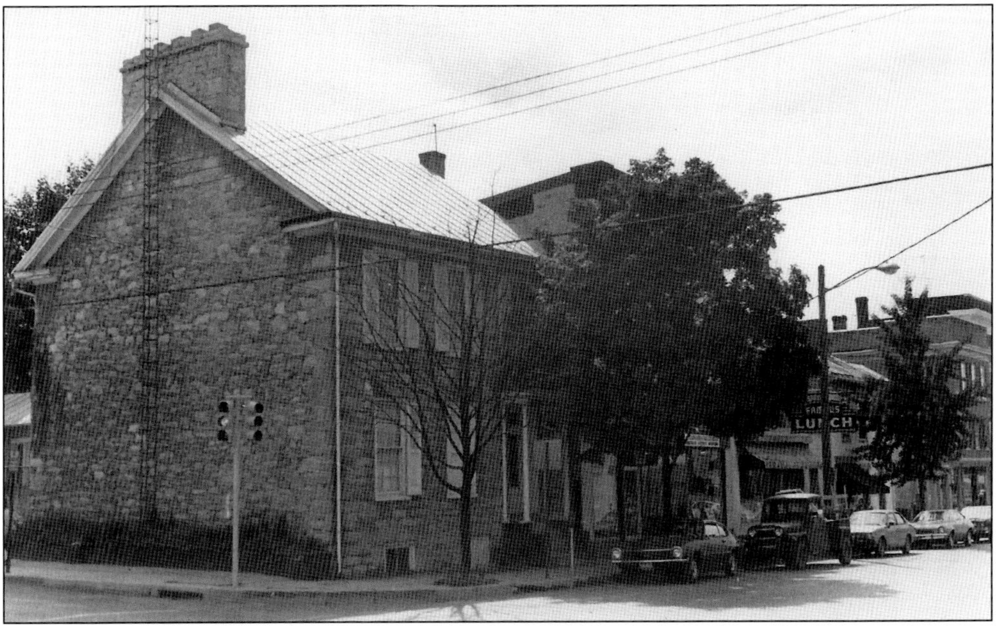

Standing at 68 East King Street on Lot No. 69 is a stone house that has been referred to as "The Doctor's House" because five physicians and a dentist have lived there over the years. The 1798 Direct Tax shows that the heirs of Robert McCall owned a 30-by-35-foot stone house on that lot. This house was recently completely renovated, but its exterior appearance remains much the same. This photograph is from the 1960s.

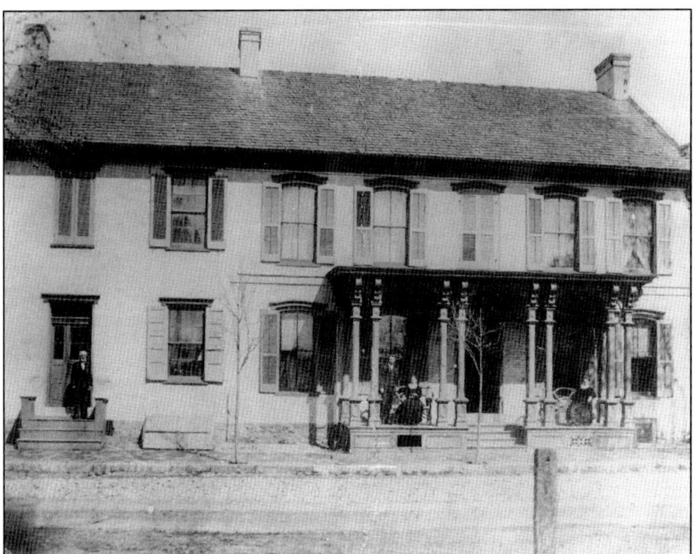

This 1870s image shows the McLean home at 49 West King Street. It was built by William McLean, a successful tanner in Shippensburg in the 19th century. In 1863, the porch on the front was used as a resting place by Confederate soldiers who occupied the town. A brick single house attached to the south side was subsequently torn down, and its former site is now a side yard of the house. The Donald and Ralma Fry family currently live there.

Wilber E. Goodhart built this stone house on Bull's Eye at 225 West King Street in the late 1950s. It was designed to provide a bomb shelter in the "duck and cover" period. Contrary to some writings, this was not the location of the stone house that was used to store supplies for Gen. Edward Braddock's 1755 expedition, nor was it the site of Fort Morris, as was once believed.

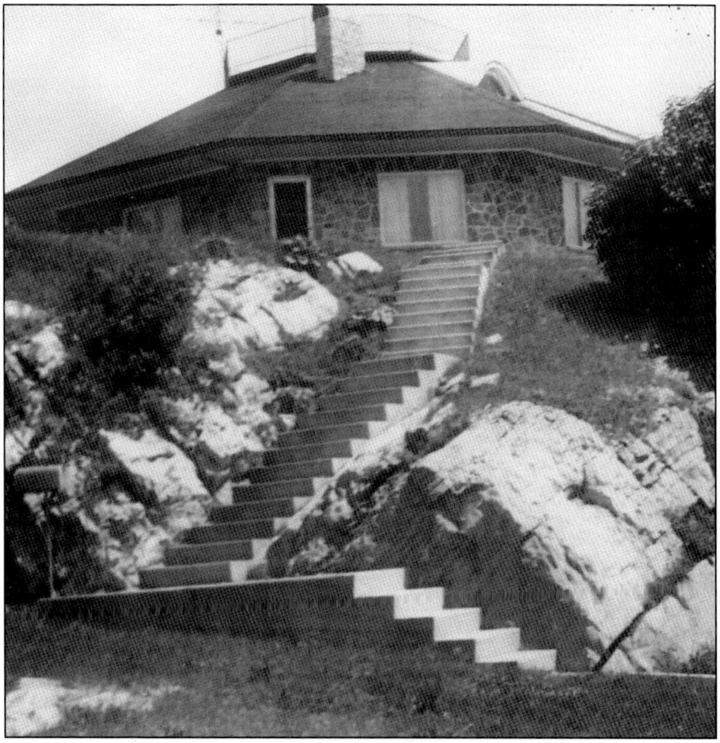

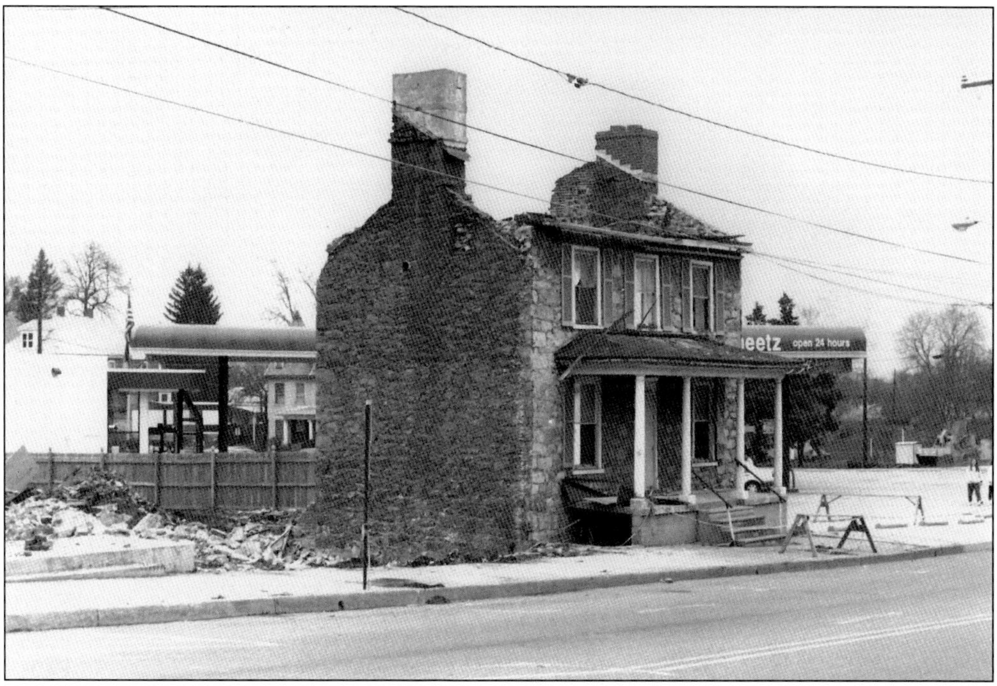

Another stone house that no longer stands was at 339–341 East King Street. This was torn down to make room for the Kwik Lube Service Center. James McCall owned and operated the Sign of Turks Head Tavern in this building from 1759 to 1765. In 1763, he received the first deed for this lot from Edward Shippen, the proprietor.

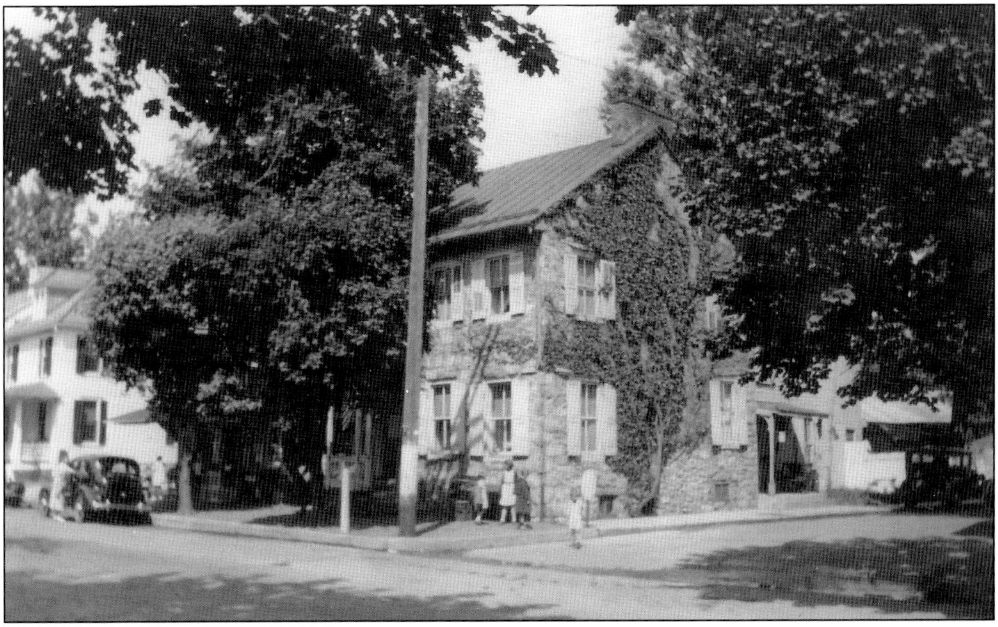

This native-limestone house occupied the northwest corner of West King and Spring Streets. In 1936, A.B. Cressler, a livestock dealer, tore the house down to open a service station. After World War II, A.B.'s son Frank Cressler tore down the service station to expand his fruit and grocery business, which became Cressler's, a local supermarket. This site is now occupied by a modern Turkey Hill convenience store.

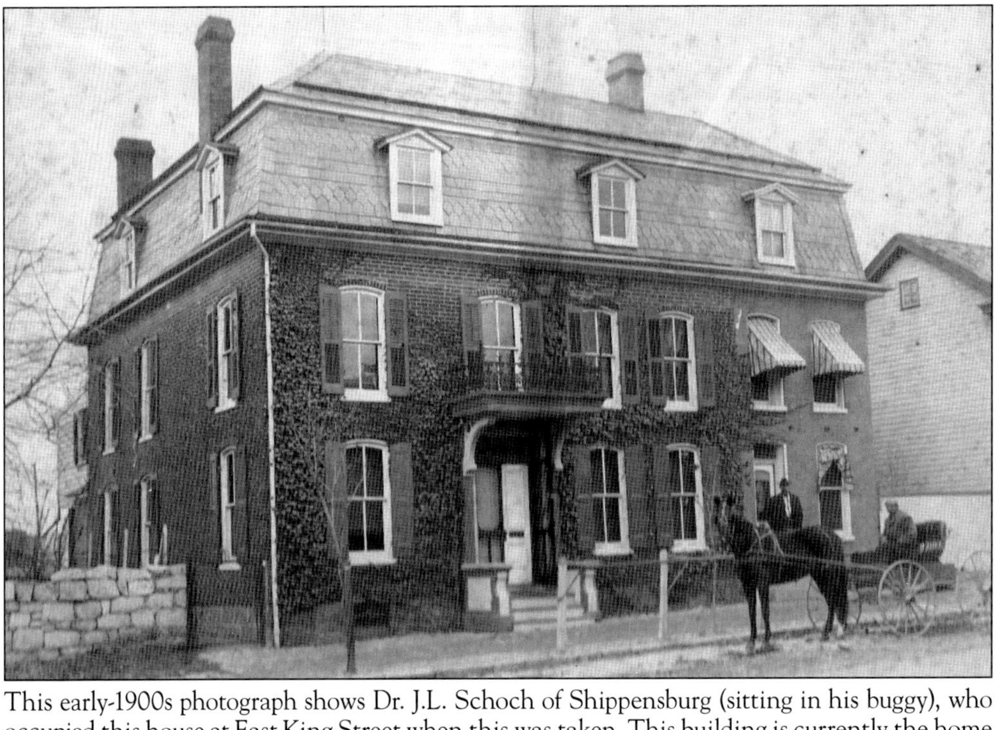

This early-1900s photograph shows Dr. J.L. Schoch of Shippensburg (sitting in his buggy), who occupied this house at East King Street when this was taken. This building is currently the home of Victorian Corner, a multifaceted business including a florist, tuxedo rental, and gifts.

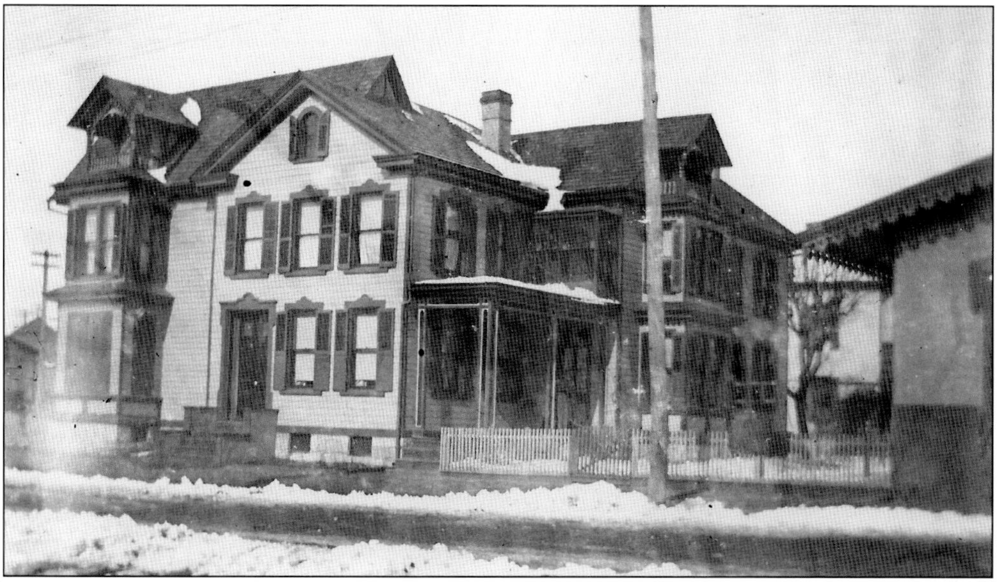

In 1886, Harry Hawk bought this lot on the corner of West Orange and South Earl Streets and sold part of it to the Cumberland Valley Railroad for the CVRR passenger station, which is visible on the right side of this photograph. The building at left was built by Hawk to house his family before he built their mansion at East Orange and South Penn Streets.

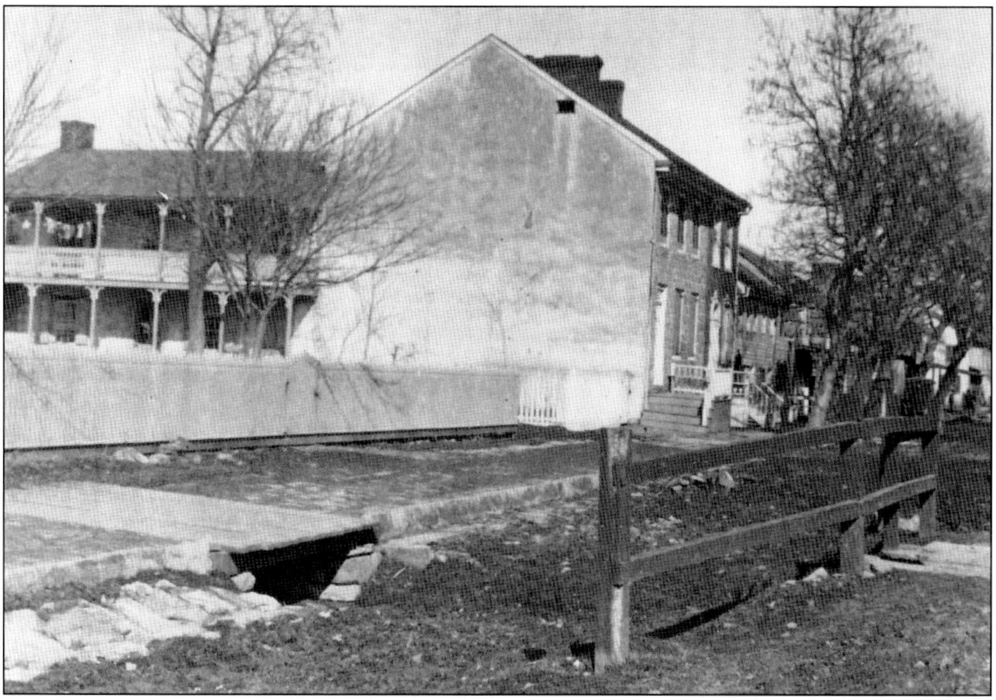

Still standing at 129 West King Street is a stone house that was recorded by the 1798 Direct Tax as measuring 24 feet by 30 feet and being owned by James Means. Samuel Rippey was the original deed owner in 1763. A brick building was added to the side of the house some time after the 1830s. Current owners are Lee (former mayor of Shippensburg) and Anne Hockersmith. This photograph is from the 1870s.

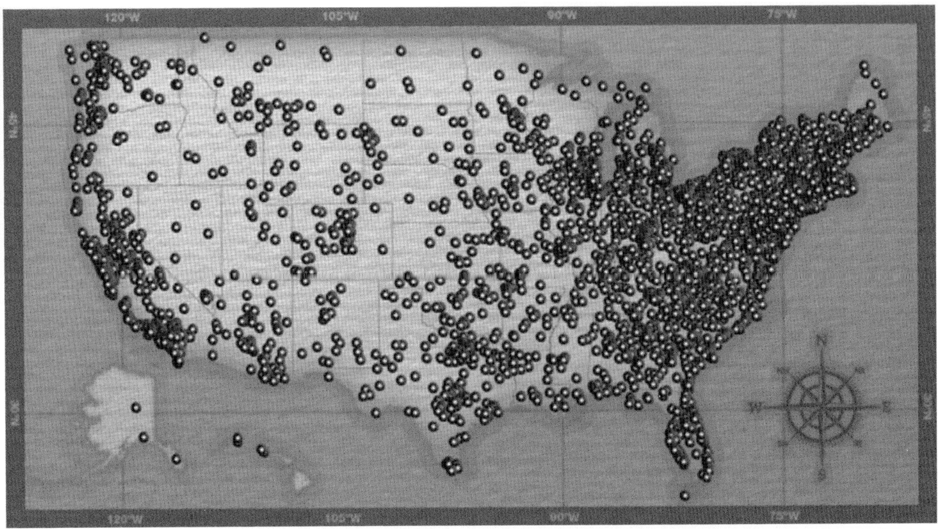

Consistent with our mission to preserve history on a local level, this book was printed in South Carolina on American-made paper and manufactured entirely in the United States. Products carrying the accredited Forest Stewardship Council (FSC) label are printed on 100 percent FSC-certified paper.

MADE IN THE USA